READING AMERICAN HORIZONS

READING AMERICAN HORIZONS

PRIMARY SOURCES FOR U.S. HISTORY IN A GLOBAL CONTEXT, VOLUME II: SINCE 1865

EDITED BY

Michael Schaller
UNIVERSITY OF ARIZONA

Robert D. Schulzinger
UNIVERSITY OF COLORADO, BOULDER

John Bezís-Selfa
WHEATON COLLEGE

Janette Thomas Greenwood
CLARK UNIVERSITY

Andrew Kirk
UNIVERSITY OF NEVADA, LAS VEGAS

Sarah J. Purcell
GRINNELL COLLEGE

Aaron Sheehan-Dean
WEST VIRGINIA UNIVERSITY

NEW YORK   OXFORD
OXFORD UNIVERSITY PRESS

Oxford University Press is a department of the University of Oxford. It furthers the University's objective
of excellence in research, scholarship, and education by publishing worldwide.

Oxford New York
Auckland Cape Town Dar es Salaam Hong Kong Karachi
Kuala Lumpur Madrid Melbourne Mexico City Nairobi
New Delhi Shanghai Taipei Toronto

With offices in
Argentina Austria Brazil Chile Czech Republic France Greece
Guatemala Hungary Italy Japan Poland Portugal Singapore
South Korea Switzerland Thailand Turkey Ukraine Vietnam

Oxford is a registered trade mark of Oxford University Press in the UK and certain other countries.

Published in the United States of America by
Oxford University Press
198 Madison Avenue, New York, NY 10016

For titles covered by Section 112 of the US Higher Education Opportunity Act,
please visit www.oup.com/us/he for the latest information about
pricing and alternate formats.

CONTENTS

PREFACE

Reading American Horizons is a Primary Sources Reader for the survey course in American history, designed to accompany the textbook *American Horizons.*

For more than four hundred years, North America has been part of a global network centered upon the exchange of peoples, goods, and ideas. Human migrations—sometimes freely, sometimes forced—have continued over the centuries, along with the evolution of commerce in commodities as varied as tobacco, sugar, and computer chips. Europeans and Africans came or were brought to the continent, where they met, traded with, fought among, and intermarried with native peoples. Some of these migrants stayed, while others returned to their home countries. Still others came and went periodically. This initial circulation of people across the oceans foreshadowed the continuous movement of people, goods, and ideas that forged the United States. These forces shaped American history, both dividing and unifying the nation. American "horizons" truly stretch beyond our nation's borders, embracing the trading networks established during and after the colonial era to the digital social networks connecting people globally today.

Reading American Horizons uses primary source materials to help tell the story of the United States, by exploring this exchange on a global scale and placing it at the center of that story. By doing so, we provide a different perspective on the history of the United States, one that we hope broadens the horizons of those who read our work and are ever mindful of the global forces that increasingly and profoundly shape our lives. At the same time, *Reading American Horizons* considers those ways in which U.S. influence reshaped the lives and experiences of people of other nations.

Understanding documents and visual artifacts from the past is vital to the study of history. *Reading American Horizons* presents a selection of these materials, all carefully selected to complement the narrative and themes presented in the accompanying *American Horizons.* It is our intention that students more deeply understand the historical narrative in the textbook by examining the original sources in this reader, and that the contextual introductions and review questions enrich the interpretations we offer in the textbook.

What qualities make the United States unique? What experiences did it share with other people around the globe? What accounts for the diversity of dialect and lifestyle across this country? How did the United States become a major player on the world stage of nations? History includes many storylines that contribute to this narrative. *Reading American Horizons* provides insight into the story of where this nation came from and how it has been shaped by its own set of shared values as well as its interaction with the rest of the world. *Reading American Horizons* depicts the intersection of storylines from many nations that influenced, and were influenced by, the United States of America.

As readers engage these materials, we encourage them to think explicitly about what makes history. What matters? What forces or events shaped how people lived their lives? What types of sources do historians rely on to explain the past? With all the sources in this book, readers should consider both what the creators hoped to accomplish and how people at the time might have read or viewed them. We encourage you to become your own historian, to read, analyze, and imagine the connections among the different voices that helped make the United States.

THE DEVELOPMENT STORY

The seven co-editors of this book specialize in a variety of time periods and methodologies. Based on our research and teaching, we all share the idea that the nation's history can best be understood by examining how, from the colonial era forward, the American experience reflected the interaction of many nations, peoples, and events. We present this idea in a format that integrates traditional narrative history with the enhanced perspective of five centuries of global interaction.

READING AMERICAN HORIZONS

CHAPTER 15

RECONSTRUCTING AMERICA, 1865–1877

15.1. JOURDON ANDERSON, LETTER TO P. H. ANDERSON (AUGUST 7, 1865)

Jourdon Anderson was one of the many ex-slaves who made their way north out of Tennessee and Kentucky into southern Ohio after the Civil War. The confused state of the labor market in the South led some masters to try to recruit former slaves back to their property to work as paid laborers.

Dayton, Ohio, August 7, 1865

To My Old Master, Colonel P. H. Anderson, Big Spring, Tennessee

Sir: I got your letter and was glad to find you had not forgotten Jourdon, and that you wanted me to come back and live with you again, promising to do better for me than anybody else can. I have often felt uneasy about you. I thought the Yankees would have hung you long before this for harboring Rebs they found at your house. I suppose they never heard about your going to Col. Martin's to kill the Union soldier that was left by his company in their stable. Although you shot at me twice before I left you, I did not want to hear of your being hurt, and am glad you are still living. It would do me good to go back to the dear old home again and see Miss Mary and Miss Martha and Allen, Esther, Green, and Lee. Give my love to them all, and tell them I hope we will meet in the better world, if not in this. I would have gone back to see you all when I was working in the Nashville Hospital, but one of the neighbors told me Henry intended to shoot me if he ever got a chance.

I want to know particularly what the good chance is you propose to give me. I am doing tolerably well here; I get $25 a month, with victuals and clothing; have a comfortable home for Mandy,—the folks here call her Mrs. Anderson),—and the children—Milly, Jane and Grundy—go to school and are learning well; the teacher says Grundy has a head for a preacher. They go to Sunday-School, and Mandy and me attend church regularly. We are kindly treated; sometimes we overhear others saying, "Them colored people were slaves" down in Tennessee. The children feel hurt when

Source: Lydia Maria Child, *The Freedmen's Book* (Boston: Tickenor and Fields, 1865), 265–67. Also see http://historymatters. gmu.edu/d/6369/.

they hear such remarks, but I tell them it was no disgrace in Tennessee to belong to Col. Anderson. Many darkies would have been proud, as I used to be, to call you master. Now, if you will write and say what wages you will give me, I will be better able to decide whether it would be to my advantage to move back again.

As to my freedom, which you say I can have, there is nothing to be gained on that score, as I got my free papers in 1864 from the Provost-Marshal-General of the Department of Nashville. Mandy says she would be afraid to go back without some proof that you are sincerely disposed to treat us justly and kindly; and we have concluded to test your sincerity by asking you to send us our wages for the time we served you. This will make us forget and forgive old scores, and rely on your justice and friendship in the future. I served you faithfully for thirty-two years and Mandy twenty years. At twenty-five dollars a month for me, and two dollars a week for Mandy, our earnings would amount to eleven thousand six hundred and eighty dollars. Add to this the interest for the time our wages has been kept back and deduct what you paid for our clothing and three doctor's visits to me, and pulling a tooth for Mandy, and the balance will show what we are in justice entitled to. Please send the money by Adams Express, in care of V. Winters, Esq., Dayton, Ohio. If you fail to pay us for faithful labors in the past we can have little faith in your promises in the future. We trust the good Maker has opened your eyes to the wrongs which you and your fathers have done to me and my fathers, in making us toil for you for generations without recompense. Here I draw my wages every Saturday night, but in Tennessee there was never any payday for the Negroes any more than for the horses and cows. Surely there will be a day of reckoning for those who defraud the laborer of his hire.

In answering this letter please state if there would be any safety for my Milly and Jane, who are now grown up and both good-looking girls. You know how it was with Matilda and Catherine. I would rather stay here and starve, and die if it comes to that, than have my girls brought to shame by the violence and wickedness of their young masters. You will also please state if there has been any schools opened for the colored children in your neighborhood, the great desire of my life now is to give my children an education, and have them form virtuous habits.

P.S. —Say howdy to George Carter, and thank him for taking the pistol from you when you were shooting at me.

From your old servant,
Jourdon Anderson

QUESTIONS

1. What do Anderson's comments reveal about the economic knowledge of former slaves?
2. What are the attributes of freedom that Anderson identifies as most important?
3. Explain the new power dynamic between Anderson and his former master. How would each of the participants have understood it?

15.2. CONGRESSMAN THADDEUS STEVENS, EXCERPTS FROM A SPEECH DELIVERED IN LANCASTER COUNTY (SEPTEMBER 6, 1865)

Thaddeus Stevens served as one of the leading radical Republicans in Congress during the Civil War and Reconstruction. A Pennsylvania native, Stevens used sarcasm, wit, and a strong command of House rules to advance his policies. Stevens supported a "hard" Reconstruction of the South that would erase the gross inequalities in wealth created by slavery, but his plans for land redistribution were not supported by more moderate members of his party.

Fellow Citizens:

In compliance with your request, I have come to give my views of the present condition of the Rebel States—of the proper mode of reorganizing the Government, and the future prospects of the Republic. During the whole progress of the war, I never for a moment felt doubt or despondency. I knew that the loyal North would conquer the Rebel despots who sought to destroy freedom. But since that traitorous confederation has been subdued, and we have entered upon the work of "reconstruction" or "restoration," I cannot deny that my heart has become sad at the gloomy prospects before us.

Four years of bloody and expensive war, waged against the United States by eleven States, under a government called the "Confederate States of America," to which they acknowledged allegiance, have overthrown all governments within those States which could be acknowledged as legitimate by the Union. The armies of the Confederate States having been conquered and subdued, and their territory possessed by the United States, it becomes necessary to establish governments therein, which shall be republican in form and principles, and form a more "perfect Union" with the parent Government. It is desirable that such a course should be pursued as to exclude from those governments every

vestige of human bondage, and render the same forever impossible in this nation; and to take care that no principles of self-destruction shall be incorporated therein. In effecting this, it is to be hoped that no provision of the Constitution will be infringed, and no principle of the law of nations disregarded. Especially must we take care that in rebuking this unjust and treasonable war, the authorities of the Union shall indulge in no acts of usurpation which may tend to impair the stability and permanency of the nation. Within these limitations, we hold it to be the duty of the Government to inflict condign punishment on the rebel belligerents, and so weaken their hands that they can never again endanger the Union; and so reform their municipal institutions as to make them republican in spirit as well as in name.... Upon the character of the belligerent, and the justice of the war, and the manner of conducting it, depends our right to take the lives, liberty and property of the belligerent. This war had its origin in treason without one spark of justice. It was prosecuted before notice of it, by robbing our forts and armories, and our navy-yards; by stealing our money from the mints and depositories, and by surrendering our forts and navies by perjurers who had sworn to support the Constitution. In its progress our prisoners, by the authority of their government, were slaughtered in cold blood.

Source: Beverly Wilson Palmer and Holly Byers Ochoa, eds., *Selected Papers of Thaddeus Stevens, Volume 2: April 1865–August 1868* (Pittsburgh: University of Pittsburgh Press, 1998), 12–25.

Ask Fort Pillow and Fort Wagner. Sixty thousand of our prisoners have been deliberately starved to death because they would not enlist in the rebel armies. The graves at Andersonville have each an accusing tongue. The purpose and avowed object of the enemy "to found an empire whose corner-stone should be slavery," rendered its perpetuity or revival dangerous to human liberty.

Surely, these things are sufficient to justify the exercise of the extreme rights of war—"to execute, to imprison, to confiscate." How many captive enemies it would be proper to execute, as an example to nations, I leave others to judge. I am not fond of sanguinary punishments, but surely some victims must propitiate the manes of our starved, murdered, slaughtered martyrs. A court-martial could do justice according to law.

But we propose to confiscate all the estate of every rebel belligerent whose estate was worth $10,000, or whose land exceeded two hundred acres in quantity. Policy if not justice would require that the poor, the ignorant, and the coerced should be forgiven. They followed the example and teachings of their wealthy and intelligent neighbors. The rebellion would never have originated with them. Fortunately those who would thus escape form a large majority of the people, though possessing but a small portion of the wealth. The proportion of those exempt compared with the punished would be I believe about nine tenths.

There are about six millions of freedmen in the South. The number of acres of land is 465,000,000. Of this, those who own above two hundred acres each number about 70,000 persons, holding, in the aggregate, (together with the States,) about 394,000,000 acres, leaving for all the others below 200 each, about 71,000,000 of acres. By thus forfeiting the estates of the leading rebels, the government would have 394,000,000 of acres, beside their town property, and yet nine-tenths of the people would remain untouched. Divide this land into convenient farms. Give, if you please, forty acres to each adult male freedman. Suppose there are one million of them. That would require 40,000,000 of acres, which, deducted from 394,000,000, leaves three hundred and fifty-four millions of acres for sale. Divide it into suitable farms, and sell it to the highest bidders. I think it, including town property, would average at least ten dollars per

acre. That would produce $3,540,000,000—three billions five hundred and forty millions of dollars.

Let that be applied as follows to wit:

1. Invest $300,000,000 in six per cent government bonds, and add the interest semi-annually to the pensions of those who have become entitled by this villainous war.
2. Appropriate $200,000,000 to pay the damages done to loyal men, North and South, by the rebellion.
3. Pay the residue, being $3,040,000,000 towards the payment of the National debt.

What loyal man can object to this? Look around you, and every where behold your neighbors, some with an arm, some with a leg, some with an eye, carried away by rebel bullets. Others horribly mutilated in every form. And yet numerous others wearing the weeds which mark the death of those on whom they leaned for support. Contemplate these monuments of rebel perfidy, and of patriotic suffering, and then say if too much is asked for our valiant soldiers....The whole fabric of southern society *must* be changed, and never can it be done if this opportunity is lost. Without this, this Government can never be, as it never has been, a true republic. Heretofore, it had more the features of aristocracy than of democracy. The Southern States have been despotisms, not governments of the people. It is impossible that any practical equality of rights can exist where a few thousand men monopolize the whole landed property. The larger the number of small proprietors the more safe and stable the government. As the landed interest must govern, the more it is subdivided and held by independent owners, the better. What would be the condition of the State of New York if it were not for her independent yeomanry? She would be overwhelmed and demoralized by the Jews, Milesians and vagabonds of licentious cities. How can republican institution, free schools, free churches, free social intercourse, exist in a mingled community of nabobs and serfs; of the owners of twenty thousand acre manors with lordly palaces, and the occupants of narrow huts inhabited by "low white trash?" If the South is ever to be made a safe republic, let her lands be cultivated by the toil of the owners or the free labor of intelligent citizens. This must be done even though it drive her nobility into exile. If they go, all the better. It will be hard to persuade the owner of ten thousand acres of land, who drives a coach and four, that he is not degraded by sitting at the same table, or in the same pew, with the embrowned and hard-handed farmer who has himself cultivated his own thriving homestead of 150 acres. This subdivision of the lands will yield ten bales of cotton to one that is made now, and he who produced it will own it and *feel himself a man.*

It is far easier and more beneficial to exile 70,000 proud, bloated and defiant rebels, than to expatriate four millions of laborers, native to the soil and loyal to the Government....Let us forget all parties and build on the broad platform of "reconstructing" the government out of the conquered territory converted into new and free States, and admitted into the Union by the sovereign power of Congress, with another plank—"THE PROPERTY OF THE REBELS SHALL PAY OUR NATIONAL DEBT, *and indemnify freed-men and*

loyal sufferers—and that under no circumstances will we suffer the National debt to be repudiated, or the interest scaled below the contract rates; nor permit any part of the rebel debt to be assumed by the nation."

Let all who approve of these principles rally with us. Let all others go with Copperheads and rebels. Those will be the opposing parties. Young men, this duty devolves on you. Would to God, if only for that, that I were still in the prime of life, that I might aid you to fight through this last and greatest battle of freedom!

QUESTIONS

1. On what basis does Stevens draw his authority for advocating a full Reconstruction of the South?
2. How does he propose to reorganize the land holdings of the South?
3. What kind of effect does he anticipate this policy will have on the region?

15.3. VISUAL DOCUMENT: THOMAS NAST, *ANDREW JOHNSON'S RECONSTRUCTION* IN *HARPER'S WEEKLY* (SEPTEMBER 1, 1866)

During the summer of 1866, Memphis and New Orleans experienced horrible race riots, in which whites murdered dozens of blacks indiscriminately. Many Northerners felt that Johnson's lenient policies fomented a recalcitrant and unapologetic white South. Thomas Nast drew political cartoons for *Harper's Weekly*, the most widely read periodical in the country. He was an early critic of Johnson and a strong proponent for a Reconstruction that treated African Americans fairly.

QUESTIONS

1. What is Nast's critique of Johnson's Reconstruction policy?
2. What do the images around the margins of the cartoon portray as Johnson's responsibility for the riots?
3. Why does Nast portray the lone black individual as a wounded Union soldier?

Source: Ben and Beatrice Goldstein Foundation Collection/Library of Congress.

15.4. JOSÉ INÁCIO BARROS COBRA, EXCERPTS FROM "SLAVE PROPERTY IS AS SACRED AS ANY OTHER" (JULY 21, 1871)

After the emancipation of slaves in the United States, Brazilian and Cuban slaveholders began to consider ways to manage the end of slavery in their own countries (the last remaining slave nations in the western hemisphere). In Brazil, the parliament considered "Free Birth" legislation, which would have freed the newborns of enslaved women as a way to gradually transition to free labor. Even this modest proposal generated criticism from slaveholders, who worked to delay the process. Barros Cobra was a member of the Brazilian parliament who delivered the speech below opposing free-birth legislation.

Gentlemen, it is true that in this country there exists a point of view that demands a solution to the great problem of slavery. The existence of this opinion is undeniable in the abstract, in principle; fortunately there is not one Brazilian who wishes the permanent preservation of slavery in the Empire; in this sense there is unanimous agreement: the cause of abolition is definitely decided upon.

To the honor of the Brazilian Empire, we do not need to overcome the difficulties, prejudices, and animosities against which the legislators of France and the United States had to struggle; the natural generosity of the Brazilian character, the religious spirit and the principles of morality and civilization decided the theoretical question a long time ago....When we attempt to solve this great question, we should not be motivated by abstractions, philosophical concepts, or sentimental inspirations, but rather by the high and venerable interests that are associated with it and that constitute the foundations of Brazilian society [*hear! hear!*]; much may be said, much may be desired in this regard, but a study and practical knowledge of our circumstances and of what can reasonably be done are what should guide us, in order that we may go forward

securely. [*Hear! Hear!*] Gentlemen, I reflected very serenely about how we might most conveniently solve this important problem, which demands full attention and challenges the deepest meditation. I considered it with total calm, far from my legislative responsibilities, and with my mind uncluttered by other concerns. Momentarily the idea of freeing the womb seemed an acceptable method (to this chamber I confess the feelings of my inner conscience); however, further thought convinced me that this idea, which at first glance is so appealing, is the most dangerous way to go in this country. [*Hear! Hear!*]

History, that great preceptress of experience, shows us that almost all the nations that tried to abolish slavery gradually did not achieve this, but were instead forced to rush headlong and disastrously toward total abolition; this was the experience of England, France, and Portugal herself. A contrary example, such as that of the United States, may be mentioned; but none of those states had a tenth of the slave population which we have, and so cannot constitute an argument in favor of the government's bill.[1] The illustrious special committee asked in their report: "What reasons do we have to fear that in our country things will go differently

Source: Robert Conrad, *Children of God's Fire: A Documentary History of Black Slavery in Brazil* (University Park: Pennsylvania State University Press, 1984), 436–46.

1 This contention is false. In 1860, Georgia had a slave population of 462,000, which was more than any Brazilian province recorded during that country's entire history.

from the way they did in countries where, after experiencing the same exaggerated fears, the same transformations were brought about?"

But those countries did not find themselves in circumstances identical to ours; they did not possess the number of slaves that we unfortunately possess, nor was agriculture almost the sole basis of their private and public wealth; nor like us did they have a free population spread out over an immense territory and, in terrifying contrast, a slave population concentrated in the main production centers. These different circumstances call for different ways to cure the evil. [*Hear! Hear!*] . . . Brazil's circumstances in this regard are very special, and we must not lose sight of them. . . . The slave born of a slave woman, who belongs to her master in virtue of principles sanctified in civil legislation, represents capital and is an instrument of labor; however, it is understood that the value of the slave is precisely dependent upon the services that he can perform [*hear! hear!*]; nobody would want an unused slave for the mere joy of possessing him. The capital here is represented by the instrument of labor, whose value is in direct proportion to the greater or lesser usefulness which as such he can render; in just the same way that the price of a slave is more or less, depending upon his capacity and fitness for work.

This being the case, which seems to me undeniable, it is entirely obvious that the intention here is to indemnify the masters with the identical thing that belongs to them by law, and which they cannot be deprived of without receiving full compensation. There is, however, a single difference: they are granted the use of the individual for thirteen years, a usufruct which, according to law, would otherwise belong to them for as long as the slave might live. It seems to me, therefore, that the right to property, sanctified and guaranteed by the Constitution of the Empire, which cannot be taken from the citizen of Brazil without prior indemnification, is in this case confiscated without any indemnification whatsoever, or with a false indemnification, which amounts to the same thing. . . .

It is known that, thanks to the generous and humane character of the Brazilians, slavery among us is so mild that the condition of our slaves is greatly preferable to that of the working classes of some European countries; on the largest agricultural establishments, order and subordination are maintained entirely by means of a prudent system of constant and severe discipline, in which careful preventive measures ordinarily make repression unnecessary. Once the proposed law is enforced, that system cannot be maintained, and it will be seriously and dangerously undermined by the simultaneous existence in those establishments of slave parents and free children, not as an exceptional or accidental situation, but as a regular and permanent reality, and by the unavoidable meddling of the authorities responsible for enforcement of the law. This situation will awaken in those who remain slaves a dangerous impatience and a terrible hopelessness which must shatter all ties of subordination and respect for their masters. . . .

QUESTIONS

1. What lessons does the speaker draw from the American experience?
2. Can you identify any other influences of U.S. emancipation on the discussion here?
3. How does the speaker's treatment of slavery compare to the opinions of U.S. authorities on the subject, such as that of James Henry Hammond, presented in Chapter 13?

15.5. GEORGES CLEMENCEAU, NOTES ON JOHNSON AND RECONSTRUCTION (SEPTEMBER 10, 1867)

By late 1867, Andrew Johnson, a wartime Republican who ascended to the presidency after Lincoln's assassination, had alienated himself from congressional Republicans because of his conservative approach to Reconstruction. Johnson turned to Northern Democrats and Southerners for support (even though many Southerners remained disenfranchised following the war). Georges Clemenceau, a French physician and journalist, covered Washington politics for a French newspaper. He served as prime minister of France during the last year of World War I and helped draft the Treaty of Versailles.

September 10, 1867. The war between the President and Congress goes on, complicated from time to time by some unexpected turn. Contrary to all that has happened, is happening, and will happen in certain countries, the legislative power here has the upper hand. That is the peculiarity of the situation, or rather of this government. Congress may, when it pleases, take the President by the ear and lead him down from his high seat, and he can do nothing about it except to struggle and shout. But that is an extreme measure, and the radicals are limiting themselves, for the present, to binding Andrew Johnson firmly with good brand-new laws. At each session they add a shackle to his bonds, tighten the bit in a different place, file a claw or draw a tooth, and then when he is well bound up, fastened, and caught in an inextricable net of laws and decrees, more or less contradicting each other, they tie him to the stake of the Constitution and take a good look at him, feeling quite sure he cannot move this time.

But then Seward, the Dalila of the piece, rises up and shouts: "Johnson, here come the radicals with old Stevens at their head; they are proud of having subjected you and are coming to enjoy the sight of you in chains." And Samson summons all his strength, and bursts his cords and bonds with a mighty effort,

and the Philistines (I mean the radicals) flee in disorder to the Capitol to set to work making new laws stronger than the old, which will break in their turn at the first test. This has been going on now for two years, and though in the course of things it is inevitable that Samson will be beaten, one must admit that he has put up a game fight. Even a sceptic, if this word has any meaning in America, would be interested in the struggle....A new amnesty has been proclaimed for the former rebels in the South, and we shall soon see the struggle begin on a new point, that is, the interpretation to be given this proclamation of amnesty and the conclusions to be drawn from it. This is the second proclamation of amnesty which Mr. Johnson has issued. Though it still insists on the obligation to swear the oath of allegiance to the Constitution and the Union, it is infinitely more liberal in its terms than the first proclamation. Instead of the fourteen classes of exceptions defined in the proclamation of amnesty of May 29, 1865, the proclamation of September 8, 1867, defines only three. None are excluded from the benefits of amnesty except the military and civil heads of the Confederate government, those who treated Federal prisoners contrary to the laws of warfare, and those who took part in the conspiracy which

Source: Fernand Baldensperger, ed., *American Reconstruction, 1865–1870, and the Impeachment of Andrew Johnson* (New York: Dial Press, 1928), 102–07.

ended in the assassination of Lincoln. The *Tribune* estimated that the first proclamation left about one hundred thousand citizens out of the amnesty, and that this one leaves out one or two thousand. There is no harm done so far, but the question will be what are the exact rights conferred by the amnesty, in other words, whether the President has the power to reinstate the former rebels in their rights and to make voters of them. The President and the Democrats say *Yes,* Congress and the Republicans say *No....*The Indians in the West have arrayed themselves against the whites, for the thousandth time. Massacres are being carried on by both sides, with brutal ferocity. The whites hunt down and drive the Indians as they formerly did the negroes in the South, and the Indians, in return, when they take prisoners, send them back to their relatives in pieces, without regard for age or sex. It is sad to be obliged to state that the first and real offenders are nearly always the white men.

QUESTIONS

1. How does Clemenceau characterize the relationship between the president and Congress?
2. How would Johnson's more liberal amnesty rules affect the landscape of postwar politics?
3. What connections exist between the Indian wars of the West and the Civil War?

15.6. SECRETARY OF WAR, LETTER ON "FREEDMEN'S AFFAIRS IN KENTUCKY AND TENNESSEE" (1868)

Founded in 1866, the Ku Klux Klan was a terrorist organization devoted to driving black people out of positions of public authority in the South. Its members operated in secret and used all manner of threats and violence to break the political alliances between blacks and whites in the Republican Party and the social institutions built by black Southerners in the postwar years.

Notice has been sent to Mrs. L. A. Baldwin, teacher of freedmen's school No. 1, Bowling Green, Kentucky, with post office dated April 27, 1868, of which the following is a copy:

Mrs. L. A. Baldwin, teacher colored school, Bonding Green, Kentucky:

KU KLUX KLANS!
BLOOD! POISON! POWDER! TORCH!
Leave in five days, or hell's your portion!
Rally, rally, watch your chance,
First blood, first premium K. K. K.

If ball, or torch, or poison fails,
The house beneath you shall be blown to hell, or move you.

K. K. K.

QUESTIONS

1. Why would the KKK attack teachers?
2. What threat did education pose to the social order?
3. How would the anonymous nature of the threat delivered to Mrs. L. A. Baldwin affect the social fabric of the Kentucky community in which she lived?

Source: Secretary of War, House Executive Document No. 329, 40th Cong., 2nd sess., 19.

15.7. U.S. SENATE, REPORTS ON "OUTRAGES COMMITTED BY DISLOYAL PERSONS" (1870)

Republican officials in the South collected evidence of Ku Klux Klan atrocities, which led to widely publicized congressional hearings in 1871. Public pressure in the North encouraged Congress to pass a series of laws that empowered the federal government and the newly created Department of Justice to crack down on conspiracies such as the KKK. A raft of prosecutions and some convictions broke up the formal organizations, but many of the members reorganized under new names and continued their campaigns of terror until Southern Republicans were driven from office.

Roxboro, Person County, North Carolina, October 7, 1870.

Dear Sir: The first victim to Ku-Klux violence was Mr. S. L. Wiles; lived four miles south of Roxboro; an industrious and, in his dealings with persons, strictly honest man. The alleged charge against him was that he was living in adultery with a colored woman. (Can't say as to the truth of the charge.) The woman's name is Harriet Bran, who also, with Wiles, was cruelly whipped, and both of them driven from the farm he had rented for the year. The next and only other instance I can call to mind was against Wm. B. Hudgens; the supposed cause was that he was living on land the title of which is in dispute. The party not in possession had ordered him to leave the premises, threatening at the same time if he failed to do so within a certain time he would be Ku-Kluxed off. He failed to leave as ordered, and was afterwards cruelly and most terribly beaten by disguised men, (26 in number,) and forced to leave the premises he had leased for two years.

Hudgens has always voted the democratic ticket; Wiles the republican. I don't think politics had anything to do with either case.

Most respectfully, & c.

P. S.—I had liked to have forgotten to mention the case of a Mr. Thomas, United States detective, who visited Roxboro on business pertaining to his duty, and, during the night, had a coffin placed at his door, with the following inscription tacked on it, to wit: "You and all other damned radicals had better leave these parts or else you will fill this furniture."

A true copy of original letter on file in executive department of North Carolina.
J. B. NEATHERY, Private Secretary.

Lincolnton, North Carolina, October 17, 1870.

Dear Sir: According to your request we send you the below list of names of persons that have been maltreated in Lincoln County:

Harriet Quickel	Black	Whipped and shot.
Sam Ward, wife, and daughter	do	Whipped.

Source: "Message of the President of the United States, Communicating, in Compliance with the Resolution of the Senate of the 16 of December, 1870, Information in Relation to Outrages Committed by Disloyal Persons in North Carolina, and Other Southern States," Senate Executive Document No. 16, 41st Cong., 3rd sess., 10–11.

Rufus Friday and Wife	do	Whipped.
James Falls	do	Whipped.
Charles Sumner	do	Whipped and robbed of $15.
John Connely	do	Whipped and shot.
William Magbee	do	Robbed in the woods of all his money.
Reuben Litton	do	Whipped and shot.
Jerry Wood	do	Whipped and drove from home; life threatened if he returned.
J. Barringer	do	Whipped and drove from home; life threatened if he returned.
Rufus Bindhardt	do	Whipped and shot dangerously.
E. Wilfong	do	Whipped and shot dangerously.
Peter Hoover	do	Whipped.
Lawson Friday	do	Whipped and shot.
S. Motz	do	Whipped.
John Miller	White	Whipped and shot.
Adeline Fisher	do	Whipped.
Mary Fisher	do	Whipped.
Sally Fisher	do	Whipped.
J. McMellen	do	Whipped.
Jeff Herndon	Black	House robbed of two guns.

There are a number of other cases, but we cannot get their names.

The colored man, Wilfong, was shot in the back and is mutilated for life.

For the sake of my family please not mention my name in this matter.

Asheboro, North Carolina, October 28, 1870.

Dear Sir: Yours of the 30th ultimo is to hand. I am sorry to have to inform you that Randolph County is almost entirely governed by the Ku-Klux. I supposed before the election that there were a good many in the county, but I had no idea that they were half so well organized; but I am proud to say that my township gave a large republican majority. The Ku-Klux have not committed many gross outrages in this county, like they have in some others. Their object seemed to be to decoy as many as possible into the organization by making them believe it was not a very bad thing. They paraded through several neighborhoods just before the election, in order to terrify the most timid republicans, and by their threats, &c., make them stay away from the election. They knew very well who was easily scared. They have not been so bold since the militia was called out. If the republicans had not (some of them, both white and colored) been so easily intimidated and staid at home, we could easily have carried Randolph. It is very hard to know whom to put confidence in. I know a great many men who laid out during the war, who were whipped, kicked, and handcuffed by the rebels during the war, who are now among the Ku-Klux, and voted for the men that abused them so badly. I don't know that any person in this county has been murdered by the Ku-Klux. I only know of two that have been whipped; one was a colored boy, I think, by the name of Cheek, who was taken to Franklinsville last spring, in the night, and tied up and whipped in the village. James Brookshire, a colored man, was whipped at his own house last spring, and his gun taken away, and he forced to leave the neighborhood. One school-house was burned in 1869; it belonged to the colored people. A great many, both white and colored, were visited by the Ku-Klux, and severe threats made against them if they voted the republican ticket.

Respectfully, yours,
JOEL ASHEWORTH.

QUESTIONS

1. Why would the KKK target an interracial couple?
2. What do these letters suggest about the Klan's social policies apart from their political objectives?
3. How would the Klan's institutionalization of violence in the postwar South reshape the political order?

15.8. VISUAL DOCUMENT: THOMAS NAST, TILDEN-HAYES CARTOON IN *HARPER'S WEEKLY* (MARCH 17, 1877)

Republicans and Democrats disputed the returns of several states in the presidential election of 1876. After a long, tense winter, an agreement was reached to count the electoral votes of Louisiana, Florida, and South Carolina for the Republican candidate, Rutherford B. Hayes, but give control of the state governments to the Democrats. Historians generally regard the election as marking the end of Reconstruction, because the three states listed above were the last states to shift back to Democratic regimes.

Mrs. U. S.—"Thanks, Mr. Tilden. I have promised to dance this set with Mr. Hayes."

QUESTIONS

1. How does Nast's representation of the two candidates signal his preference?

2. Why does the cartoon avoid the controversy that surrounded the election?

3. Does the cartoon "naturalize" Hayes's victory?

Source: The Granger Collection, NYC.

CHAPTER 16

FORGING A TRANSCONTINENTAL NATION, 1877–1900

16.1. FREDERICK JACKSON TURNER, EXCERPTS FROM THE "TURNER THESIS" (JULY 12, 1893)

The 1893 Chicago World's Columbian Exposition presented fairgoers from all over the world with an exciting vision of an American future. A few exposition attendees opted to hear historian Frederick Jackson Turner offer a new theory on the American past. The "Turner Thesis" lamented the "closing" of the frontier and presented a powerful and influential interpretation of how the conquest and settlement of the frontier shaped American history.

In a recent bulletin of the Superintendent of the Census for 1890 appear these significant words: "Up to and including 1880 the country had a frontier of settlement, but at present the unsettled area has been so broken into by isolated bodies of settlement that there can hardly be said to be a frontier line. In the discussion of its extent, its westward movement, etc., it can not, therefore, any longer have a place in the census reports." This brief official statement marks the closing of a great historic movement. Up to our own day American history has been in a large degree the history of the colonization of the Great West. The existence of an area of free land, its continuous recession, and the advance of American settlement westward, explain American development.

Behind institutions, behind constitutional forms and modifications, lie the vital forces that call these organs into life and shape them to meet changing conditions. The peculiarity of American institutions is, the fact that they have been compelled to adapt themselves to the changes of an expanding people—to the changes involved in crossing a continent, in winning a wilderness, and in developing at each area of this progress out of the primitive economic and political conditions of the frontier into the complexity of city life. Said Calhoun in 1817, "We are great, and rapidly—I was about to say fearfully—growing!" So saying, he touched the distinguishing feature of American life. All peoples show development; the germ theory of politics has been sufficiently

Source: Frederick Jackson Turner, "The Significance of the Frontier in American History" in *The Frontier In American History* (New York: Henry Holt and Company, 1921).

emphasized. In the case of most nations, however, the development has occurred in a limited area; and if the nation has expanded, it has met other growing peoples whom it has conquered. But in the case of the United States we have a different phenomenon. Limiting our attention to the Atlantic coast, we have the familiar phenomenon of the evolution of institutions in a limited area, such as the rise of representative government; into complex organs; the progress from primitive industrial society, without division of labor, up to manufacturing civilization. But we have in addition to this a recurrence of the process of evolution in each western area reached in the process of expansion. Thus American development has exhibited not merely advance along a single line, but a return to primitive conditions on a continually advancing frontier line, and a new development for that area. American social development has been continually beginning over again on the frontier. This perennial rebirth, this fluidity of American life, this expansion westward with its new opportunities, its continuous touch with the simplicity of primitive society, furnish the forces dominating American character. The true point of view in the history of this nation is not the Atlantic coast, it is the Great West. Even the slavery struggle, which is made so exclusive an object of attention by writers like Professor von Holst, occupies its important place in American history because of its relation to westward expansion.

QUESTIONS

1. Why does Turner say the frontier is "closed?"
2. Why does he think that this closing is significant in American history?
3. What does Turner mean when he says: "American social development has been continually beginning over again on the frontier"?

16.2. VISUAL DOCUMENTS: COWBOYS AND PRESIDENTS—THEODORE ROOSEVELT (c. 1885) AND RONALD REAGAN (FEBRUARY 1977)

In the 19th century, cowboys were transformed from their humble beginnings as itinerant Spanish *vaqueros* into mythic figures and internationally recognized symbols of America. U.S. presidents from Theodore Roosevelt to George W. Bush used the powerful symbolism of the cowboy to portray themselves and their administrations to the nation and the world. In the 20th century, foreign governments and American critics reimagined the cowboy as a reckless and arrogant figure. Whether they were sinister "black hat" cowboys or rugged "white hat" cowboys symbolizing freedom, the image of the American cow-worker is one of the most recognizable in the world.

Theodore Roosevelt, perhaps more than any other American president, capitalized on the symbolism of the cowboy. Ronald Reagan was one of a number of 20th-century American presidents who portrayed himself as a cowboy.

Sources: Theodore Roosevelt (1858–1919). 26th President of the United States. Posing as a cowboy while living as a gentleman rancher in North Dakota, 1885. Courtesy The Granger Collection; Ronald Reagan on his Ranch. © Tony Korody/Sygma/Corbis.

Theodore Roosevelt posing as a cowboy while living as a gentleman rancher in North Dakota, 1885.

Ronald Reagan on his ranch, 1977.

QUESTIONS

1. Why did cow-workers become symbols of American freedom and individualism?
2. Look carefully at the two presidential photos. Notice the different ways that Roosevelt and Reagan wear frontier and cowboy symbols. Are these photos simply moments captured in time or artifacts of political image creation?
3. Why do you think these two presidents, from two very different times, decided to adopt the identity of the cowboy?

16.3. COMPETING VISIONS OF THE WEST: EXCERPTS FROM FITZ HUGH LUDLOW'S "SEVEN WEEKS IN THE GREAT YO-SEMITE" (1870) AND RICHARD F. BURTON'S *CITY OF THE SAINTS* (1861)

Many 19th-century Americans viewed the West as the garden of the world, an ideal place for Eastern farmers to make a new start in an Edenic site, a region of unbounded potential for settlement, prosperity, and the expansion of democratic ideals. The garden of the world myth, depicted alongside portrayals of an adventurous Wild West and in opposition to the myth of the American Desert, dominated 19-century representations of the region. Albert Bierstadt, one of America's most famous landscape artists and a transcontinental traveler, created a number of popular canvasses depicting the West as an idyllic place. These depictions influenced government legislation with respect to the West and contributed to the mass westward migrations and the corresponding displacements

Albert Bierstadt, *The Sierra Nevada in California,* oil on canvas, 1868. Courtesy of the Granger Collection.

Sources: Fitz Hugh Ludlow, "Seven Weeks in the Great Yo-Semite," in *The Heart of the Continent: A Record of Travel across the Plains and in Oregon, with an Examination of the Mormon Principle* (New York: Hurd & Houghton, 1870), 412, 425–26, 434; Richard F. Burton, *City of the Saints among the Mormons and across the Rocky Mountains to California* (Santa Barbara, CA: Narrative Press, 2003), 61–62, 369.

of Native peoples in the mid- and late-19th century. Beyond promoting the region for settlement, some, including Bierstadt's fellow-traveler, author Fitz Hugh Ludlow, promoted the West's aesthetic appeal, which he compared favorably to European geography and architecture in hopes of furthering American cultural independence. For Ludlow, the West's unmatched scenic beauty was most abundantly evident in Yosemite. In contrast to these imperialistic, nationalistic, and exceptionalistic portrayals, other writers, including world traveler Sir Richard F. Burton, described the West differently, using comparative frameworks to highlight similarities between the West and other regions of the globe. Burton crossed the continent a few years before Ludlow, but his weariness outweighed his interest in exploring Ludlow's Edenic California.

SEVEN WEEKS IN THE GREAT YO-SEMITE

If report was true, we were going to the original site of the Garden of Eden,—into a region which out-Bendemered Bendemere, out-valleyed the valley of Rasselas, surpassed the Alps in its waterfalls, and the Himmal'yeh in its precipices. As for the two former subjects of comparison, we never met any tourist who could adjust the question from his own experience; but the superiority of the Yo-Semite to the Alpine cataracts was a matter put beyond doubt by repeated judgments; and a couple of English officers who had explored the wildest Himmal'yeh scenery told Starr King that there was no precipice in Asia to be compared for height or grandeur with Tutoch-anula and Tis-sa-ack.

We were going into the vale whose giant domes and battlements had months before thrown their photographic shadow through Watkins's camera across the mysterious wide Continent, causing exclamations of awe at Goupil's window, and ecstasy in Dr. Holmes's study. At Goupil's counter and in Starr King's drawing-room we had gazed on them by the hour already, — I, let me confess it, half a Thomas-a Didymus to Nature, unwilling to believe the utmost true of her till I could put my finger in her very prints. Now we were going to test her reported largess for ourselves....

Our dense leafy surrounding hid us from the feet of our approach to the Valley's tremendous battlement, till our trail turned at a sharp angle, and we stood on "Inspiration Point."

That name had appeared pedantic, but we found it only the spontaneous expression of our own feelings on the spot. We did not so much seem to be seeing from that crag of vision a new scene on the old familiar globe, as a new heaven and a new earth into which the creative spirit had just been breathed. I hesitate now, as I did then, at the attempt to give my vision utterance. Never were words so beggared for an abridged translation of any Scripture of Nature....

Sitting in their divine workshop, by a little after sunrise our artists [including Bierstadt] began labor in that only method which can ever make a true painter or a living landscape,—color-studies on the spot; and though I can not here speak of their results, I will assert that during their seven weeks' camp in the Valley they learned more and gained greater material for future triumphs than they had gotten in all their lives before at the feet of the greatest masters.

CITY OF THE SAINTS

"Scott's Bluffs," situated 285 miles from Fort Kearney and 51 from Fort Laramie, was the last of the great marl formations which we saw on this line, and was of all by far the most curious. In the dull uniformity of the prairies it is a striking and attractive object, far excelling the castled crag of Drachenfels or any of the beauties of romantic Rhine. From a distance of a day's march it appears in the shape of a large blue mound, distinguished only by its dimensions from the detached fragments of hill around. As you approach within four or five miles, a massive medieval city gradually defines itself, clustering, with a wonderful fullness of detail, round a colossal fortress, and crowned with a royal castle....At a nearer aspect again, the quaint illusion vanishes: the lines of masonry become yellow layers of boulder and pebble imbedded in a mass of stiff, tamped, bald marly clay; the curtains and angles change to the gashings of the rains of ages, and the warriors are metamorphosed into dwarf cedars and dense shrubs, scattered singly over the surface. Travelers have compared this glory of the *mauvaises terres* to Gibraltar, to the Capitol at Washington, to Stirling Castle. I could think of nothing in its presence but the Arabs' "City of Brass," that mysterious abode of bewitched infidels, which often appears at a distance to the wayfarer toiling under the burning sun, but ever eludes his nearer search....

I spent ten pleasant days at San Francisco. There remained some traveller's work to be done: the Giant Trees, the Yosemite or Yohamite Falls,—the highest cataracts yet known in the world,—and the Almaden Cinnabar Mines, with British Columbia, Vancouver's Island, and Los Angeles temptingly near. But in sooth I was aweary of the way; for eight months I had lived on board steamers and railroad cars, coaches, and mules; my eyes were full of sight-seeing, my pockets empty, and my brain stuffed with all manner of useful knowledge.

QUESTIONS

1. How does Bierstadt's painting depict the West? How might this and similar depictions have impacted government legislation and westward migration?
2. How does Ludlow's Yosemite compare with the great geographical features of Europe? Why would Ludlow want to describe the West favorably in relation to Europe?
3. Englishman Sir Richard Burton, like Ludlow, compares Western geography with Eastern geography, but how does his comparison differ? How can we account for these differences?

16.4. JOHN WESLEY POWELL, EXCERPTS FROM *REPORT ON THE LANDS OF THE ARID REGION* (1879)

Starting in 1869, one-armed Civil War veteran John Wesley Powell led a series of important surveys of the Colorado River system. Setting out at Green River, Wyoming, in four boats, the Powell expedition followed the Colorado River through the Flaming Gorge, Desolation, Marble, and Grand Canyons, crossing the confluences of the Yampa, Green, and little Colorado Rivers. In a second expedition in 1872, Powell explored the expansive Colorado Plateau. Powell was the first government scientist to understand the Colorado River's critical importance for the southwest. His insightful 1879 *Report on the Lands of the Arid Region* recommended an alternative pattern of settlement based on his scientific findings about aridity. Powell warned that traditional settlement patterns and agricultural practices would fail in the arid West and counseled cautious settlement guided by hydrology and climate.

Source: John Wesley Powell, *Report on the Lands of the Arid Region of the United States* (Washington: Government Printing Office, 1879).

John K. Hillers, *The Heart of Lodor.* Hiller's photograph of Frederick Samuel Dellenbaugh in Ladore Canyon on the Colorado River (1872). Courtesy National Archives and Records Administration.

It was my intention to write a work on the Public Domain. The object of the volume was to give the extent and character of the lands yet belonging to the Government of the United States. Compared with the whole extent of these lands, but a very small fraction is immediately available for agriculture; in general, they require drainage or irrigation for their redemption.

It is true that in the Southern States there are some millions of acres, chiefly timber lands, which at no remote time will be occupied for agricultural purposes. Westward toward the Great Plains, the lands in what I have, in the body of this volume, termed the Humid Region have passed from the hands of the General Government. To this statement there are some small exceptions here and there—fractional tracts, which, for special reasons, have not been considered desirable by persons in search of lands for purposes of investment or occupation.

In the Sub-humid Region settlements are rapidly extending westward to the verge of the country where agriculture is possible without irrigation.

In the Humid Region of the Columbia the agricultural lands are largely covered by great forests, and for this reason settlements will progress slowly, as the lands must be cleared of their timber.

The redemption of the Arid Region involves engineering problems requiring for their solution the greatest skill. In the present volume only these lands are considered. Had I been able to execute the original plan to my satisfaction, I should have treated of the coast swamps of the South Atlantic and the Gulf slopes, the Everglade lands of the Floridian Peninsula, the flood plain lands of the great rivers of the south, which have heretofore been made available only to a limited extent by a system of levees, and the lake swamp lands found about the headwaters of the Mississippi and the region of the upper Great Lakes. All of these lands require either drainage or protection from overflow, and the engineering problems involved are of diverse nature. These lands are to be redeemed from excessive aridity. When the excessively humid lands are redeemed, their fertility is almost inexhaustible, and the agricultural capacity of the United States will eventually be largely increased by the rescue of these lands from their present valueless condition. In like manner, on the other hand, the arid lands, so far as they can be redeemed by irrigation, will perennially yield bountiful crops, as the means for their redemption involves their constant fertilization.

To a great extent, the redemption of all these lands will require extensive and comprehensive plans, for the execution of which aggregated capital or cooperative labor will be necessary. Here, individual farmers, being poor men, cannot undertake the task. For its accomplishment a wise prevision, embodied in carefully considered legislation, is necessary. It was my purpose not only to consider the character of the lands themselves, but also the engineering problems involved in their redemption, and further to make suggestions for the legislative action necessary to inaugurate the enterprises by which these lands may eventually be rescued from their present worthless state. When I addressed myself to the broader task as indicated above, I found that my facts in relation to some of the classes of lands mentioned, especially the coast swamps of the Gulf and some of the flood plain lands of the southern rivers, were too meager for anything more than general statements. There seemed to be no immediate necessity for the discussion of these subjects; but to the Arid Region of the west thousands of persons are annually repairing, and the questions relating to the utilization of these lands are of present importance. Under these considerations I have decided to publish that portion of the volume relating to the arid lands, and to postpone to some future time that part relating to the excessively humid lands....

In the preparation of the contemplated volume I desired to give a historical sketch of the legislation relating to swamp lands and executive action thereunder;

another chapter on bounty lands and land grants for agricultural schools, and still another on land grants in aid of internal improvements—chiefly railroads. The latter chapter has already been prepared by Mr. Willis Drummond, jr., and as the necessary map is ready I have concluded to publish it now, more especially as the granted lands largely lie in the Arid Region. Mr. Drummond's chapter has been carefully prepared and finely written, and contains much valuable information.

To the late Prof. Joseph Henry, secretary of the Smithsonian Institution, I am greatly indebted for access to the records of the Institution relating to rainfall. Since beginning my explorations and surveys in the far west, I have received the counsel and assistance of the venerable professor on all important matters relating to my investigations ; and whatever of value has been accomplished is due in no small part to his wisdom and advice. I cannot but express profound sorrow at the loss of a counselor so wise, so patient, and so courteous.

I am also indebted to Mr. Charles A. Schott, of the United States Coast Survey, to whom the discussion of the rain gauge records has been intrusted by the Smithsonian Institution, for furnishing to me the required data in advance of publication by himself. Unfortunately, the chapters written by Messrs. Gilbert, Dutton, Thompson, and Drummond have not been proof-read by themselves, by reason of their absence during the time when the volume was going through the press; but this is the less to be regretted from the fact that the whole volume has been proof-read by Mr. J. C. Pilling, whose critical skill is all that could be desired.

QUESTIONS

1. Why does Powell think that rainfall is an important consideration for the settlement of the West?
2. Who might be capable of achieving the "extensive and comprehensive plans" needed to make the arid West agriculturally productive and suitable for settlement?
3. Who does he indicate is not able to achieve these plans alone?
4. How do Powell's descriptions and Hillers's photograph differ from Ludlow's portrayals and Bierstadt's painting?

16.5. *SOUTHERN WORKMAN AND HAMPTON SCHOOL RECORD* AND EDNA DEAN PROCTOR, "COLUMBIA'S ROLL CALL" (JUNE 1892) AND "THE INDIANS' APPEAL" (JANUARY 1892)

The establishment of Indian boarding schools became an official U.S. policy with the passage of the Dawes Act on February 8, 1887. Indian education was a simple idea proposed by reformers who thought they were providing a humanitarian alternative to violence. Indian children were taken away from their "ignorant" parents and "backward" communities and trained to be Americans who cherished individualism and republicanism over tribal life.

Indian boarding schools commemorated the passage of the Dawes Act with a special holiday and an elaborate pageant designed to reinforce the ideals of Indian assimilation. The Hampton School celebrated with a stage production, "Columbia's Roll Call."

COLUMBIA'S ROLL CALL

The platform was cleared for the scenic representation of "Columbia's Roll Call," a reproduction, with some abbreviation, of that given on Indian Citizenship day, of which our March number contained a full account. The characters were taken by the same students as then, so far as possible, and they entered into it with equal spirit. Juanita presided with queenly dignity as Columbia, "from her century terraced height;" the heroes who had made her great, summoned forth from the past by the Heralds of Fame and History, took their stand at her right hand—Columbus, Capt. John Smith; Miles Standish and the Puritan maiden; John Elliot, Apostle to the Indians, William Penn and a sister of peace, and the great Washington. Again the "Indian Petitioner" threw herself at the foot of the throne, beseeching a share for her people with Columbia's children, and, to justify her plea, Fame and History summoned those who could balance the roll of pale face heroes—the friend of Columbus from San Salvador; Pocahontas the savior of Capt. John Smith, Samoset, welcomer of the pilgrims; one of Eliot's Indian converts; Taminend,

friend of William Penn, and the White Mingo, friend of Washington. The double line of heroes, in the varied beautiful costumes of the old world and the wilderness, made a brilliant setting for Columbia's throne, the keystone of the arch. Every word spoken by the characters was distinct and clear, and very sweetly the voices of the Pilgrims blended in Mrs. Heman's song of "The Breaking Waves Dashed High." But Columbia was not satisfied with past records. Had she not conferred her citizenship already on one other race? The Afro-American Student of Hampton stepped forward with the stars and stripes. What can the petitioner match with that? She is ready with "The Hampton Indian Student," who bearing the School's banner took stand opposite. "This is well for the present, what of the future?" "Who is ready to pledge our future?" "Speak for yourselves?" A rush from the ranks of the Indian school, and gathering under the Hampton flag they respond, in the song, "Spirit of Peace." "Brothers, we come at your altars to pray." "It is enough. Take my banner," says Columbia, "and your place as my citizens." "Speed our Republic, O Father on High!" What can close the scene but a gen-

Sources: "Columbia's Roll Call," *Southern Workman and Hampton School Record* 21, no. 6 (June 1892), 82; Edna Dean Proctor, "The Indians' Appeal," *Southern Workman and Hampton School Record* 21, no. 1 (January 1892), 11.

eral chorus of "My Country, 'tis of Thee." The Indian actors linger to listen to a representative of whom they may well be proud. A fitting close and beautiful addition to the tableau of Columbia's Roll Call was made, as before the half-circle of brilliantly costumed heroes of the past of two races, stepped the dignified, erect, high-souled woman, the representative and product of the best progress of one, the best philanthropy of the other—LaFlesche, the Arrow—Arrow of the Future from the bow of the Past strained by the cord of the Present.

THE INDIANS' APPEAL

You have taken our rivers and fountains And the
    plains where we loved to roam,—
Banish us not to the mountains
And the lonely wastes for home!
No! let us dwell among you;
Cheer us with hope again;
For the life of our fathers has vanished,
And we long by your side to be men.

Our clans that were strongest and bravest
Are broken and powerless through you;
Let us join the great tribe of the white men,
As brothers to dare and to do!
We will fight to the death in your armies;
As scouts we will distance the deer

Trust us, and witness how loyal
Are the ranks that are stranger to fear!

And the still ways of peace we would follow—
Sow the seed and the sheaves gather in,
Share your labor, your learning, your worship,
A life larger, better, to win.
Then, foeman no longer nor aliens,
But brothers indeed we will be,
And the sun find no citizens truer
As he rolls to the uttermost sea.

You have taken our rivers and fountains
And the plains where we loved to roam,—
Banish us not to the mountains
And the lonely wastes for home!
No! let us dwell among you;
Cheer us with hope again;
For the life of our fathers has vanished,
And we long by your side to be men.

QUESTIONS

1. What was the message of Indian Citizenship Day?
2. What does the first passage ask of the students who recited these words?
3. What do Anglo-American attempts to reform Native American peoples imply about the former's view of themselves?

16.6. HORACE GREELEY, EXCERPT FROM *AN OVERLAND JOURNEY FROM NEW YORK TO SAN FRANCISCO* (1860)

In 1859, Horace Greeley, editor of the *New York Tribune*, crossed the continent to outline a possible route for the transcontinental railroad and determine the possibilities for settlement along the route. Greeley joined a chorus of writers and politicians encouraging the construction of a transcontinental railroad.

Source: Horace Greeley, *An Overland Journey from New York to San Francisco in the Summer of 1859* (Lincoln: University of Nebraska Press, 1999), 368, 386.

Brochure of Alice's Adventures in the New Wonderland: The Yellowstone National Park (1885), University of Wyoming American Heritage Center, Toppan Library.

NEW YORK, Oct. 20, 1859.

I PROPOSE in this letter to present such considerations as seem to me pertinent and feasible, in favor of the speedy construction of a railroad, connecting at some point our eastern network of railways with the waters of the Pacific ocean....

Men and brethren! let us resolve to have a railroad to the Pacific—to have it soon. It will add more to the strength and wealth of our country than would the acquisition of a dozen Cubas. It will prove a bond of union not easily broken, and a new spring to our national industry, prosperity and wealth. It will call new manufactures into existence, and increase the demand for the products of those already existing.

It will open new vistas to national and to individual aspiration, and crush out filibusterism by giving a new and wholesome direction to the public mind. My long, fatiguing journey was undertaken in the hope that I might do something toward the early construction of the Pacific Railroad; and I trust that it has not been made wholly in vain.

QUESTIONS

1. What purposes, according to Greeley, will a transcontinental railroad serve?
2. How does the portrayal of "The Wonderland Route" depict the West, and more specifically, Yellowstone?

16.7. FRANK H. MAYER, "WE KILL THE GOLDEN GOOSE"

On the plains in the 1870s, cattle drives, ranching, overland migration, and depletion of resources contributed to the decline of the buffalo, but hunting and a short-lived but expansive world market for buffalo hides proved to be even more significant factors in the animal's disappearance.

I found it out every day when I went out scouting for something to shoot. A couple of years before it was nothing to see[—]5,000, 10,000 buff[alo] in a day's ride. Now if I saw 50 I was lucky. Presently all I saw was rotting red carcasses or bleaching white bones. We had killed the golden goose.

During my runner's years I, quite naturally, wasn't interested in overall figures on total number killed, shipped, and so forth. I was a runner, not a statistician. But if I'd had sense enough in those days I could have realized in a few minutes' time that the game was on the way out. I couldn't have done anything about it, but I could have foreseen that my future was rather dim as a buffalo runner.

Completely accurate figures will likely never be compiled, but here are some authentic ones from the Southwest Historical Society which will show how thoroughly we killed the golden goose.

Dodge City, Kansas, was known as the buffalo city, and more hides were shipped from there than from anywhere else. The shipments started in earnest in 1871, but figures for that year are missing. During the

Approximately 40,000 buffalo hides piled up in Rath and Wright's Buffalo Hide Yard, Dodge City, Kansas (1878), © Bettmann/CORBIS.

Source: Frank H. Mayer with Charles B. Roth, *The Buffalo Harvest* (Chicago: Sage Press, 1958), 86–87

winter of 1872–1873, one firm alone out of Dodge City shipped 200,000 hides. During the same year the same firm handled 1,617,000 pounds of buffalo meat, and $2,500,000 worth of buffalo bones. Now, that was big business in a small frontier town; and remember Dodge, although largest handler of buffalo hides and meat, was only one of a dozen cities that were on rails and shipping buffalo.

But notice how swiftly the traffic dropped. The buffalo years were only seven, 1871 to 1878. The last big shipment was in 1878. It consisted of 40,000 hides, only a fifth of the number handled by the same firm from the same railhead seven years before. After that there weren't enough buffalo left to make handling profitable, so agents shut up their offices and got into some other racket, usually cattle, for fast on the heels of the buffalo came the cattle drives. Again Dodge assumed importance, took on a leading role.

Here are some other figures confirming the Dodge City figure I just cited.

In 1872, figures show that 1,491,489 buffalo were killed. In 1873, the high year, the figure given is 1,508,568. Now note this: in 1874, the total is only 158,583—the buffalo was decimated in just one year. Tragic picture, don't you think?

If you want to add the total killed during those three years you will see it comes to 3,158,730. But the Indian was getting his share, too, and Indian kills are set down by men who study records carefully enough to be listened to and believed, at 405,000 a year, or 1,215,000 in the three-year period.

Add the Indian crop to the white runners' crop and you will have a total kill for years 1872, 1873, and 1874 of 4,373,730 animals; in three years' time. No one can say how many were killed during the seven-year period the buffalo harvest lasted, but it must have been well over five million and might even have been close to six. Who knows?

I once, some years ago, sought a definite answer to that question by consulting railroads, because all the buffalo shipped from the ranges went by rail, and I figured if anyone would have the correct answer it would be the roads themselves. Everywhere I went I got the rather naive answer that the railroads couldn't

answer my question, because they kept no records! Since when did railroads stop keeping records?

The Santa Fe got the lion's share of the business, and about a third of the hides went out over the Santa Fe. But the Santa Fe didn't keep records either, I was told!

What happens whenever the law of diminishing returns sets to work, increased efficiency, happened on the buffalo ranges. I know when I started in we were wasteful. We shot only cows. Their fur was softer; their skins were thinner; they were more in demand. If we killed a bull or two and we killed more than one or two just for the devil of it, we didn't bother to skin him; just left him lay for the wolves and coyotes to come along and do our job for us. Later on, we were glad to kill bulls, calves, anything.

We were wasteful of hides, too, and I have figures showing how we got over that and increased our efficiency in handling. In 1872, for instance, every hide that reached market represented three or four buffalo killed. The others were wasted by improper handling, rotting on the ground, and similar shiftlessnesses. The next year we began to tighten up a little: for every hide reaching railhead two buffalo gave their only lives. And in 1874, each hide represented the death of one and a-fourth buffalo. Yes, we became efficient, economical when we had nothing to be efficient or economical about. Our efficiency came too late. We learned our profession, but had no chance to practice it, which is always a tragedy.

One by one we runners put up our buffalo rifles, sold them, gave them away, or kept them for other hunting, and left the ranges. And there settled over them a vast quiet, punctuated at night by the snarls and howls of prairie wolves as they prowled through the carrion and found living very good. Not a living thing, aside from these wolves and coyotes stirred.

The buffalo was gone.

QUESTIONS

1. How does Mayer account for the wastefulness of the buffalo hunt?
2. According to Mayer, who or what was responsible for the destruction of the buffalo?
3. Why does he take the time to give such detailed figures?

16.8. COLONEL WILLIAM F. CODY, EXCERPTS FROM *THE LIFE AND ADVENTURES OF "BUFFALO BILL"* (1917)

No single person blended history and myth better than William "Buffalo Bill" Cody. A legend in his own time, Cody was simultaneously a real person and a fictional character of international fame. Cody's heavily embellished life story of migration west as a youth from LeClaire, Iowa, over the plains and through the Rockies in the 1850s encompassed all of the experiences global audiences recognized as part of western frontier life: buffalo hunting, Indian fighting, bronco busting, gunslinging, and military scouting. In the 1880s, Cody's "Wild West" shows featured real life Westerners recreating idealized versions of contemporary western events. Cody traveled the world introducing Indian resistance leaders like Sitting Bull to various queens, the young German Kaiser Wilhelm, and hordes of peasants from Paris to Poland.

His Story shows his Devotion to Duty as a Child when Supporting his Widowed Mother, his Valuable Services to the Government while riding in the Famous "Pony Express" and Vividly Portrays his Thrilling Experiences as Hunter and Scout while acting as Guide to the Army and Trains of Prairie Schooners-His many Hair-breadth Escapes and Fights with Indians, Desperadoes and while Hunting Buffalo and other Wild Animals, as well as his Later Triumphs in Conducting the Tours of his Great Wild West Exhibition in the United States and Europe.

The whole work comprising an Authentic History of many Events inseparably interwoven with the Exploration, Settlement and Development of our Great Western Plains.

1917

DEDICATION

To the American and English publics, at whose generous hands have received so many favors, hospitable attention and numerous special kindnesses;

and

To the army of the frontier, the brave comrades and pioneers whose valorous deeds, though unwritten in their country's annals, and whose graves are unmarked save by the soughing oak or the modest daisy, but who have left the heritage of a million happy and prosperous homes in the redeemed West,

THIS BOOK

Is inscribed, by one who holds their courageous lives in grateful remembrance.

W. F. Cody (Buffalo Bill)

INTRODUCTION

The evolution of government and of civilisation, and the adaptation of one to the other, are interesting to the student of history; but particularly fascinating is the story of the reclamation of the Great West and the supplanting of the wild savages that from primeval days were lords of the country but are now become wards of the Government, whose guardianship they were forced to recognize. This story is one well calculated to inspire a feeling of

Source: Colonel William F. Cody, *The Life and Adventures of "Buffalo Bill"* (Chicago: John R. Stanton Co., 1917), ii-vi.

pride even in the breasts of those whose sentimentality impels to commiserate the hard lot of the poor Indian; for, rising above the formerly neglected prairies of the West are innumerable monuments of thrift, industry, intelligence, and all the contributory comforts and luxuries of a peaceful and God-fearing civilisation; those evidences that proclaim to a wondering world the march of the Anglo-Saxon race towards the attainment of perfect citizenship and liberal, free and stable government.

For the small part I have taken in redeeming the West from savagery, I am indebted to circumstances rather than to a natural, inborn inclination for the strifes inseparable from the life I was almost forced to choose. But to especially good fortune must I make my acknowledgments, which protected me or preserved my life a hundred times when the very hand of vengeful fate appeared to lower its grasp above my head, and hope seemed a mockery that I had turned my back upon. Good fortune has also stood ever responsive to my call since I first came before the public, and to the generous American and English peoples, as well as to kind fortune, I here pour out a full measure of profound thanks and hearty appreciation, and shall hold them gratefully in my memory as a remembrance of old friends, until the drum taps "lights out" at the close of the evening of my eventful life.

QUESTIONS

1. How does Cody make his personal story a national narrative?
2. Why do you think his story became an international sensation?
3. Cody worked closely with Indians most of his life. What tensions do you see between his desire for "civilization" and his concerns about Indian culture, as revealed by this brief sample of his autobiography?

CHAPTER 17

A NEW INDUSTRIAL AND LABOR ORDER, 1877–1900

17.1. VISUAL DOCUMENT: SINGER SEWING MACHINE ADVERTISEMENT (c. 1890)

This advertisement for the Singer Sewing Machine Company was published around 1890.

QUESTIONS

1. Who is the audience for this advertisement?
2. Why did Singer choose the slogan, "All Nations Use Singer Sewing Machines"? What point is the company trying to make?
3. How does the company depict the people from around the world using their sewing machines?

17.2. VISUAL DOCUMENT: *FRANK LESLIE'S ILLUSTRATED NEWSPAPER*, "THE FEMALE SLAVES OF NEW YORK—'SWEATERS' AND THEIR VICTIMS" (NOVEMBER 3, 1888)

This illustration appeared in *Frank Leslie's Illustrated Newspaper* on November 3, 1888. *Frank Leslie's* was a popular periodical that illustrated news and events with drawings in the years before photographs could be published cheaply and clearly.

Source: Frank Leslie's Illustrated Newspaper, November 3, 1888/Library of Congress.

QUESTIONS

1. What do you notice first about these drawings?
2. What are the main points that the artist is trying to make about sweatshops? How does he make his point of view clear?
3. Based on this source, what conclusions can you draw about work in the sweatshops?

17.3. EMMA E. BROWN, EXCERPTS FROM "CHILDREN'S LABOR: A PROBLEM" (DECEMBER 1880)

One of the most industrialized states in the country, Massachusetts passed several child labor laws in the 19th century limiting the employment of children. The law made it illegal to employ children under the age of 10 and established educational requirements, including mandatory certification from school committees, for employed children between the ages of 10 and 14. In 1880, journalist Emma E. Brown reported on the effectiveness of the law in an article published in the *Atlantic Monthly*.

During the past year some hundred and sixty factories in the State that had been inspected give an average of only two per cent where strict compliance was found....In one factory the inspector was shown a file of certificates which gave the names of thirteen children employed in the mills, but no data on their ages. Singling out, at random, a bright little fellow busily at work as a "doffer," the inspector asked him his name and age. "John Donnelly, sir, and I'm goin' on twelve years," was the ready response.

"But how is this?" said the officer, running over the list of certificates he still held in his hand. "There's no such name here as 'John Donnelly' and—Well, who is that little girl tubing the machine by the window?"

"Oh, her's Maggie Sweeney," said the little doffer, thrusting a huge square of tobacco into his mouth and hurrying back to his work, as if to avoid further questioning.

No Maggie Sweeney, either, was to be found among the names on the certificates, and the officer's suspicions being now fully aroused, he questioned a number of little operatives, whereupon it appeared that *not one half* of the children employed in the factory were represented upon the certificates. Further investigation also proved that a large proportion of these children were under ten years of age....

In another factory, where the certificates seemed to show a compliance with the laws, a fine, well-developed girl of fourteen was found who could neither read nor write. "She had worked in the mills ever since she could remember,—had *never had no time* to go to school."

In still another factory, the very first child interviewed was under ten years of age....

Systematic investigation has shown that of the 13,000 children employed in various factories

Source: Emma E. Brown, "Children's Labor: A Problem," *Atlantic Monthly*, December 1880, 787–92.

throughout the State in 1878 only 4575 received the legal amount of schooling; and that among the 282,485 children in Massachusetts between the ages of five and fifteen there are no less than 25,000 children who never have been present in either our public or private schools.

An overseer in one of the print works in the State says: "There seems to be a growing disposition on the part of parents to put their children to work before they are of the legal age, and to avoid sending them to school the length of time required by law. Scarcely a day passes but mothers come to the mills and beg us to use our influence in procuring employment for their children."

"We endeavor to comply with the school law," said a prominent mill owner to one of the inspectors, "but find it extremely difficult, as parents again and again give false statements regarding their children's ages."...

"Please, sir, could Denise have a permit to stay in the mills a month longer? It's time she was in school, I know but the father is all drawn up with rheumatis', and they've took him to the 'ospital, and I don't know how ever in the world we're goin' to git along if Denise has to leave the mills!"

It was all said in one breath, and the superintendent of the schools, glancing up from his books, saw a woman of thirty-five or thereabouts, with a peculiar, dazed expression, and eyes as dull and faded as the old gray waterproof she was nervously twitching with one finger.

He answered, not unkindly, "We cannot give any such permit. Besides, you are liable to a fine of fifty dollars, if the child is kept out of school. How old did you say she was?"

"Eleven years, sir."...

"Has she ever been to school?"

"Oh, yes, sir. Tell the gentleman, Denise, what reader you were in last."

"'Twas the First Reader,—the primer, you know," whispered the little girl, hanging down her head.

"A child of eleven years ought to be farther advanced than that!" remarked the superintendent.

"I suppose so," acknowledged the mother, with a sigh; "but I couldn't spare her to go to school when she was a earnin' twenty cents a day."

"Has your husband been a drinking man?"

"Oh, no. Not but that he would take a glass, now and then, but it never got the better of him,—oh no! He's always been a good husband, and we got along nicely whilst he was well and a gittin' fair wages. Denise never worked a day in the mills, sir, till the rheumatis' took *him*. He was a shoemaker by trade, and I've been a takin' in sewing, off and on, as I could git it; but work is scarce now, sir, and they say at the 'ospital as how he may never be able to use his hands agin, sir, and it's more nor I know what ever's a goin' to become of us!..."

The superintendent shook his head. "I am really very sorry for you, madam, but according to the law your little girl must enter school to-morrow."...

My friend, who had happened in at the superintendent's office and heard the whole conversation, resolved to investigate the case. She found the woman's story true in every particular....

My friend left the office in a brown study. "Can it be a normal state of things," she said to a certain political economist, "when children of eleven years are reckoned among the bread winners of a State?"

"Something must be wrong," he answered, "when an organic law of production is violated, as is the case in Massachusetts, where children between the ages of ten and fifteen constitute forty-four percent of the whole number of working people, and yet produce but twenty-four percent of the income!"

"But is it not possible for a strong, able-bodied man, if he is temperate and provident, to earn enough to support his family and keep his children in school till they are fifteen?"

"It certainly ought to be, but with the present relation of wages to cost of living in Massachusetts it seems that a laboring man with a family cannot keep out of debt with a yearly income of *less* than $600. Now, the fact is that the majority of workingmen earn *less* than $600 a year. I know of one Irish family where both the father and eldest son, a child of about twelve, work in the mills. Their combined earnings amount to $564....The family numbers six, and one of the four children the parents have kept in school. They dress shabbily, occupy a tenement of four rooms in one of the most unhealthy localities in the city, and are in a wretched condition generally. Knowing that the family were constantly running in debt, I inquired into their items of expense, and found the yearly amount to be [$589]....This total of $589 is a larger expenditure than is warranted by the income of $564. Subtract from this income the child's wages, which amount to $132, and you find the father's income to be only $432. What would be the financial condition of this family without the child's labor? I cannot tell how provident they are, but it is difficult to see where their expenses could be lessened."...

"It would seem, then, that without children's assistance, other things remaining equal, the majority of workingmen's families in Massachusetts would be in poverty or in debt?"

"That would seem, indeed, to be the true statement of the case."

In England, the over-working and under-schooling of minors is now a subject of heavy penalties; but past generations of factory children have already given rise to an almost distinct class of English working people,—pale, sallow, and stunted both in physical and mental growth.

How long will it be before a deteriorated race like the Stockinger, Leicester, and Manchester spinners springs up on our New England soil?...

QUESTIONS

1. How would the author of this article answer her own question regarding child labor: "Who is to blame"?
2. According to the author, what are the short-term and long-term consequences of child labor?
3. How would an industrialist of this era have responded to this article?

17.4. VISUAL DOCUMENT: BERNHARD GILLAM, *THE PROTECTORS OF OUR INDUSTRIES*, IN *PUCK* (FEBRUARY 7, 1883)

This cartoon, entitled "The Protectors of Our Industries," was published in *Puck*, a popular magazine that commented on politics and culture, in 1883.

QUESTIONS

1. What do each of the characters and symbols in the cartoon represent?
2. Who, according to the cartoonist, are "The Protectors of our Industries"?
3. What is the cartoonist trying to say about American society in the 1880s?

Source: The Granger Collection, NYC.

THE PROTECTORS OF OUR INDUSTRIES.

17.5. JOHN BROPHY, EXCERPTS FROM A *MINER'S LIFE* (1964)

Born the son of a coal miner in industrial Lancashire, England, in 1883, John Brophy immigrated to the coal fields of Pennsylvania with his parents when he was nine years old and entered the mines at the age of 12. Brophy dedicated his life to labor unions and rose to prominence as a leader in the United Mine Workers, the Committee for Industrial Organization (CIO), and the AFL-CIO. In this excerpt from his autobiography, Brophy discusses the tradition of labor activism that British miners carried with them to the Pennsylvania coal fields in the late 19th century and the obstacles they faced.

Source: John Brophy, *A Miner's Life* (Madison: University of Wisconsin Press, 1964).

probably learned as much, if not more, about America sitting out under the apple tree in my uncle's garden as I did in school. In the warm weather, people would gather there to talk about the old country and the new, and I was always there, taking in everything that was said. People would talk about conditions of work in the mines of central Pennsylvania. Talk of hard times and grievances led to discussion of the need for a union. These British miners had had a good union at home, and they saw the need for one in Pennsylvania, too. The Knights of Labor had had some following, but were declining. Local Assemblies of the miners in the Knights of Labor had been brought together into District Assembly 135, the nearest thing to a national union allowed by the structure of the Knights, and I heard many discussions of its ideals and purposes. The national leadership stressed co-operation and education—self-improvement, you might call it—as the solution to the workers' problems, and discouraged strikes and even boycotts against unfair employers. The high point of the movement had been reached in 1886, before our arrival in America, and I heard many discussions of the bomb explosion at Haymarket Square in Chicago that year, which was blamed on the Knights and contributed to their downfall. Closer to us, in time and distance, was the Homestead steel strike of 1892. These tales of violence made it clear even to me that it would take more than talk to win decent conditions from the employers....

In January, 1890, District 135 of the Knights of Labor and the National Progressive Union of Miners and Mine Laborers merged into the United Mine Workers of America, but the merger was largely on paper. The Pennsylvania locals kept alive their interest in the Knights of Labor. At best, the new union was not very strong, and the depression of the early nineties did it no good. All through 1892 and 1893, prices were falling, wages being cut, and miners being thrown out of work altogether, or kept on at part-time work only. Public appeals for help for the miners met with no response in the capitals of the mining states. The leaders of the union decided to follow the strategy used by the English miners a few years before—to call a suspension of work until the glut of coal on the market was eliminated, and then try to restore the wage

rates prevailing in May, 1893. On April 1, 1894, the suspension began. Although the national union had barely 13,000 dues-paying members and less than $3000 in the treasury at the time, 125,000 miners in eight states answered the call. Eight weeks after the strike began, the union claimed that strikers numbered 180,000, but the effort failed to achieve its purpose. Prolonged depression, with coal consumption at a minimum, had created a terribly glutted market to begin with. And the stoppage had not had the desired effect in reducing surpluses, because of increased activity in the anthracite fields untouched by the strike, and in unorganized Virginia, Maryland, and West Virginia. By the end of July, the strike was lost. In most districts, including central Pennsylvania, the union disappeared completely.

Both my father and my uncle were active in the strike. They picketed mines which tried to operate with scabs. Most of the latter were native [born] Americans from the back country, known as "buckwheaters," because their little patches of land would grow buckwheat, but not much else. A few recent immigrants from central Europe were brought in as strikebreakers. To help maintain morale, the miners would parade to other towns and hold mass meetings. There was no money for relief, of course, but the miners helped each other out as much as they could, which was not much, and some storekeepers donated flour and other food. In spite of efforts to divide the miners along lines of national origin, they held together very well.

During the strike, the press used the argument that the strike was a foreign conspiracy, because many leaders of the union were British immigrants. This gave superpatriots a chance to fight the Revolutionary War all over again and drive the agents of British imperialism away from our shores. It is strange how often this kind of "patriotism" has been used successfully against just such agents of foreign imperialism as my father and uncle....

Our lot was hard enough during the strike, though we had the consolation that we were suffering to improve things for the miners. But with the end of the strike, something close to despair descended upon us. Both my uncle and father were blacklisted and denied work at their old places in the Pardee mine....

QUESTIONS

1. What ideas and strategies concerning labor unions did British miners bring with them when they immigrated to the United States?

2. What obstacles did the unionized miners face in attempting to better their condition?

17.6. TWO VIEWS OF THE HOMESTEAD LOCKOUT: EXCERPTS FROM *THE MANUFACTURER AND BUILDER* (AUGUST 1892) AND *NEW ENGLAND MAGAZINE* (SEPTEMBER 1892)

Americans drew different conclusions about the violent Homestead Lockout that occurred in 1892 and the subsequent victory of Carnegie Steel over its union workers. The following two editorials represent two opposing views. The first of these editorials was published in *The Manufacturer and Builder*, which, as its name suggests, was a trade journal for industrialists and other businessmen. The second editorial was published in *New England Magazine*, which was a general interest illustrated monthly published in Boston.

THE HOMESTEAD AFFAIR

As indicated last month in our comments on the Homestead incident, the conflict is virtually ended, and the works are now being operated by non-union workmen. The disappointed and desperate leaders of the subdued rioters, it is true, continue to talk of the fight for the recognition of their union as still going on, but this silly opposition to the logic of facts deceives no one but the more ignorant and unthinking of the rank and file of their following. In fact, the fight was lost to the men from the moment when they placed themselves, at the outset, in the position of law-breakers, and gave the American people an object lesson in the practical application of the principles of trades unionism, which they are not likely soon to forget. On the whole, and barring the reckless sacrifice of human life involved in this episode, it may prove in the end to be a blessing, if it shall teach the greatly-needed lesson to the authorities everywhere throughout the land that lawlessness is a crime against the liberty and prosperity of every law-abiding citizen, and is none the less criminal because committed in the name of an irresponsible labor organization; if it shall teach the great body of intelligent citizens that sympathy for law-breakers means direct encouragement to lawlessness; and more than all, if they shall be brought to a realizing sense of the infamous tyranny that is practiced by that small fraction of the working force of the country that is "organized," wherever it has had the opportunity of exhibiting its power, upon the great body of workmen

Sources: The Manufacturer and Builder, "The Homestead Affair," August 1892, 185; *New England Magazine*, "Editor's Table," September 1892, 130–35.

who prefer to exercise their rights, as freemen and sell their labor at their own price....

In contemplating these facts, these questions obtrude themselves: Has the non-union workman no rights that the unionist or amalgamationist is bound to respect? Will the people of this country continue to permit an organized band of ruffians to interfere with the indefensible right of every freeman to earn his living by selling his labor where and to whom he pleases? And, lastly, how long will the employers of labor continue to suffer the insolence and interference of advisory committees, walking delegates, and other creations of trades unionism?

EDITOR'S TABLE

The attitude of the better newspapers of the country with reference to the recent unhappy affair at Homestead has been such as to afford some encouraging indication that the American people are gradually getting educated upon industrial questions, and getting clearer ideas of relative justice and of some simple matters of right and wrong. The clear headed men of the press have seen plainly, as most men of the pulpit have said... that whatever else is to be said about the Homestead strike and its results, the one matter of serious moment and the one great wrong, so great as almost to excuse inattention to all else, was the organization of a private military force by the Carnegie Company, or its manager for the time, a private little army of its own, and the attempt to smuggle this armed force into its fortified works, on its own account, to cope with the disaffected workmen, instead of calling for such protection as was needed upon the constituted authorities of the State....

We have seen exhibitions of "Pinkerton men" in some previous struggles between employers and employees in this country....But we have never had a wholesale exhibition of the character of that which has just been witnessed at Homestead,—and for the credit of the republic it is to be hoped that we shall never have another....No one who is familiar with the government and the social conditions of England or France or Germany can conceive of a great corporation in Liverpool or Lyons or Leipzig, whose property was in any real danger, doing anything but apply to the State for protection and suppression of disor-

der....The Fort Frick and Pinkerton exhibition which we have just been witnessing at Homestead shows that we are not in advance of the nations of western Europe, but in important respects behind them, in the securities for liberty, equality, and real democracy. It is an exhibition befitting only the feudal middle age....It is insufferable and a thing not to be endured in a democracy, that any men or any companies of men, for whatever purposes incorporated, should have the power of organizing and arming military and police forces of their own, to act in the settlement of affairs in which they are themselves interested parties, and to shoot men when and how they direct....

The American workingmen are not Anarchists, the men of the American labor unions are not Anarchists,—the sooner all good people take that fact peaceably to heart, the better....Not one brick of the Carnegie property was damaged through all the tumult. Not one of the thousands of striking men, we are authoritatively told, was once found drunk. Of what company of four thousand bankers or railroad magnates, suddenly thrown into a month's idleness at New York or Newport, could as much be said?...Let none of us need any second prompting to declare that if any man is indeed piling up millions out of the labor of discontented men, with whom he has driven sharp bargains about wages, and out of the profits is building schools or libraries or hospitals or churches, the title of "Christian philanthropist," which it tickles him this week to wear, shall not outlast the week, but shall give place to the plain and homely label, stuck fatally upon his forehead by the lightning of God—*An unjust man!* Let every one of us hold to strictest account the rich and privileged man.

QUESTIONS

1. What lessons did each magazine draw from the Homestead Lockout? What did Homestead symbolize for each?
2. According to each magazine, who committed acts of lawlessness?
3. Do these two perspectives share any common ground?
4. What do these contrasting views suggest about the relationship of labor and capital in the Gilded Age?

CHAPTER 18

CITIES, IMMIGRANTS, CULTURE, AND POLITICS, 1877–1900

18.1. WIKTORYA AND ANTONI OSINSKI, EXCERPTS FROM LETTERS FROM POLAND TO CHILDREN WHO MIGRATED TO THE UNITED STATES (1902–1908)

These letters were dictated by Wiktorya and Antoni Osinski and written by a literate acquaintance to their sons: Jan, who migrated to America first, and Michal (Michalek), who soon followed. The family lived in Poland near the German frontier in an area where residents regularly emigrated to Germany for seasonal work and where emigration to the United States had been occurring for many years.

January 3, 1902

Dear Son,

We thank you nicely for the 10 roubles. You wrote us, dear son, that we might make [from this money] a better Christmas tree and make ourselves merry during the holidays. I should be much merrier if you came here.... This money has been of use to us, for we were owing 8 roubles to the carpenter, so your father gave them back at once. He brought 2 roubles home. Of these two we gave 8 zloty for a holy mass, and the rest we took for our Christmas festival. Father says so [to you] "Economize as much as you can so that no one [of your creditors] may drum at your windows when you come back." If our Lord Jesus allows us to get rid of our debts, we shall remember you, for our debts amount to 70 roubles. If God grants us health in this New Year we hope to pay them back, for last year there were only expenses, and no income at all.

Now inform us whether you are near a church, and whether you have already been in it a few times, and how is the divine service celebrated, whether there are sermons and teachings like those in our country. And inform me how do you like America, whether you like it as much as our country. Describe everything, for it is difficult for me [to write you long letters], since I cannot write myself to you. Now I admonish you, dear

Source: William I. Thomas and Florian Znaniecki, *The Polish Peasant in Europe and America: Monograph of An Immigrant Group,* vol. 1 (Boston: Gorham Press, 1918), 404–06, 413, 417–18.

son, live in the New Year honestly and religiously, for I pray our Lord Jesus for you every day, when going to bed and rising.

May 25, 1902

Dear Son,

You asked me to send you one *gomolka*.[1] When they read it to me, I laughed. It is true that I had none when she left [a cousin going to America], but if she would have taken it, I would have found one. So instead of cheese I send you a godly image—you will have a token—and from every member of the family I send you a small medal. When you receive this image, kiss it, that it may bless you in your work and your health and guard you against a mortal sin.... Michal sends you a package of tobacco and Aleksander a package of cigarettes....

You wrote to your father asking, what he would send you. Well, he sends you these words: "Remember always the presence of God...." Now I send you other words: "Work and economize as much as you can."...

I can send you nothing more, dear son, except my heart. If I could take it away from my breast and divide it into four parts, as you are four whom our Lord Jesus keep for me still, I would give a part to every one, from love.

July 29, 1903

Dear Son,

You wrote us, dear son, to take a maid-servant, but the worst is that none is to be found; they all go to America. Probably we shall manage alone until you come back. Aleksander can already help me in the heaviest work, he can already reach the sheaves to the cart and then pull them back, and Frania also works as she can. So instead of sending money for the servant, if you have any, send them a little for *okrezne*.[2] Then they will be still more willing to work, and when you come back we shall give you whatever you can.... Father was ill for a week; now he has already recovered.... I was so grieved, for father lay ill, and Michalek was on the journey—such is my luck, that I am always at work and in grief....

As to Michal, we tried by all means to persuade him not to go, particularly I told him about his journey, how it would be, and that he would be obliged to work heavily. But he always answered that he is ready to work, but he wants to get to America and to be with you. Now I beg you, dear son, if he is in grief, comfort him as much as you can and care for him. You wrote me, dear son, not to grieve about you, but my heart is always in pain that we are not all together or at least all in our country, that we might visit one another.

September 24, 1904

Dear Son,

We are very glad that you are in good health and that you succeed well, so that you even want to take us to America. But for us, your parents, it seems that there is no better America than in this country. Your father says he is too weak and sickens too often. I should be glad to see you, but it is impossible to separate ourselves in our old age. I have also no health; particularly my arms are bad...and you wrote that in America one must work hard, and often cannot get work even if he wants it, while here we have always work.

October 29, 1906

Dear Son [Michal],

We received your letter.... We are glad that you are in good health for we thought that you all were dead.[3] You had written, dear son, that you would write us something curious, so we waited impatiently thinking that perhaps you were already journeying home.... So now when we read this letter of yours we were very much grieved, for we remember you ten times a day and it is very painful to us that you evidently forget us. Dear son, since you did not come, surely we shan't see one another in this world, for this year a penalty was established, that if anybody who belongs to the army went away, his father must pay big money for him, and when he comes back after some years, he must serve his whole time in a disciplinary battalion....

Dear son, you write that you are getting on well enough. Thanks to God for this, but we beg you, we your parents, not to forget about God, then God won't

---

1 A small, homemade cheese.
2 Harvest festival.
3 Because they had not written home.

forget about you. It is very hard for us that we cannot see you. More than once we shed bitter tears that we have brought you up and now we cannot be with you.... May we at least merit to be in heaven together.

April 26, 1908

Dear Children,

We received your letter and the post-notification on Good Friday evening when we came back from the passion....

Dear children, you write that you think about taking Aleksander to America. But we and our work, for whom would it be left? You would all be there and we here. While if he goes to the army for 3 years and God keeps him and brings him happily back, he would help us as he does now. Well, perhaps Frania could remain upon this [farm]; but even so we could see him

no more. Moreover, now whole throngs of people are coming back from America...and the papers write that it won't be better, but worse.

QUESTIONS

1. What is the tone of these letters? What are the parents' chief concerns for their children who have immigrated to the United States?
2. Based on these letters, what impact did immigration have on the family and other villagers who remained in Poland?
3. Choose one of the letters and, based on your general knowledge of immigrant life in this era, write a response from one of the sons to his parents, addressing their concerns and describing his life in the United States.

18.2. VISUAL DOCUMENT: F. VICTOR GILLAM, *THE INEVITABLE RESULT TO THE AMERICAN WORKINGMAN OF INDISCRIMINATE IMMIGRATION*, IN *JUDGE* (DECEMBER 24, 1892)

This cartoon appeared in the periodical *Judge* in 1892 in the era when immigration to the United States was at its height.

THE INEVITABLE RESULT TO THE AMERICAN WORKINGMAN OF INDISCRIMINATE IMMIGRATION.

QUESTIONS

1. What does each of the main figures in the cartoon represent?
2. How do the cartoon's two settings—Ellis Island and the workingman's home—compare to one another?
3. What point is the cartoonist trying to make?
4. How might an immigrant laborer from this era respond to this cartoon? How would he or she defend his or her decision to immigrate to the United States?

Source: Judge, December 24, 1892.

18.3. DILLINGHAM COMMISSION, EXCERPT FROM REPORTS OF THE IMMIGRATION COMMISSION: EMIGRATION CONDITIONS IN EUROPE (1911)

In 1907, pressured by anti-immigration forces, the U.S. Senate formed a commission to study the sources of immigration and its impact on the United States. Known as the Dillingham Commission because of the leadership of Senator William Paul Dillingham of Vermont, the commission's report ultimately consisted of 42 volumes. The excerpt below comes from the volume that examined conditions in Europe that led to immigration to the United States and focuses on immigrants who returned to their home countries.

INFLUENCE OF RETURNED IMMIGRANTS

Emigrants who have returned for a visit to their native land are also great promoters of emigration. This is particularly true of southern and eastern European immigrants, who, as a class, make more or less frequent visits to their old homes. Among the returning emigrants are always some who have failed to achieve success in America, and some who through changed conditions of life and employment return in broken health. It is but natural that these should have a slightly deterrent effect on emigration, but on the whole this is relatively unimportant, for the returning emigrant, as a rule, is one who has succeeded and, as before stated, is inclined to exaggerate rather than minimize his achievements in the United States. . . .

The investigators of the Bureau of Immigration were impressed by the number of men in Italy and in various Slavic communities who speak English and who exhibit a distinct affection for the United States. The unwillingness of such men to work in the fields at 25 to 30 cents a day; their tendency to acquire property; their general initiative; and most concretely, the money they can show, make a vivid impression. They are dispensers of information, and are often willing to follow up the inspiration by loans to prospective emigrants.

The Commission was informed that one-third of the emigrants from Syria return for a time to their native country and later go back to the United States; but that in the meantime many of them build houses much superior to those of their neighbors and by such evidence of prosperity add to the desire for emigration among their countrymen. A man who left a little village in Transylvania in 1904 with the proceeds of the sale of two heads of cattle came back two years later with $500, and was the source of a genuine fever of emigration among his acquaintances, which has increased ever since. It is not be to wondered at that young men of spirit and ambition should want to emulate successful friends, and one can easily feel the truth of a statement made by a large land proprietor to the Royal Italian Agricultural Commission . . . : "Emigration is spontaneous. It becomes like a contagious disease. Even the children speak of going to America." . . .

Source: U.S. Senate, *Reports of the Immigration Commission: Emigration Conditions in Europe* (Washington: Government Printing Office, 1911), 58, 232–33.

EMIGRATION CONDITIONS IN EUROPE: ITALY

In many instances the Commission observed that the standard of living among repatriated Italians was noticeably higher than among peasants generally. Their houses were conspicuously better, as was the general appearance of their premises. The pigs, donkeys, and chickens had been banished from the houses, and there was about their homes and themselves an appearance of prosperity which was lacking among their nonemigrant neighbor.

In its report on Basilicata and Calabria the Royal Italian Agricultural Commission frequently refers to the returned emigrant, his changed views of life, and his effect upon his countrymen. The report says that—

> The first idea of the emigrants who return is to improve their houses. Many families that in times past have lived in one room only, and perhaps with a pig, now have two or three rooms, besides a kitchen and stable. In America they have had their standard of living raised. Those who return from America purchase a house with a small estate; when this is not sufficient they hire some lands or work on shares. The "Americans" come back improved, more clever, and intelligent....
>
> At the post offices [of Albano di Lucania] are deposited 60,000 lire as savings of the so-called Americans. * * * Returned countrymen do not adapt

themselves to the hardest labors to which they were subjected in other times, except in the case they work on their own estates. Many emigrants, not accustomed to possess money, after returning from America squander it....

A large proprietor, on being asked why the people emigrate, replied: "They see their countrymen returning well dressed, with an overcoat, a cigar in the mouth, and therefore they all wish to go away." It is evident that "Americans" live better and have cleaner houses. Emigration has created in Lagonegro a small bourgeois class that is called "American." They have returned from the United States and from Argentina; they have an income of from 3 to 5 lire (60 cents to $1) daily; they don't work; and they live like old employers in retreat, with their only ambition to become either councilors of the municipality or foremen in some labor society....

QUESTIONS

1. According to this report, what role did immigrants who returned to their villages in Europe play in the ongoing migration to the United States?
2. What new ideas and concepts did returned immigrants carry back with them to Europe?
3. What impact, if any, did returning immigrants have on the culture and social organization of their native villages?

18.4. VISUAL DOCUMENT: THOMAS NAST, *THE CHINESE QUESTION*, IN *HARPER'S WEEKLY* (FEBRUARY 18, 1871)

This cartoon by Thomas Nast appeared in *Harper's Weekly*, a popular magazine, in February 1871. The caption reads: "The Chinese Question—Columbia—Hands off, Gentlemen! America Means Fair Play for All Men."

QUESTIONS

1. Who does each figure in the cartoon represent? Which characters are depicted sympathetically? Which are represented critically?

2. How do the words describing the Chinese in the posters contrast and compare with the actions of the men on the right?

3. What is the point of view of the cartoonist regarding "The Chinese Question"? Is he for or against Chinese exclusion?

Source: Harper's Weekly, February 1871.

18.5. VISUAL DOCUMENT: "HOMELESS CHILDREN" ADVERTISEMENT IN *TECUMSEH CHIEFTAIN* (JULY 8, 1893)

In the late 19th century, American cities swarmed with children, some of whom were orphaned, others homeless. This ad appeared in Nebraska's *Tecumseh Chieftain* newspaper on July 8, 1893, notifying readers of the availability of 13 children under the auspices of the Children's Home Society. Founded in 1883 by the Reverend Martin Van Arsdale, the Children's Home Society sought to place street children in homes, rather than in poor houses and work farms.

QUESTIONS

1. How does this advertisement appeal to potential foster or adoptive parents?
2. What key descriptive words does the ad use to describe the children, and what do they suggest?

Source: Nebraska State Historical Society Library/Archives Division.

18.6. EXCERPTS FROM "CHEERED MARY E. LEASE" IN *NEW YORK WORLD* (AUGUST 11, 1896)

On August 11, 1896, the *New York World* reported on a speech given by the Populist speaker Mary Elizabeth Lease at New York's Cooper Union Hall. Lease, one of the most popular Populist speakers, gave her address in the midst of the highly contested 1896 presidential campaign.

CHEERED MARY E. LEASE
The Crowd Liked Her Denunciation of Cleveland and Whitney
SOCIALISM RAMPANT AND NOISY
Every Reference to Wealth and Its Owners Received with Wild Delight.
ATTACKED THE ENTIRE SOCIAL SYSTEM

Charmed by the seductive oratory of Mrs. Mary Elizabeth Lease, the free silver mass-meeting at Cooper Union last night nursed itself into all the semblance of a Socialistic gathering. From the beginning to the end, from the first sentence of introduction until the Kansas woman had concluded in a sonorous period, Socialism predominated. Every mention of gold or wealth was greeted with shouts and jeers, and the names of Whitney and Cleveland, of Vanderbilt and Rothschild were hailed with hisses and cat-calls....

It was very warm in the hall, and Mrs. Lease felt it. She was dressed in a light, lace-trimmed waist and black satin skirt, and her hair was neatly coiled. A winning smile was upon her face, and again and again she bowed to the plaudits of the crowd.

"I accept this splendid greeting from this splendid audience," she began, and the crowd howled appreciation of the compliment, "in evidence that there is no Mason and Dixon's line between the East and West. I accept it as an evidence of the fact that the people of the East and West are battling for common cause against a common foe. Not since the bleeding years of the war have party lines been so nearly obliterated, and the obedience to party leaders so refused as at the present time...."

At this point Mrs. Lease took the opportunity offered by cheering to wipe a fugitive drop from her ear....

"We stand to-day at the beginning of one of those revolutionary periods that mark an advance of the race. We stand at the period that marks a reformation.

"All history is illustrated by the fact that new liberties cannot exist with old tyrannies. New ideals ever seek new manifestations. The ideas of Christ could not live under the tyrannies of the Roman government. The ideals of the founders of this Government could not exist under the tyrannies of royal rule."

Striding to the edge of the platform, Mrs. Lease stretched out her hand, clenched her fingers and then roared with masculine energy:

"The grand principles of Socialism and the brotherhood of man cannot live under old forms of tyranny—neither under the forms of Old-World tyranny nor of British gold."

The demonstration that followed this announcement was remarkable. Two thousand throats sent up a shout that showed the sentiment of the meeting, and it was at least two minutes before absolute quiet prevailed. When Mrs. Lease proceeded, she spoke of the great prosperity this country had seen.

"Yet to-day," she cried, "our splendid theory of government is confronted by a great peril. We have become blind to evils that menace us. We are confronted with glutted markets and idle labor. It is a con-

Source: http://projects.vassar.edu/1896/leasespeech.html.

dition that makes it possible for a few men to become landlords of a proud city like this while God's poor are packed in the slums."

"Hooray!" yelled a man far back in the hall, "Hooray—ki—yi!"

The crowd took up the cry, and back and forth the cheers and yells and cat-calls rattled.

"Such a condition is not only a menace to Republican institutions, but a travesty upon the gospel of Jesus Christ..."

"Horray, horray!" yelled the man in the crowd again, and once more the hall resounded with the expression of the audience's temper....

"A condition by which the wealth accumulated by the common people is poured into lard tubs and oil wells to enable Mr. Rockefeller to found a college and Mr. Whitney to buy a diamond tiara for his daughter is a disgrace to the country.

"Once we made it our boast that this nation was not founded upon any class distinction. But now we are not only buying diamonds for their wives and daughters and selling our children to titled debauchees, but we are setting aside our Constitution and establishing a gold standard to help the fortunes of our hereditary foe.

"To-day, a determined and systematic effort is being made by our financiers to perpetuate a gold standard. Every influence that moulds public opinion has been bought up, and the great dailies in the employ of the gold syndicate have fallen into line. The whole power of the government administration is being used to deceive the people. We hear sound money and honest dollar applied to the most dishonest money that ever cursed a nation or enslaved a people...."

"An organized effort is making to deceive the people. There are two great enemies of thought and progress, the aristocracy of royalty and the aristocracy of gold...."

"But here in this country we find in place of an aristocracy of royalty an aristocracy of wealth...."

"We have advanced scientifically, ethically and otherwise," she said, "but in finance we have followed the barbaric methods of our ancestors and the teachings of college-bred idiots who tell us that gold is the only desirable coin."

This bon mot was delivered fiercely, and was as fiercely applauded. "College-bred idiots" hit the crowd....

Mrs. Lease then took a shy at the "crime of '73." She told how the Government had made contracts on a bimetallic basis and then had changed it to a single standard. Lincoln, she declared, had called such acts as that a crime against posterity.... During all the evening she made various flings at the press, but most of her speech was specially directed at the press seats.... [A] man shouted:

"Make 'em take it down! Make 'em take it down!" He meant the reporters.

"Yes, yes," roared the crowd, "make 'em take it down!"

Mrs. Lease smiled happily and brushed away the perspiration...and then she went at it....

"They say this question is so deep," said Mrs. Lease... "that the common people are not fit to decide it. They say 'leave it to the financiers.' We have left it to them too long, and while we have been sinking into bankruptcy our financiers have been growing millionaires."

After a few other remarks about gold and Great Britain and robbery Mrs. Lease made a ball of her handkerchief, dabbed her face once or twice and sat down. Great applause followed.

During the meeting resolutions were read by Secretary Barr. The resolutions applauded the work of the Democratic and Populistic conventions....They denounced also the application of the epithet "anarchist" to them by the capitalists and agents of capital. The sudden affection for the laborer evinced by certain newspapers was also condemned as suspicious. Government ownership of telegraph and railroad lines was also advocated.

When the resolutions were read and put to vote many cried "No! no!" to them. At this a man in the back of the hall demanded a rising vote and almost precipitated a fight. He was subdued, however and the resolutions were declared adopted.

QUESTIONS

1. Was the writer of this article supportive or critical of Lease and the Populists? What specific words does he use to describe Lease and her audience?

2. What key phrases from Lease's speech seem to best encapsulate her message?

3. Based on Lease's speech, what accounted for her popularity as a speaker? What would some Americans find appealing in her speech? Why would others reject her ideas?

CHAPTER 19

THE UNITED STATES EXPANDS ITS REACH, 1892–1912

19.1. MARY ELIZABETH LAME, "AWAKE UNITED STATES" SHEET MUSIC AND LYRICS (1898)

This sheet music was published in 1898, after the sinking of the U.S.S. *Maine*. Before the invention of radio or television, middle-class Americans purchased sheet music, gathered around their pianos, and played and sang the popular tunes of the day as entertainment.

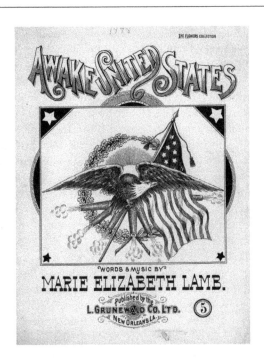

Source: Courtesy of the David M. Rubenstein Rare Book & Manuscript Library, Duke University.

How proudly sailed the warship Maine,
A nation's pride, without stain!
A wreck she lies, her sailors slain
By trech'rous butchers paid by Spain!

Awake! Thy Stars and Stripes unfurl!
And shot and shell and vengeance hurl!
Though clouds may gather, they will go
And sunlight follow after woe.

Awake! It is no dream
Dost hear the sailors scream?
Comrades will you go?
Avenge the cruel blow!

Not many suns shall rise and set
Before in battle we have met,

And made the Spanish butcher reel,
And downed the banners of Castile!

Stay their cruel hand,
In justice to our land.
Change their cruel art,
And crush their marble heart!

QUESTIONS

1. What does this song suggest about the mood of the country after the explosion of the *Maine*?
2. What images does the songwriter use to depict the United States and Spain?
3. Why would someone choose to buy this music and sing this song?

19.2. TWO VIEWS ON THE PHILIPPINES QUESTION: EXCERPTS FROM ANDREW CARNEGIE, "DISTANT POSSESSIONS" (AUGUST 1898) AND ALBERT BEVERIDGE, "THE MARCH OF THE FLAG" (SEPTEMBER 16, 1898)

In August 1898, war with Spain ended and Americans began to debate the question of whether to colonize the Philippines. Two views on this issue are presented below. Steel magnate and outspoken anti-imperialist Andrew Carnegie published the first essay in the *North American Review* in August 1898 shortly after the end of the war. Congressman Albert Beveridge of Indiana delivered the second essay as a speech on September 16, 1898—a month after Carnegie published his anti-imperialist essay—to a Republican meeting in Indianapolis.

DISTANT POSSESSIONS

Twice only have the American people been called upon to decide a question of such vital import as that now before them.

Is the Republic, the apostle of Triumphant Democracy, of the rule of the people, to abandon her political creed and endeavor to establish in other lands the rule of the foreigner o ver the people, Triumphant Despotism?

Sources: Andrew Carnegie, "Distant Possessions—The Parting of the Ways," *North American Review*, August 1898, 239–48; Albert Beveridge, "The March of the Flag," September 16, 1898, http://www.fordham.edu/halsall/mod/1898beveridge.asp.

Is the Republic to remain one homogeneous whole, one united people, or to become a scattered and disjointed aggregate of widely separated and alien races?

Is she to continue the task of developing her vast continent until it holds a population as great as that of Europe, all Americans, or to abandon that destiny to annex, and to attempt to govern, other far distant parts of the world as outlying possessions, which can never be integral parts of the Republic?

Is she to exchange internal growth and advancement for the development of external possessions which can never be really hers in any fuller sense than India is British, or Cochin-China French? Such is the portentous question of the day. Two equally important questions the American people have decided wisely, and their flag now waves over the greater portion of the English-speaking race; their country is the richest of all countries, first in manufactures, in mining and in commerce (home and foreign), first this year also in exports. But, better than this, the average condition of its people in education and in living is the best.... In international affairs her influence grows so fast and foreshadows so much, that one of the foremost statesmen has recently warned Europe that it must combine against her if it is to hold its own in the industrial world. The Republic remains one solid whole,... united, impregnable, triumphant; clearly destined to become the foremost power of the world, if she continues to follow the true path. Such are the fruits of wise judgment in deciding the two great issues of the past, Independence and The Union....

There are two kinds of national possessions, one colonies, the other dependencies. In the former we establish and reproduce our own race. Thus Britain has peopled Canada and Australia with English-speaking people, who have naturally adopted our ideas of self-government....

With "dependencies" it is otherwise. The most grievous burden which Britain has upon her shoulders is that of India, for there it is impossible for our race to grow. The child of English-speaking parents must be removed and reared in Britain. The British Indian official must have long respites in his native land. India means death to our race....

Inasmuch as the territories outside our own continent which our country may be tempted to annex cannot be "colonies," but only "dependencies," we need not dwell particularly upon the advantages or disadvantages of the former....

Some of the organs of manufacturing interests, we observe, favor foreign possessions as necessary or helpful markets for our products. But the exports of the United States this year are greater than those of any other nation in the world. Even Britain's exports are less, and Britain "possesses," it is said, a hundred "colonies" and "dependencies" scattered all over the world. The fact that the United States has none does not prevent her products and manufactures from invading Japan, China, Australia, New Zealand, Canada, and all parts of the world in competition with those of Britain. "Possession" of colonies or dependencies is not necessary for trade reasons....

As long as we remain free from distant possessions, we are impregnable against serious attack; yet, it is true, we have to consider what obligations may fall upon us of an international character requiring us to send our forces to points beyond our own territory. Up to this time we have disclaimed all intention to interfere with affairs beyond our own continent, and only claimed the right to watch over American interests according to the Monroe Doctrine, which is now firmly established.... I am no "Little" American, afraid of growth, either in population or territory, provided always that the new territory be American and that it will produce Americans, and not foreign races bound in time to be false to the Republic in order to be true to themselves....

To reduce it to the concrete, the question is: Shall we attempt to establish ourselves as a power in the Far East and possess the Philippines for glory? The glory we already have, in Dewey's victory.... The Philippines have about seven and a half millions of people, composed of races bitterly hostile to one another, alien races, ignorant of our language and institutions. Americans cannot be grown there.... But, if we take the Philippines, we shall be forced to govern them as generously as Britain governs her dependencies, which means that they will yield us nothing, and probably be a source of annual expense. Certainly, they will be a grievous drain upon revenue if we consider the enormous army and navy which we shall be forced to maintain upon their account. . . .

The aspirations of a people for independent existence are seldom repressed, nor, according to American ideas hitherto, should they be. . . . Is it possible that the Republic is to be placed in the position of the suppressor of the Philippine struggle for independence? Surely, that is impossible. With what face shall we hang in the schoolhouses of the Philippines the Declaration of our own Independence, and yet deny independence to them? . . . President McKinley's call for volunteers to fight for Cuban independence against the cruel dominion of Spain meets with prompt response, but who would answer the call of the President of an "imperial" republic for free citizens to fight . . . and slaughter the patriots of some distant dependency which struggles for independence? . . .

Let another phase of the question be carefully weighed. Europe is to-day an armed camp . . . because of fear of aggressive action upon the part of other nations touching outlying "possessions." . . .

It has never been considered the part of wisdom to thrust one's hand into the hornet's nest, and it does seem as if the United States must lose all claim to ordinary prudence and good sense if she enters this arena, and become involved in the intrigues and threats of war which make Europe an armed camp.

If we are to compete with other nations for foreign possession we must have a navy like theirs. . . . While the immense armies of Europe need not be duplicated, yet we shall certainly be too weak unless our army is at least twenty times what it has been—say 500,000 men. Even then we will be powerless as against three of our rivals. . . .

This drain upon the resources of these countries has become a necessity from their respective positions, largely as graspers for foreign possessions. The United States, happily, to-day has no such necessity, her neighbors being powerless against her, since her possessions are concentrated and her power is one solid mass. . . .

From every point of view we are forced to the conclusion that the past policy of the Republic is her true policy for the future; for safety, for peace, for

happiness, for progress, for wealth, for power—for all that makes a nation blessed.

THE MARCH OF THE FLAG

It is a noble land that God has given us; a land that can feed and clothe the world; a land whose coastlines would inclose half the countries of Europe; a land set like a sentinel between the two imperial oceans of the globe, a greater England with a nobler destiny.

It is a mighty people that He has planted on this soil; a people sprung from the most masterful blood of history. . . .

It is a glorious history our God has bestowed upon His chosen people; a history heroic with faith in our mission and our future; a history of statesmen who flung the boundaries of the Republic out into unexplored lands and savage wilderness; a history of soldiers who carried the flag across blazing deserts and through the ranks of hostile mountains, even to the gates of sunset; a history of a multiplying people who overran a continent in half a century; a history of prophets who saw the consequences of evils inherited from the past and of martyrs who died to save us from them; a history divinely logical, in the process of whose tremendous reasoning we find ourselves to-day.

Therefore, in this campaign, the question is larger than a party question. It is an American question. It is a world question. Shall the American people continue their march toward the commercial supremacy of the world? Shall free institutions broaden their blessed reign as the children of liberty wax in strength, until the empire of our principles is established over the hearts of all mankind?

Have we no mission to perform, no duty to discharge to our fellow-man? Has God endowed us with gifts beyond our deserts and marked us as the people of His peculiar favor, merely to rot in our own selfishness, as men and nations must, who take cowardice for their companion and self for their deity—as China has, as India has, as Egypt has? . . .

Hawaii is ours; Porto Rico is to be ours; at the prayer of her people Cuba finally will be ours; in the islands of the East, even to the gates of Asia, coaling stations are to be ours at the very least; the flag of a liberal government is to float over the Philippines, and may it be the banner that Taylor unfurled in Texas and Fremont carried to the coast.

The Opposition tells us that we ought not to govern a people without their consent. I answer, The rule of liberty that all just government derives its authority from the consent of the governed, applies only to those who are capable of self-government. We govern the Indians without their consent, we govern our territories without their consent, we govern our children without their consent. How do they know that our government would be without their consent? Would not the people of the Philippines prefer the just, humane, civilizing government of this Republic to the savage, bloody rule of pillage and extortion from which we have rescued them?

They ask us how we shall govern these new possessions. I answer: Out of local conditions and the necessities of the case methods of government will grow. If England can govern foreign lands, so can America. If Germany can govern foreign lands, so can America. If they can supervise protectorates, so can America. Why is it more difficult to administer Hawaii than New Mexico or California? Both had a savage and an alien population; both were more remote from the seat of government when they came under our dominion than the Philippines are to-day....

There are so many real things to be done—canals to be dug, railways to be laid, forests to be felled, cities to be builded, fields to be tilled, markets to be won, ships to be launched, peoples to be saved, civilization to be proclaimed and the flag of liberty flung to the eager air of every sea. Is this an hour to waste upon triflers with nature's laws? Is this a season to give our destiny over to word-mongers and prosperity-wreckers?

No! It is an hour to remember our duty to our homes. It is a moment to realize the opportunities fate has opened to us. And so it is an hour for us to stand by the Government.

Wonderfully has God guided us. Yonder at Bunker Hill and Yorktown His Providence was above us. At New Orleans and on ensanguined seas His hand sustained us. Abraham Lincoln was His minister and His was the altar of freedom the Nation's soldiers set up on a hundred battle-fields. His power directed Dewey in the East and delivered the Spanish fleet into our hands, as He delivered the elder Armada into the hands of our English sires two centuries ago. The American people can not use a dishonest medium of exchange; it is ours to set the world its example of right and honor. We can not fly from our world duties; it is ours to execute the purpose of a fate that has driven us to be greater than our small intentions. We can not retreat from any soil where Providence has unfurled our banner; it is ours to save that soil for liberty and civilization.

QUESTIONS

1. Why does Carnegie believe that the United States should refrain from colonizing the Philippines, and why does Beveridge think the United States should make the Philippines a colony?

2. How do both Carnegie and Beveridge use history to make their claims?

3. Who do you think makes the most convincing case overall? Why?

4. How do Carnegie and Beveridge define "American"? What role does race play in the arguments of each man?

19.3. VISUAL DOCUMENT: PEARS' SOAP ADVERTISEMENT IN *THE COSMOPOLITAN* (1899)

This advertisement for a popular soap appeared in *The Cosmopolitan* in 1899. Spanish-American-Philippines war hero Admiral George Dewey appears at the center of the ad.

QUESTIONS

1. How do the makers of Pears' Soap use the Spanish-American-Philippines War to sell their product?

2. What does this ad reveal—in words and images—about racial attitudes and imperialism at the turn of the 20th century?

Source: Library of Congress Prints and Photographs Division

19.4. *RICHMOND PLANET* AND *WISCONSIN WEEKLY ADVOCATE*, EXCERPTS FROM LETTERS FROM AFRICAN AMERICAN SOLDIERS IN THE PHILIPPINES (1899–1900)

Black soldiers serving in the Philippines to put down the insurgency against the United States sent letters to African American newspapers relating their experiences on the islands. Some disheartened soldiers found that the color line extended far beyond the boundaries of the United States, while others saw action in the Philippines as a chance to prove their patriotism and their equality. The first and third letters below were published in the *Richmond Planet* on December 30, 1899, and December 22, 1900, respectively. The second letter was published in the Milwaukee newspaper *Wisconsin Weekly Advocate* on May 17, 1900.

Dear Mr. Editor:

We received copies of the *Planet* sent to us at this point. You can imagine how much we appreciated them when we had not seen a paper of any kind for weeks, and as for an Afro-American paper, I can not remember when I last laid eyes on one....

The whites have begun to establish their diabolical race hatred in all its home rancor in Manila, even endeavoring to propagate the phobia among the Spaniards and Filipinos so as to be sure of the foundation of their supremacy when the civil rule that must necessarily follow the present military regime, is established.

I felt it worth the while to probe the Filipino as to his knowledge and view of the American colored man that we might know our position intelligently. What follows is a condensed account of the results. The questions were put to the intelligent, well-educated Filipinos....

Ques. Do the Filipinos hold a different feeling toward the colored American from that of the white?

Ans. "Before American occupation of the islands and before colored troops came to the Philippines, Filipinos knew little if anything of the colored people of America....All were simply Americans to us. This view was held up to the time of the arrival of the colored regiments in Manila, when the white troops, seeing your acceptance on a social plane by the Filipino and Spaniard was equal to, if not better than theirs,...began to tell us of the inferiority of the American blacks—of your brutal natures, your cannibal tendencies—how you would rape our senioritas, etc. Of course, at first we were a little shy of you, after being told of the difference between you and them; but we studied you, as results have shown. Between you and him, we look upon you as the angel and him as the devil.

Of course, you are both Americans, and conditions between us are constrained, and neither can be our friends in the sense of friendship, but the affinity of complexion between you and me tells, and you exercise your duty so much more kindly and manly in dealing with us. We can not help but appreciate the differences between you and the whites."

Interview of Senor Tordorica Santos, a Filipino physician. By the difference in "dealing with us" expressed is meant that the colored soldiers do not push them

Source: Willard B. Gatewood, Jr., *Smoked Yankees and the Struggle for Empire: Letters from Negro Soldiers, 1898–1902* (Fayetteville, AK: University of Arkansas Press, 1987), 251–55, 279–81, 284–85.

off the streets, spit at them, call them damned "niggers," abuse them in all manner of ways, and connect race hatred with duty, for the colored soldiers has none such for them.

The future of the Filipino, I fear, is that of the Negro in the South. Matters are almost to that condition now. No one (white) has any scruples as regards respecting the rights of a Filipino. He is kicked and cuffed at will and he dare not remonstrate....

Yours truly,
John W. Galloway
Sgt. Major,
24th U.S. Infantry

Editor, New York Age

I have mingled freely with the natives and have had talks with American colored men here in business and who have lived here for years, in order to learn of them the cause of their (Filipino) dissatisfaction and the reason for this insurrection, and I must confess they have a just grievance. All this never would have occurred if the army of occupation would have treated them as people. The Spaniards, even if their laws were hard, were polite and treated them with consideration; but the Americans, as soon as they saw that the native troops were desirous of sharing in the glories as well as the hardships of the hard-won battles with the Americans, began to apply home treatment for colored peoples: cursed them as damned niggers, steal [from] and ravish them, rob them on the street of their small change, take from the fruit vendors whatever suited their fancy, and kick the poor unfortunate if he complained, desecrate their church property, and after fighting began, looted everything in sight, burning, robbing the graves.

This may seem a little tall—but I have seen with my own eyes carcasses lying bare in the boiling sun, the results of raids on receptacles for the dead in search of diamonds. The [white] troops, thinking we would be proud to emulate their conduct, have made bold of telling their exploits to us. One fellow, member of the 13th Minnesota, told me how some fellows he knew had cut off a native woman's arm in order to get a fine inlaid bracelet. On upbraiding some fellows one morning, whom I met while out for a walk (I think they belong to a Nebraska or Minnesota regiment,

and they were stationed on the Malabon road) for the conduct of the American troops toward the natives and especially as to raiding, etc., the reply was: "Do you think we could stay over here and fight these damn niggers without making it pay all it's worth? The government only pays us $13 per month: that's starvation wages. White men can't stand it." Meaning they could not live on such small pay. In saying this they never dreamed that Negro soldiers would never countenance such conduct. They talked with impunity of "niggers" to our soldiers, never once thinking that they were talking to home "niggers" and should they be brought to remember that at home this is the same vile epithet they hurl at us, they beg pardon and make some effeminate excuse about what the Filipino is called.

I want to say right here that if it were not for the sake of the 10,000,000 black people in the United States, God alone knows on which side of the subject I would be. And for the sake of the black men who carry arms for them as their representatives, ask them to not forget the present administration at the next election. Party be damned! We don't want these islands, not in the way we are to get them, and for Heaven's sake, put the party [Democratic] in power that pledged itself against this highway robbery. Expansion is too clean a name for it.

[Unsigned]

Sir:

I have the honor to address you as to the present situation in the Philippines. Two battalions of the 25th Infantry, colored, arrived in Manila Bay on July 31st, 1899....Since our landing on the Island of Luzon we have executed some of as hard and effective work as any other regiment in the Philippines, also made some of the more important captures of the campaign....

Wherever we have been stationed on the islands we have made friends with the natives and they always express regret when we are ordered from amongst them, especially if we have been stationed near them for any length of time.

Our officers and men always make it a rule wherever we are stationed to treat the natives with civility and we have always complied with this rule....

We treat them with due consideration, insurgent prisoners as well as peaceable natives; but whenever they show fight, they are greeted with a warm reception and they soon learn to their discontent what kind of fighting material, the seemingly peaceable black fighters of Uncle Sam's regular army are made out of.

We have been stationed in Zambales Province longer than in any other one place on the Island. We were the first U.S. soldiers to enter the province where we were met with strong resistance, but the Filipinos never once had the nerve to stand their ground when they were charged upon by the dusky fighters. They never have once scored a victory over the 25th Infantry....

We were jubilant over the prospects of going to China a few weeks ago, but...our wise Excellency, the President, has restored peace, which he always does whenever his good and wise judgment is called into play. The 25th would like to have had China added to her list, but we will be contented with our past accomplishments; but whenever duty calls us we will not be weighed and found wanting. Our courage has won us fame; our moral principles and kindness have won us friends; our good workmanship and how to deal with the enemy have won us fear; our good discipline has won us praise from our superiors....

I have read a good many accounts, by discharged volunteers and regulars through the American newspapers, of depredations committed upon Filipinos by our men in the field, which reports are false....The prisoners as well as the peaceable [natives] are treated with great consideration. Our officers take great pride in protecting [the natives]....

If a person were to search the roots of these reports they could easily see where they originate. Some men came into the army for pleasure and some for adventure, but when they enlist and are presented their field equipment and commence camp life, their expectation of feather mattresses...ham and eggs, quail on toast and other such delicacies are not realized, they commence to cry to go home; they generally turn [out] to be chronic kickers and newspaper correspondents.

It seems as if they expect to campaign in a Pullman Palace Car. The American Army is better off without such men....They should be corralled up and fed on beeftea and chicken broth until they can be given back to their parents....

Respectfully yours,
James Booker
Co. H, 25th Infantry

QUESTIONS

1. Based on these letters, what conclusions can you draw about the experiences of black soldiers in the Philippines?

2. What evidence suggests that these black soldiers experienced the war differently than white soldiers? What evidence suggests that their wartime experience was the same?

3. Several letters remark on violence perpetrated on Filipinos by American soldiers, whereas one letter claims these events never happened. What might account for this difference? What additional sources would you seek out to substantiate how soldiers treated Filipinos during the war?

CHAPTER 20

AN AGE OF PROGRESSIVE REFORM, 1890–1920

20.1. CONGRESSMAN GEORGE H. WHITE, EXCERPTS FROM FAREWELL ADDRESS TO CONGRESS (JANUARY 29, 1901)

With the rise of segregation, disfranchisement, and a vicious white supremacy campaign in his home state of North Carolina, Congressman George H. White, the only black Congressman at the turn of the 20th century, chose not to run for a third term, seeing his chances of being reelected as hopeless. He gave his last speech on the floor of Congress on January 29, 1901. It would be another 28 years before another black representative sat in Congress.

I want to enter a plea for the colored man, the colored woman, the colored boy, and the colored girl of this country. I would not thus digress from the question at issue and detain the House in a discussion of the interests of this particular people at this time but for the constant and the persistent efforts of certain gentlemen upon this floor to mold and rivet public sentiment against us as a people and to lose no opportunity to hold up the unfortunate few who commit crimes and depredations and lead lives of infamy and shame, as other races do, as fair specimens of representatives of the entire colored race....

In the catalogue of members of Congress in this House perhaps none have been more persistent in their determination to bring the black man into disrepute and, with a labored effort, to show that he was unworthy of the right of citizenship than my colleague from North Carolina, Mr. Kitchin. During the first session of this Congress...he labored long and hard to show that the white race was at all times and under all circumstances superior to the Negro by inheritance if not otherwise, and...that an illiterate Negro was unfit to participate in making the laws of a sovereign state and the administration and execution of them; but an illiterate white man living by his side, with no more or perhaps not as much property, with no more exalted character, no higher thoughts of civilization, no more knowledge of the handicraft of government, had by

Source: George H. White, speech addressed to the U.S. House of Representatives, on January 29, 1901, 56th Cong., 2d sess., *Congressional Record* 34, pt. 2:1635–38.

birth, because he was white, inherited some peculiar qualification....

In the town where this young gentleman was born, at the general election last August..., Scotland Neck had a registered white vote of 395, most of whom of course were Democrats, and a registered colored vote of 534, virtually if not all of whom were Republicans, and so voted. When the count was announced, however, there were 831 Democrats to 75 Republicans; but in the town of Halifax, same county, the result was much more pronounced.

In that town the registered Republican vote was 345, and the total registered vote of the township was 539, but when the count was announced it stood 990 Democrats to 41 Republicans, or 492 more Democratic votes counted than were registered votes in the township. Comment here is unnecessary....

It would be unfair, however, for me to leave the inference upon the minds of those who hear me that all of the white people of the State of North Carolina hold views with Mr. Kitchin and think as he does. Thank God there are many noble exceptions to the example he sets, that, too, in the Democratic party; men who have never been afraid that one uneducated, poor, depressed Negro could put to flight and chase into degradation two educated, wealthy, thrifty white men. There never has been, nor ever will be, any Negro domination in that State, and no one knows it any better than the Democratic party. It is a convenient howl, however, often resorted to in order to consummate a diabolical purpose by scaring the weak and gullible whites into support of measures and men suitable to the demagogue....

I trust I will be pardoned for making a passing reference to one more gentleman—Mr. Wilson of South Carolina—who, in the early part of this month, made a speech, some parts of which did great credit to him....But his purpose was incomplete until he dragged in the reconstruction days and held up to scorn and ridicule the few ignorant, gullible, and perhaps purchasable Negroes who served in the State legislature of South Carolina over thirty years ago....These few ignorant men who chanced at that time to hold office are given as a reason why the black man should not be permitted to participate in the affairs of the Government which he is forced to pay taxes to support....

If the gentleman to whom I have referred will pardon me, I would like to advance the statement that the musty records of 1868...as to what the Negro was thirty-two years ago, is not a proper standard by which the Negro living on the threshold of the twentieth century should be measured. Since that time we have reduced the illiteracy of the race at least 45 percent. We have written and published nearly 500 books. We have nearly 300 newspapers, 3 of which are dailies. We have now in practice over 2,000 lawyers, and a corresponding number of doctors. We have accumulated over $12,000,000 worth of school property and about $40,000,000 worth of church property. We have about 140,000 farms and homes, valued in the neighborhood of $750,000,000, and personal property valued about $170,000,000. We have raised about $11,000,000 for educational purposes, and the property per-capita for every colored man, woman and child in the United States is estimated at $75.

We are operating successfully several banks, commercial enterprises among our people in the South land, including one silk mill and one cotton factory. We have 32,000 teachers in the schools of the country; we have built, with the aid of our friends, about 20,000 churches, and support 7 colleges, 17 academies, 50 high schools, 5 law schools, 5 medical schools, and 25 theological seminaries. We have over 600,000 acres of land in the South alone. The cotton produced, mainly by black labor, has increased from 4,669,770 bales in 1860 to 11,235,000 in 1899. All this we have done under the most adverse circumstances.

We have done it in the face of lynching, burning at the stake, with the humiliation of "Jim Crow" cars, the disfranchisement of our male citizens, slander and degradation of our women, with the factories closed against us, no Negro permitted to be conductor on the railway cars...no Negro permitted to run as engineer on a locomotive, most of the mines closed against us. Labor unions—carpenters, painters, brick masons, machinists, hackmen and those supplying nearly every conceivable avocation for livelihood—have banded themselves together to better their condition, but, with few exceptions, the black face has been left out. The Negroes are seldom employed in our mercantile stores....

With all these odds against us, we are forging our way ahead, slowly, perhaps, but surely. You may tie us and then taunt us for lack of bravery, but one day we will break the bonds. You may use our labor for two and a half centuries and then taunt us for our poverty, but let me remind you we will not always remain poor. You may withhold even the knowledge of how to read God's word and...then taunt us for our ignorance, but we would remind you that there is plenty of room at the top, and we are climbing....

Now Mr. Chairman, before concluding my remarks I want to submit a brief recipe for the solution of the so-called American negro problem. He asks no special favors, but simply demands that he be given the same chance for existence, for earning a livelihood, for raising himself in the scales of manhood and womanhood, that are accorded to kindred nationalities. Treat him as a man; go into his home and learn his social conditions; learn of his cares, his troubles, and his hopes for the future; gain his confidence; open the doors of industry to him; let the word "negro," "colored," and "black" be stricken from all the organizations enumerated in the federation of labor. Help him to overcome his weaknesses, punish the crime-committing class by the courts of the land, measure the standard of the race by its best material, cease to mold prejudicial and unjust public sentiment against him, and my word for it, he will learn to support, hold up the hands of, and join in with that political party, that institution, whether secular or religious, in every community where he lives, which is destined to do the greatest good for the greatest number. Obliterate race hatred, party prejudice, and help us to achieve nobler ends, greater results and become satisfactory citizens to our brother in white.

This, Mr. Chairman, is perhaps the negroes' temporary farewell to the American Congress; but let me say, Phoenix-like he will rise up some day and come again....

The only apology I have to make for the earnestness with which I have spoken is that I am pleading for the life, the liberty, the future happiness, and manhood suffrage for one-eighth of the entire population of the United States.

QUESTIONS

1. According to Congressman White, how did the Democrats manage to push blacks out of office?
2. How, according to the speech, did white Democrats mischaracterize history in order to regain power in North Carolina?
3. How does Congressman White use history to defend the right of black Americans to vote and hold office?

20.2. VISUAL DOCUMENT: PROGRESSIVE "BULL MOOSE" PARTY CAMPAIGN POSTER (1912)

This campaign poster summarizes the platform of the Progressive, or "Bull Moose," Party in 1912. Disaffected by Taft's conservative presidency, some progressive Republicans split off to create a new party and nominated former president Theodore Roosevelt as its candidate for president and Hiram Johnson as its candidate for vice president.

"Thou Shalt Not Steal"

Roosevelt & Johnson

The men whom the crooked politicians fear above all things.

The men who will lead the Progressive Party to success in November.

The Party of the Common People.

The Party which the "Invisible Government" and the "Bosses" are fighting tooth and nail. Why?

Because it is the Party of the Laboring Classes and they are demanding a change so their vote will be counted fairly for the People's Interests. No more stealing of Delegates by the "Bosses" in Convention.

The Party will revise the Tariff and Method of Tariff making.

The Party which will stop Child Labor and the abuses of our factory system.

The Party which declares women are human beings and should have equal rights with men.

The Party which Penrose, Murphy, Lorimer, Barnes, Taggart, Crane, Smoot, Stevenson, Root, Parker, Ryan & Company are trying to defeat. If these men are against the Progressive Party, you and I must vote for it to protect ourselves.

The Party which demands a "Square Deal" for all, may they be poor or rich.

The Party which is causing the Trusts to have "Buck Fever."

The Party which believes in the emancipation of the laboring classes from infantile employment, unfair hours of labor and insufficient wage for subsistence, as Lincoln believed in the emancipation of the black race in 1860.

If Abraham Lincoln were alive today, he would be with the Progressive Party.

"Pass Prosperity Around"

QUESTIONS

1. Why do you think the party chose to title this poster "Thou Shall Not Steal"?
2. What did the Progressive Party stand for?
3. What language and images from this poster do you think were most effective in appealing to voters? Why?

Source: Courtesy of the David M. Rubenstein Rare Book & Manuscript Library, Duke University.

20.3. HELEN KELLER, EXCERPTS FROM "STRIKE AGAINST WAR" (JANUARY 5, 1916)

Helen Keller was one of the most famous people of her era. Born blind and deaf in 1880, Keller managed to graduate from Radcliffe College in 1904 and lived her life as an activist for a number of causes. In addition to fighting for rights for the disabled, she embraced feminism and socialism. She gave this speech to the Women's Peace Party in New York on January 5, 1916, as the First World War raged in Europe and the United States continued to maintain its neutrality while preparing for war.

To begin with, I have a word to say to my good friends, the editors, and others who are moved to pity me. Some people are grieved because they imagine I am in the hands of unscrupulous persons who lead me astray and persuade me to espouse unpopular causes and make me the mouthpiece of their propaganda. Now, let it be understood once and for all that I do not want their pity; I would not change places with one of them. I know what I am talking about. My sources of information are as good and reliable as anybody else's. I have papers and magazines from England, France, Germany and Austria that I can read myself. Not all the editors I have met can do that....All I ask, gentlemen, is a fair field and no favor. I have entered the fight against preparedness and against the economic system under which we live. It is to be a fight to the finish, and I ask no quarter.

The future of the world rests in the hands of America. The future of America rests on the backs of 80,000,000 working men and women and their children. We are facing a grave danger in our national life. The few who profit from the labor of the masses want to organize the workers into an army which will protect the interests of capitalists....It is in your power to refuse to carry the artillery and the dreadnoughts and to shake off some of the burdens, too, such as limousines, steam yachts and country estates. You do not need to make a great noise about it. With the silence and dignity of creators you can end wars and the system of selfishness and exploitation that causes wars. All you need to do to bring about this stupendous revolution is to straighten up and fold your arms....

Congress is not preparing to defend the people of the United States. It is planning to protect the capital of American speculators and investors in Mexico, South America, China and the Philippine Islands. Incidentally this preparation will benefit the manufacturers of munitions and war machines....

Every modern war has had its root in exploitation. The Civil War was fought to decide whether the slaveholders of the South or the capitalists of the North should exploit the West. The Spanish-American War decided that the United States should exploit Cuba and the Philippines. The South African War decided that the British should exploit the diamond mines. The Russo-Japanese War decided that Japan should exploit Korea. The present war is to decide who shall exploit the Balkans, Turkey, Persia, Egypt, India, China, Africa....

All the machinery of the system has been set in motion. Above the complaint and din of the protest from the workers is heard the voice of authority.

Source: American Foundation for the Blind, http://www.afb.org/section.asp?SectionID=1&TopicID=193&SubTopicID=21&DocumentID=1154.

"Friends," it says… "fellow workmen, patriots; your country is in danger! There are foes on all sides of us. There is nothing between us and our enemies except the Pacific Ocean and the Atlantic Ocean. Look at what has happened to Belgium. Consider the fate of Serbia. Will you murmur about low wages when your country, your very liberties, are in jeopardy? What are the miseries you endure compared to the humiliation of having a victorious German army sail up the East River? Quit your whining, get busy and prepare to defend your firesides and your flag…."

Will the workers walk into this trap? Will they be fooled again? I am afraid so….

The clever ones, up in the high places know how childish and silly workers are. They know that if the government dresses them up in khaki and gives them a rifle and starts them off with a brass band and waving banners, they will go forth to fight valiantly for their own enemies. They are taught that brave men die for their country's honor. What a price to pay for an abstraction—the lives of millions of young men; other millions crippled and blinded for life; existence made hideous for still more millions of human beings; the achievement and inheritance of generations swept away in a moment—and nobody the better off for all the misery! This terrible sacrifice would be comprehensible if the thing you die for and call country fed, clothed, housed and warmed you, educated and cherished your children. I think the workers are the most unselfish of the children of men; they toil and live and die for other people's country, other people's sentiments, other people's liberties and other people's happiness! The workers have no liberties of their own; they are not free when they are compelled to work twelve or ten or eight hours a day. They are not free when they are ill paid for their exhausting toil. They are not free when their children must labor in mines, mills and factories or starve, and when their women may be driven by poverty to lives of shame. They are not free when they are clubbed and imprisoned because they go on strike for a raise of wages and for elemental justice that is their right as human beings.

We are not free unless the men who frame and execute the laws represent the interests of the lives of the people and no other interest. The ballot does not make a free man out of a wage slave. There has never existed a truly free and democratic nation in the world….

As civilization has grown more complex the workers have become more and more enslaved, until today they are little more than parts of the machines they operate. Daily they face the dangers of railroad, bridge, skyscraper, freight train, stokehold, stockyard, lumber raft and mine….And what is their reward? A scanty wage, often poverty, rents, taxes, tributes and war indemnities….

It is your duty to insist upon still more radical measures. It is your business to see that no child is employed in an industrial establishment or mine or store, and that no worker is needlessly exposed to accident or disease. It is your business to make them give you clean cities, free from smoke, dirt, and congestion. It is your business to make them pay you a living wage. It is your business to see that this kind of preparedness is carried into every department of the nation, until every one has a chance to be well born, well nourished, rightly educated, intelligent and serviceable to the country at all times.

Strike against all ordinances and laws and institutions that continue the slaughter of peace and the butcheries of war. Strike against war, for without you no battles can be fought. Strike against manufacturing shrapnel and gas bombs and all other tools of murder. Strike against preparedness that means death and misery to millions of human beings. Be not dumb, obedient slaves in an army if destruction. Be heroes in the army of construction.

QUESTIONS

1. For what kind of "preparedness" does Keller advocate instead of preparation for war?
2. What are the connections between international and national security, according to Keller?
3. How does she use a global perspective to criticize both the war effort and domestic problems?

20.4. WILLIAM G. SHEPHERD, "EYEWITNESS AT THE TRIANGLE" (MARCH 27, 1911)

United Press reporter William G. Shepherd happened to be in New York's Washington Square when the Triangle Shirtwaist Factory fire broke out. As the tragedy played out before his eyes, he reported this account by telephone, and it was subsequently telegraphed and reported in newspapers around the country. This account appeared in the *Milwaukee Journal* on March 27, 1911.

I was walking through Washington Square when a puff of smoke issuing from the factory building caught my eye. I reached the building before the alarm was turned in. I saw every feature of the tragedy visible from outside the building. I learned a new sound—a more horrible sound than description can picture. It was the thud of a speeding, living body on a stone sidewalk.

Thud—dead, thud—dead, thud—dead, thud—dead. Sixty-two thud—deads. I call them that, because the sound and the thought of death came to me each time, at the same instant. There was plenty of chance to watch them as they came down. The height was eighty feet.

The first ten thud—deads shocked me. I looked up—saw that there were scores of girls at the windows. The flames from the floor below were beating in their faces.

Somehow I knew that they, too, must come down, and something within me—something that I didn't know was there—steeled me.

I even watched one girl falling. Waving her arms, trying to keep her body upright until the very instant she struck the sidewalk, she was trying to balance herself. Then came the thud—then a silent, unmoving pile of clothing and twisted, broken limbs.

As I reached the scene of the fire, a cloud of smoke hung over the building....I looked up to the seventh floor. There was a living picture in each window—four screaming heads of girls waving their arms.

"Call the firemen," they screamed—scores of them. "Get a ladder," cried others. They were all as alive and whole and sound as were we who stood on the sidewalk. I couldn't help thinking of that. We cried to them not to jump. We heard the siren of a fire engine in the distance. The other sirens sounded from several directions.

"Here they come," we yelled. "Don't jump; stay there."

One girl climbed onto the window sash. Those behind her tried to hold her back. Then she dropped into space. I didn't notice whether those above watched her drop because I had turned away. Then came that first thud. I looked up, another girl was climbing onto the window sill; others were crowding behind her. She dropped. I watched her fall, and again the dreadful sound. Two windows away two girls were climbing onto the sill; they were fighting each other and crowding for air. Behind them I saw many screaming heads. They fell almost together, but I heard two distinct thuds. Then the flames burst out through the windows on the floor below them, and curled up into their faces.

The firemen began to raise a ladder. Others took out a life net and, while they were rushing to the sidewalk with it, two more girls shot down. The firemen held it under them; the bodies broke it; the grotesque simile of a dog jumping through a hoop struck me. Before they could move the net another girl's body

Source: Leon Stein, ed., *Out of the Sweatshop: The Struggle for Industrial Democracy* (New York: Quadrangle/New York Times Book Co., 1977), 188–93.

flashed through it. The thuds were just as loud, it seemed, as if there had been no net there. It seemed to me that the thuds were so loud that they might have been heard all over the city.

I had counted ten. Then my dulled senses began to work automatically. I noticed things that it had not occurred to me before to notice. Little details that the first shock had blinded me to. I looked up to see whether those above watched those who fell. I noticed that they did; they watched them every inch of the way down and probably heard the roaring thuds that we heard.

As I looked up I saw a love affair in the midst of all the horror. A young man helped a girl to the window sill. Then he held her out, deliberately away from the building and let her drop. He seemed cool and calculating. He held out a second girl the same way and let her drop. Then he held out a third girl who did not resist. I noticed that. They were as unresisting as if her were helping them onto a streetcar instead of into eternity. Undoubtedly he saw that a terrible death awaited them in the flames, and his was only a terrible chivalry.

Then came the love amid the flames. He brought another girl to the window. Those of us who were looking saw her put her arms about him and kiss him. Then he held her out into space and dropped her. But quick as a flash he was on the window sill himself. His coat fluttered upward—the air filled his trouser legs. I could see that he wore tan shoes and hose. His hat remained on his head.

Thud—dead, thud—dead—together they went into eternity. I saw his face before they covered it. You could see in it that he was a real man. He had done his best.

We found out later that, in the room in which he stood, many girls were being burned to death by the flames and were screaming in an inferno of flame and heat. He chose the easiest way and was brave enough to even help the girl he loved to a quicker death, after she had given him a goodbye kiss. He leaped with an energy as if to arrive first in that mysterious land of eternity, but her thud—dead came first.

The firemen raised the longest ladder. It reached only to the sixth floor. I saw the last girl jump at it and miss it. And then the faces disappeared from the window. But now the crowd was enormous, though all this had occurred in less than seven minutes, the start of the fire and the thuds and deaths.

I heard screams around the corner and hurried there. What I had seen before was not so terrible as what had followed. Up in the [ninth] floor girls were burning to death before our very eyes. They were jammed in the windows. No one was lucky enough to be able to jump, it seemed. But, one by one, the jams broke. Down came the bodies in a shower, burning, smoking—flaming bodies, with disheveled hair trailing upward. They had fought each other to die by jumping instead of by fire.

The whole, sound, unharmed girls who had jumped on the other side of the building had tried to fall feet down. But these fire torches, suffering ones, fell inertly, only intent that death should come to them on the sidewalk instead of in the furnace behind them.

On the sidewalk lay heaps of broken bodies. A policeman later went about with tags, which he fastened with wires to the wrists of the dead girls, numbering each with a lead pencil, and I saw him fasten tag no. 54 to the wrist of a girl who wore an engagement ring. A fireman who came downstairs from the building told me that there were at least fifty bodies in the big room on the seventh floor. Another fireman told me that more girls had jumped down an air shaft in the rear of the building. I went back there, into the narrow court, and saw a heap of dead girls....

The floods of water from the firemen's hose that ran into the gutter were actually stained red with blood. I looked upon the heap of dead bodies and I remembered these girls were the shirtwaist makers. I remembered their great strike of last year in which these same girls had demanded more sanitary conditions and more safety precautions in the shops. These dead bodies were the answer.

QUESTIONS

1. How does the author convey the horrors of the Triangle fire? Which images do you think are most powerful?

2. How do you think that American reading this report in 1911 would have reacted?

20.5. JANE ADDAMS, EXCERPTS FROM "WOMEN AND INTERNATIONALISM" (1915)

In 1915, Jane Addams led a delegation of American women to The Hague in the Netherlands, where, in the midst of the war, she presided over the International Congress of Women, made up of women from both European countries at war with each other, such as Germany and Great Britain, and neutral countries, such as the United States. This essay, written by Jane Addams in 1915, advocates for the continuing role of women in international affairs.

The fifteen hundred women who came to the Congress in the face of such difficulties must have been impelled by some profound and spiritual forces. During a year when the spirit of internationalism had apparently broken down, they came together to declare the validity of the internationalism which surrounds and completes national life,...to insist that internationalism does not conflict with patriotism....

The belief that a woman is against war simply because she is a woman and not a man cannot of course be substantiated. In every country there are women who believe that war is inevitable and righteous; the majority of women as well as men in the nations at war doubtless hold that conviction. On the other hand...women, who have brought men into the world and nurtured them until they reach the age for fighting, must experience a peculiar revulsion when they see them destroyed, irrespective of the country in which these men may have been born....

The International Congress of Women at The Hague passed a resolution to hold a meeting "in the same place and at the same time as the Conference of Powers which shall frame the terms of the peace settlement after the war, for the purpose of presenting practical proposals to that Conference."...

Within the borders of every country at war there is released a vast amount of idealism, without which war could never be carried on; a fund which might still be drawn upon when the time for settlement arrives. If the people knew that through final negotiations Europe would be so remade and internationalized that further wars would be impossible, many of them would feel that the death of thousands of young men had not been in vain, that the youth of our generation had thus contributed to the inauguration of a new era in human existence.... [T]he women in the Hague Congress considered it feasible to urge a declaration that "the exclusion of women from citizenship is contrary to the principles of civilization and human right," as one of the fundamental measures embodied in their resolutions for permanent peace.

But perhaps our hopes for such action are founded chiefly upon the fact that the settlement at the end of this war may definitely recognize a fundamental change in the functions of government taking place in all civilized nations, a change evoked as the result of concrete, social, and economic conditions, approximating similarity all over the world. The recent entrance of women into citizenship so rapidly not only in the nations of Europe and America, but discernible in certain Asiatic nations as well, is doubtless one manifestation of this change, and the so-called radical or progressive element in each nation, whether they like it or not, recognize it as such. Nevertheless, there are men in each of these countries even among those who would grant the franchise to women in the city and

Source: Jane Addams, Emily G. Balch, and Alice Hamilton, *Women at the Hague: The International Congress of Women and Its Results* (New York: Macmillan, 1915), 124–42.

state, to whom it is still repugnant that women should evince an interest in international affairs. These men argue that a woman's municipal vote may be cast for the regulation of contagious diseases, her state vote for protection of working children, and that war no longer obtains between cities or even between states; but because war is still legitimate in settling international difficulties, and because international relations are so much a matter of fortified boundaries and standing armies, that it is preposterous for women who cannot fight, to consider them....Only in time of war is government thrown back to its primitive and sole function of self-defence, belittling for the moment the many other real interests of which it is the guardian....

But because this primitive conception of the function of government and of the obsolete division between the lives of men and women has obtained during the long months of the European war, there is obviously great need at the end of the war that women should attempt, in an organized capacity, to make their contribution to that governmental internationalism between the nations which shall in some measure approximate the genuine internationalism already developed in so many directions among the peoples....

An organized and formal effort on the part of women would add but one more to that long procession of outstanding witnesses who in each generation have urged juster and more vital international relations between Governments. Each exponent in

this long effort to place law above force was called a dreamer and a coward, but each did his utmost to express clearly the truth that was in him, and beyond that human effort cannot go.

This tide of endeavor has probably never been so full as at the present moment. Religious, social, and economic associations, many of them organized since the war began, are making their contributions to the same great end....

Out of the present situation, which certainly "presents the spectacle of the breakdown of the whole philosophy of nationalism, political, racial, and cultural," may conceivably issue a new birth of internationalism, founded not so much upon arbitration treaties, to be used in time of disturbance, as upon governmental devices designed to protect and enhance the fruitful processes of cooperation in the greatest experiment if living together in a world become conscious of itself.

QUESTIONS

1. How does Addams justify the unpopular position that women have a special role to play in international affairs?
2. Do you agree with Addams that women have a "peculiar revulsion" to war? Why or why not?
3. Why do you think that she was so confident that internationalism, rather than nationalism, was the wave of the future?

CHAPTER 21

AMERICA AND THE GREAT WAR, 1914–1920

21.1. VISUAL DOCUMENTS: PROPAGANDA POSTERS (1914–1918)

Propaganda posters issued by U.S. government agencies and voluntary organizations reached and informed millions of Americans during World War I. These posters urged men to join the armed forces, women to take war production jobs, citizens to buy war bonds, people on the home front to send cigarettes to soldiers, and the public to support the proposed League of Nations.

James Montgomery Flagg, Send Smokes to Sammy! (1918).   Howard Chandler, Clear the Way!! (c. 1918).

QUESTIONS

1. How did this poster art simplify complex questions?

2. To what emotions did propaganda posters appeal?

Souces: James Montgomery Flagg, *Send Smokes to Sammy! Our Boys in France Tobacco Fund* (1918) © Swim Ink 2, LLC/CORBIS; Howard Chandler Christy, *Clear The Way!! Buy Bonds, Fourth Liberty Loan* (c. 1918) © CORBIS.

21.2. COMMITTEE ON PUBLIC INFORMATION, "GENERAL SUGGESTIONS TO SPEAKERS" (MAY 22, 1917) AND "SPEECH BY A FOUR MINUTE MAN" (OCTOBER 8, 1917)

The government's Committee on Public Information (CPI) organized pro-war educational activities at home and abroad during World War I. The CPI recruited 75,000 amateur orators called "Four Minute Men" to give brief speeches in movie theaters, schools, churches, and union halls in English and dozens of other languages ranging from Yiddish and Italian to Sioux. These speeches warned of enemy efforts to subvert the war effort and the importance of national unity.

GENERAL SUGGESTIONS TO SPEAKERS

The speech must not be longer than four minutes, which means there is no time for a single wasted word.

Speakers should go over their speech time and time again until the ideas are firmly fixed in their mind and can not be forgotten. This does not mean that the speech needs to be written out and committed,[1] although most speakers, especially when limited in time, do best to commit.

Divide your speech carefully into certain divisions, say 15 seconds for final appeal; 45 seconds to describe the bond; 15 seconds for opening words, etc., etc. Any plan is better than none, and it can be amended every day in the light of experience.

There never was a speech yet that couldn't be improved. Never be satisfied with success. Aim to be more successful, and still more successful. So keep your eyes open. Read all the papers every day, to find a new slogan, or a new phraseology, or a new idea to replace something you have in your speech. For instance, the editorial page of the *Chicago Herald* of May 19 is crammed full of good ideas and phrases. Most of the article is a lit-

tle above the average audience, but if the ideas are good, you should plan carefully to bring them into the experience of your auditors. There is one sentence which says, "No country was ever saved by the other fellow; it must be done by you, by a hundred million yous, or it will not be done at all." Or again, Secretary McAdoo says, "Every dollar invested in the Liberty Loan is a real blow for liberty, a blow against the militaristic system which would strangle the freedom of the world," and so on. Both the *Tribune* and the *Examiner*, besides the *Herald*, contain President Wilson's address to the nation in connection with the draft registration. The latter part is very suggestive and can be used effectively. Try slogans like "Earn the right to say, I helped to win the war," and "This is a Loyalty Bond as well as a Liberty Bond," or "A cause that is worth living for is worth dying for, and a cause that is worth dying for is worth fighting for." Conceive of your speech as a mosaic made up of five or six hundred words, each one of which has its function.

If you come across a new slogan, or a new argument, or a new story, or a new illustration, don't fail to send it to the Committee. We need your help to make the Four-Minute Men the mightiest force for arousing patriotism in the United States.

Sources: Committee on Public Information, *Four Minute Men Bulletin* 1, May 22, 1917; Committee on Public Information, *Four Minute Men Bulletin* 17, October 8, 1917.

1. Memorized.

SPEECH BY A FOUR MINUTE MAN

Ladies and Gentlemen:

I have just received the information that there is a German spy among us—a German spy watching *us*.

He is around, here somewhere, reporting upon you and me—sending reports about us to Berlin and telling the Germans just what we are doing with the Liberty Loan. From every section of the country these spies have been getting reports over to Potsdam—not general reports but details—where the loan is going well and where its success seems weak, and what people are saying in each community.

For the German Government is worried about our great loan. Those Junkers fear its effect upon the German *morale*. They're raising a loan this month, too.

If the American people lend their billions now, one and all with a hip-hip-hurrah, it means that America is united and strong. While, if we lend our money half-heartedly, America seems weak and autocracy remains strong.

Money means everything now; it means quicker victory and therefore less bloodshed. We are *in* the war, and now Americans can have but *one* opinion, only *one* wish in the Liberty Loan.

Well, I hope these spies are getting their messages straight, letting Potsdam know that America is *hurling back* to the autocrats these answers:

For treachery here, attempted treachery in Mexico, treachery everywhere—*one billion*.

For murder of American women and children—*one billion more*.

For broken faith and promise to murder more Americans—*billions and billions more*.

And then we will add:

In the world fight for Liberty, our share—*billions and billions and billions and endless billions*.

Do not let the German spy hear and report that *you* are a slacker.

QUESTIONS

1. What topics were speakers encouraged to raise in their public speaking?
2. What information sources did speakers use?

21.3. U.S. ARMY, INTELLIGENCE TEST, ALPHA (1921)

After the United States entered the Great War in April 1917, millions of men quickly joined or were drafted into military service. Psychologist Robert M. Yerkes convinced the army he could assess the intelligence of raw recruits and select those suitable for officer training by administering a standardized "IQ" test. The tests clearly favored those men from wealthier, educated backgrounds and were later used as evidence to claim that most Eastern European immigrants and African Americans were "subnormal."

TEST 8

Notice the sample sentence:

People **hear** *with* **the eyes** <u>ears</u> **nose mouth**

The correct word is **ears**, because it makes the truest sentence.

In each of the sentences below you have four choices for the last word. Only one of them is correct. In each sentence draw a line under the one of these four words which makes the truest sentence. If you can not be sure, guess. The two samples are already marked as they should be.

SAMPLES   *People* **hear** *with the* **eyes** <u>ears</u> **nose mouth**

France is in <u>Europe</u> **Asia Africa Australia**

1   **America** was discovered by **Drake Hudson Columbus Balboa**
2   **Pinochle** is played with **rackets cards pins dice**
3   The most prominent industry of **Detroit** is **automobiles brewing flour packing**
4   The **Wyandotte** is a kind of **horse fowl cattle granite**
5   The **U. S. School for Army Officers** is at **Annapolis West Point New Haven Ithaca**
6   **Food products** are made by **Smith & Wesson Swift & Co. W. L. Douglas B. T. Babbitt**
7   **Bud Fisher** is famous as an **actor author baseball player comic artist**
8   The **Guernsey** is a kind of **horse goat sheep cow**
9   **Marguerite Clark** is known as a **suffragist singer movie actress writer**
10   **"Hasn't scratched yet"** is used in advertising a **duster flour brush cleanser**
11   **Salsify** is a kind of **snake fish lizard vegetable**
12   **Coral** is obtained from **mines elephants oysters reefs**
13   **Rosa Bonheur** is famous as a **poet painter composer sculptor**
14   The **tuna** is a kind of **fish bird reptile insect**
15   **Emeralds** are usually **red blue green yellow**
16   **Maize** is a kind of **corn hay oats rice**
17   **Nabisco** is a **patent medicine disinfectant food product tooth paste**
18   **Velvet Joe** appears in advertisements of **tooth powder dry goods tobacco soap**
19   **Cypress** is a kind of **machine food tree fabric**
20   **Bombay** is a city in **China Egypt India Japan**
21   The **dictaphone** is a kind of **typewriter multigraph phonograph adding machine**
22   The **pancreas** is in the **abdomen head shoulder neck**
23   **Cheviot** is the name of a **fabric drink dance food**
24   **Larceny** is a term used in **medicine theology law pedagogy**

Source: Carl C. Brigham, *A Study of American Intelligence* (London: Oxford University Press, 1923), 29.

25 The **Battle of Gettysburg** was fought in **1863 1813 1778 1812**

26 The **bassoon** is used in **music stenography bookbinding lithography**

27 **Turpentine** comes from **petroleum ore hides trees**

28 The number of a **Zulu's legs** is **two four six eight**

29 The **scimitar** is a kind of **musket cannon pistol sword**

30 The **Knight engine** is used in the **Packard Lozier Stearns Pierce Arrow**

31 The author of "**The Raven**" is **Stevenson Kipling Hawthorne Poe**

32 **Spare** is a term used in **bowling football tennis hockey**

33 A **six-sided figure** is called a **scholium parallelogram hexagon trapezium**

34 **Isaac Pitman** was most famous in **physics shorthand railroading electricity**

35 The **ampere** is used in measuring **wind power electricity water power rainfall**

36 The **Overland car** is made in **Buffalo Detroit Flint Toledo**

37 **Mauve** is the name of a **drink color fabric food**

38 The **stanchion** is used in **fishing hunting farming motoring**

39 **Mica** is a **vegetable mineral gas liquid**

40 **Scrooge** appears in **Vanity Fair The Christmas Carol Romola Henry IV**

QUESTIONS

1. How do such intelligence tests show a cultural or class bias?

2. How could the results of these tests be misused?

21.4. THEODORE ROOSEVELT, "THE HUN WITHIN OUR GATES" (1917)

Former President Theodore Roosevelt criticized President Woodrow Wilson's reluctance to enter World War I. Once the United States did so in April 1917, Roosevelt launched a campaign against all Americans who he deemed less enthusiastic war supporters than himself. In this article he published in 1917, Roosevelt denounced many politicians, ethnic Americans, labor activists, pacifists, and others whom he accused of being German agents.

The Hun within our gates is the worst of the foes of our own household, whether he is the paid or the unpaid agent of Germany. Whether he is pro-German or poses as a pacifist, or a peace-at-any-price man, matters little. He is the enemy of the United States. Senators and Congressmen like Messrs. Stone, La Follette and Maclemore belong in Germany and it is a pity they cannot be sent there.... Such men are among the worst of the foes of our own household; and so are the sham philanthropists and sinister agitators and the wealthy creatures without patriotism who support and abet them. Our Government has seemed afraid to grapple with these people. It is permitting thousands of allies of Berlin to sow the seeds of treason and sedition in this country. The I.W.W. boasts its defiance of all law, and many of its members exultingly proclaim that in their war against industry in the United States they are endeavoring to give the Government so much

Source: Theodore Roosevelt, *The Foes of Our Own Household* (New York: George H. Doran Co., 1917), 293–95.

to do that it will have no troops to spare for Europe. Every district where the I.W.W. starts rioting should be placed under martial law, and cleaned up by military methods. The German-language papers carry on a consistent campaign in favor of Germany against England. They should be put out of existence for the period of this war. The Hearst papers, more ably edited than the German sheets, play the Kaiser's game in a similar way. When they keep within the law they should at least be made to feel the scorn felt for them by every honest American. Wherever any editor can be shown to be purveying treason in violation of law he should be jailed until the conflict is over. Every disloyal German-born citizen should have his naturalization papers recalled and should be interned during the term of the war. Action of this kind is especially necessary in order to pick out the disloyal but vociferous minority of citizens of German descent from the vast but silent majority of entirely loyal citizens of German descent who otherwise will suffer from a public anger that will condemn all alike. Every disloyal native-born American should be disfranchised and interned. It is time to strike our enemies at home heavily and quickly. Every copperhead in this country is an enemy to the Government, to the people, to the army and to the flag, and should be treated as such.

This pro-German, anti-American propaganda has been carried on for years prior to the war, and its treasonable activities are performed systematically today....These men support and direct the pro-German societies. They incite disloyal activities among the Russian Jews. They finance the small groups of Irish-Americans whose hatred for England makes them traitors to the United States. They foment seditious operations among the German–American socialists and the I.W.W.'s. They support the German-language periodicals. Their campaigns range from peace movements and anti-draft schemings to open efforts in favor of sedition and civil war.

These traitors are following out the vicious teachings of Prussian philosophers; there is no cause for surprise at their treasonable course. Unfortunately there is cause for surprise at the license which the Administration extends to their detestable activities. In this attitude the Administration is repeating its course of indifference to world-threatening aggression, and of submission to studied acts of murderous violence, which resulted, after two and a half years of injury and humiliation, in our being dragged unprepared into war.

If during those two and a half years a policy of courage, and of consistent and far-sighted Americanism, had been followed, either the brutal invasion of our national rights would have been checked without war or else if we had been forced into war we would have brought it instantly to a victorious end. Our failure to prepare is responsible for our failure now efficiently to act in the war. In exactly the same fashion it may be set down as certain that continuance of the present craven policy of ignoring sedition and paltering with treason will encourage and aid German autocracy, and will be translated either into terrible lists of Americans slain and crippled on the battlefield or else into an ignoble peace which will leave Germany free at some future time to resume its campaign against America and against liberty-loving mankind.

QUESTION

1. Who did Roosevelt believe threatened the United States during World War I?

21.5. HO CHI MINH (NGUYEN AI QUOC), PETITION TO WOODROW WILSON (1919)

During the 1919 peace conference in Paris following World War I, numerous individuals and groups from European and Japanese colonies petitioned the Great Powers to either grant independence or put them on a path toward self-determination, as promised by President Woodrow Wilson in his "14 Points" speech of January 1918. Among these petitioners was Nguyen Ai Quoc, better known to Americans in the 1960s as North Vietnamese leader Ho Chi Minh. Ho Chi Minh presented this appeal to Secretary of State Robert Lansing in the vain hope that the United States would pressure France to liberate Vietnam, then called Annam.

To his Excellency, the Secretary of State of the Republic of the United States, Delegate to the Peace Conference

Excellency,

We take the liberty of submitting to you the accompanying memorandum setting forth the claims of the Annamite people on the occasion of the Allied victory.

We count on your great kindness to honor our appeal by your support whenever the opportunity arises.

We beg your Excellency graciously to accept the expression of our profound respect.

For the Group of Annamite Patriots
Nguyen Ai Quoc
56, rue Monsieur le Prince, Paris

CLAIMS OF THE ANNAMITE PEOPLE

Since the victory of the Allies, all the subject peoples are frantic with hope at the prospect of an era of right and justice which should begin for them by virtue of the formal and solemn engagements, made before the whole world by the various powers of the entente in the struggle of civilization against barbarism.

While waiting for the principle of national self-determination to pass from ideal to reality through the effective recognition of the sacred right of all peoples to decide their own destiny, the inhabitants of the ancient Empire of Annam, at the present time French Indochina, present to the noble Governments of the entente in general and in particular to the honorable French Government the following humble claims:

1. General amnesty for all the native people who have been condemned for political activity.
2. Reform of Indochinese justice by granting to the native population the same judicial guarantees as the Europeans have, and the total suppression of the special courts which are the instruments of terrorization and oppression against the most responsible elements of the Annamite people.
3. Freedom of press and speech.
4. Freedom of association and assembly.
5. Freedom to emigrate and to travel abroad.
6. Freedom of education, and creation in every province of technical and professional schools for the native population.
7. Replacement of the regime of arbitrary decrees by a regime of law.

Sources: Department of State, National Archives, Washington, DC, 851G.00/1.

8. A permanent delegation of native people elected to attend the French parliament in order to keep the latter informed of their needs.

The Annamite people, in presenting these claims, count on the worldwide justice of all the Powers, and rely in particular on the goodwill of the noble French people who hold our destiny in their hands and who, as France is a republic, have taken us under their protection. In requesting the protection of the French people, the people of Annam, far from feeling humiliated, on the contrary consider themselves honored, because they know that the French people stand for liberty and justice and will never renounce their sublime ideal of universal brotherhood. Consequently, in giving heed to the voice of the oppressed, the French people will be doing their duty to France and to humanity.

In the Name of the Group of Annamite Patriots
Nguyen Ai Quoc

QUESTIONS

1. What American ideals did Ho/Nguyen invoke in appealing for Vietnamese independence?
2. How radical or moderate were Ho's demands?

21.6. A. MITCHELL PALMER, EXCERPTS FROM "THE CASE AGAINST THE REDS: (1920)

Following Germany's defeat in November 1918, much of the hostility directed toward alleged pro-German Americans was redirected against radical labor organizers and others accused of being agents of the Bolshevik, or communist, regime in Russia. Attorney General A. Mitchell Palmer published this article in 1920 to justify his order to arrest and deport thousands of resident aliens and naturalized citizens in the so-called Palmer Raids of 1919–1920. Note his appeal to anti-Semitism by referring to Bolshevik leader Leon Trotsky by his original name, Leon Bronstein, and mentioning that he once lived in New York City's Lower East Side, a Jewish neighborhood.

Like a prairie-fire, the blaze of revolution was sweeping over every American institution of law and order a year ago. It was eating its way into the homes of the American workmen, its sharp tongues of revolutionary heat were licking the altars of the churches, leaping into the belfry of the school bell, crawling into the sacred corners of American homes, seeking to replace marriage vows with libertine laws, burning up the foundations of society.

Robbery, not war, is the ideal of communism. This has been demonstrated in Russia, Germany, and in America. As a foe, the anarchist is fearless of his own life, for his creed is a fanaticism that admits no respect of any other creed. Obviously it is the creed of any criminal mind, which reasons always from motives impossible to clean thought. Crime is the degenerate factor in society.

The whole mass of evidence, accumulated from all parts of the country, was scrupulously scanned, not merely for the written or spoken differences of viewpoint as to the Government of the United States, but, in spite of these things, to see if the hostile declarations might not be sincere in their announced motive to improve our social order. There was no hope of such a thing.

By stealing, murder and lies, Bolshevism has looted Russia not only of its material strength but of its moral force. A small clique of outcasts from the East Side of New York has attempted this, with what success we

Source: A. Mitchell Palmer, "The Case Against the 'Reds,'" *Forum* 63 (1920): 173–85.

all know. Because a disreputable alien—Leon Bronstein, the man who now calls himself Trotzky—can inaugurate a reign of terror from his throne room in the Kremlin, because this lowest of all types known to New York can sleep in the Czar's bed, while hundreds of thousands in Russia are without food or shelter, should Americans be swayed by such doctrines?

Such a question, it would seem, should receive but one answer from America.

My information showed that communism in this country was an organization of thousands of aliens who were direct allies of Trotzky. Aliens of the same misshapen caste of mind and indecencies of character, and it showed that they were making the same glittering promises of lawlessness, of criminal autocracy to Americans, that they had made to the Russian peasants. How the Department of Justice discovered upwards of 60,000 of these organized agitators of the Trotzky doctrine in the United States is the confidential information upon which the Government is now sweeping the nation clean of such alien filth....

WILL DEPORTATION CHECK BOLSHEVISM?

Behind, and underneath, my own determination to drive from our midst the agents of Bolshevism with increasing vigor and with greater speed, until there are no more of them left among us, so long as I have the responsible duty of that task, I have discovered the hysterical methods of these revolutionary humans with increasing amazement and suspicion. In the confused information that sometimes reaches the people they are compelled to ask questions which involve the reasons for my acts against the "Reds." I have been asked, for instance, to what extent deportation will check radicalism in this country. Why not ask what will become of the United States Government if these alien radicals are permitted to carry out the principles of the Communist Party as embodied in its so-called laws, aims and regulations?

There wouldn't be any such thing left. In place of the United States Government we should have the horror and terrorism of bolsheviki tyranny such as is destroying Russia now. Every scrap of radical literature demands the overthrow of our existing government. All of it demands obedience to the instincts of criminal minds, that is, to the lower appetites, material and

moral. The whole purpose of communism appears to be a mass formation of the criminals of the world to overthrow the decencies of private life, to usurp property that they have not earned, to disrupt the present order of life regardless of health, sex or religious rights. By a literature that promises the wildest dreams of such low aspirations, that can occur to only the criminal minds, communism distorts our social law....

It has been inferred by the "Reds" that the United States Government, by arresting and deporting them, is returning to the autocracy of Czardom, adopting the system that created the severity of Siberian banishment. My reply to such charges is that in our determination to maintain our government we are treating our alien enemies with extreme consideration. To deny them the privilege of remaining in a country which they have openly deplored as an unenlightened community, unfit for those who prefer the privileges of Bolshevism, should be no hardship. It strikes me as an odd form of reasoning that these Russian Bolsheviks who extol the Bolshevik rule should be so unwilling to return to Russia. The nationality of most of the alien "Reds" is Russian and German. There is almost no other nationality represented among them.

It has been impossible in so short a space to review the entire menace of the internal revolution in this country as I know it, but this may serve to arouse the American citizen to its reality, its danger, and the great need of united effort to stamp it out, under our feet, if needs be. It is being done. The Department of Justice will pursue the attack of these "Reds" upon the Government of the United States with vigilance, and no alien, advocating the overthrow of existing law and order in this country, shall escape arrest and prompt deportation.

It is my belief that while they have stirred discontent in our midst, while they have caused irritating strikes, and while they have infected our social ideas with the disease of their own minds and their unclean morals we can get rid of them and not until we have done so shall we have removed the menace of Bolshevism for good.

QUESTIONS

1. What was the Communist threat to the United States that Palmer perceived?
2. How did Palmer justify deporting radical aliens?

CHAPTER 22

A NEW ERA, 1920–1930

22.1. HENRY FORD, EXCERPTS FROM *MY LIFE AND WORK* (1922)

The United States led the world in mass industrial production in the 1920s. In these selections from his autobiography, Henry Ford, owner of the Ford Motor Company, explains the development of the factory assembly line as a means of employing unskilled workers to produce high-quality goods cheaply.

It is self-evident that a majority of the people in the world are not mentally—even if they are physically—capable of making a good living. That is, they are not capable of furnishing with their own hands a sufficient quantity of the goods which this world needs to be able to exchange their unaided product for the goods which they need. I have heard it said, in fact I believe it is quite a current thought, that we have taken skill out of work. We have not. We have put in skill. We have put a higher skill into planning, management, and tool building, and the results of that skill are enjoyed by the man who is not skilled. This I shall later enlarge on.

We have to recognize the unevenness in human mental equipments. If every job in our place required skill the place would never have existed. Sufficiently skilled men to the number needed could not have been trained in a hundred years. A million men working by hand could not even approximate our present daily output. No one could manage a million men. But more important than that, the product of the unaided hands of those million men could not be sold at a price in consonance with buying power....I cannot see how under such conditions the men could possibly be paid more than ten or twenty cents a day—for of course it is not the employer who pays wages. He only handles the money. It is the product that pays the wages and it is the management that arranges the production so that the product may pay the wages....

The first step forward in assembly came when we began taking the work to the men instead of the men to the work. We now have two general principles in all operations—that a man shall never have to take more than one step, if possibly it can be avoided, and that no man need ever stoop over.

The principles of assembly are these:

1. Place the tools and the men in the sequence of the operation so that each component part shall travel the least possible distance while in the process of finishing.

Source: Henry Ford, *My Life and Work* (New York: Doubleday, Page and Co., 1922), 77–80.

2. Use work slides or some other form of carrier so that when a workman completes his operation, he drops the part always in the same place—which place must always be the most convenient place to his hand—and if possible have gravity carry the part to the next workman for his operation.

3. Use sliding assembling lines by which the parts to be assembled are delivered at convenient distances.

The net result of the application of these principles is the reduction of the necessity for thought on the part of the worker and the reduction of his movements to a minimum. He does as nearly as possible only one thing with only one movement.

QUESTIONS

1. How would you describe Ford's view of workers? How do his "principles of assembly" especially reflect his attitudes about his workers?

2. Based on this excerpt, what do you think it was like to work in a Ford plant?

22.2. ELLISON DURANT SMITH, EXCERPTS FROM " 'SHUT THE DOOR': A SENATOR SPEAKS FOR IMMIGRATION RESTRICTION" (APRIL 9, 1924)

During the 1924 Congressional debate over immigration restriction, South Carolina Senator Ellison DuRant Smith expressed opposition to any new immigration to the United States. He drew upon popular pseudo-scientific racial stereotypes to conclude that recent immigrants threatened American prosperity and democracy.

I think that we have sufficient stock in America now for us to shut the door, Americanize what we have, and save the resources of America for the natural increase of our population. We all know that one of the most prolific causes of war is the desire for increased land ownership for the overflow of a congested population. We are increasing at such a rate that in the natural course of things in a comparatively few years the landed resources, the natural resources of the country, shall be taken up by the natural increase of our population. It seems to me the part of wisdom now that we have throughout the length and breadth of continental America a population which is beginning to encroach upon the reserve and virgin resources of the country to keep it in trust for the multiplying population of the country....

I think we now have sufficient population in our country for us to shut the door and to breed up a pure, unadulterated American citizenship. I recognize that there is a dangerous lack of distinction between people of a certain nationality and the breed of the dog. Who is an American? Is he an immigrant from Italy? Is he an immigrant from Germany? If you were to go abroad and some one were to meet you and say, "I met a typical American," what would flash into your mind as a typical American, the typical representative of that new Nation? Would it be the son of an Italian immigrant, the son of a German immigrant, the son of any of the breeds from the Orient, the son of the denizens of Africa? We must not get our ethnological distinctions mixed up with out anthropological distinctions. It is the breed of the dog in which I am

Source: Ellison DuRant Smith, speaking to the U.S. Senate, on April 9, 1924, 68th Cong., 1st sess., *Congressional Record* 65, 5961–62. See also http://historymatters.gmu.edu/d/5080.

interested. I would like for the Members of the Senate to read that book just recently published by Madison Grant, *The Passing of a Great Race.* Thank God we have in America perhaps the largest percentage of any country in the world of the pure, unadulterated Anglo-Saxon stock; certainly the greatest of any nation in the Nordic breed. It is for the preservation of that splendid stock that has characterized us that I would make this not an asylum for the oppressed of all countries, but a country to assimilate and perfect that splendid type of manhood that has made America the foremost Nation in her progress and in her power, and yet the youngest of all the nations. I myself believe that the preservation of her institutions depends upon us now taking counsel with our condition and our experience during the last World War....

The great desideratum of modern times has been education—not alone book knowledge, but that education which enables men to think right, to think logically, to think truthfully, men equipped with power to appreciate the rapidly developing conditions that are all about us, that have converted the world in the last 50 years into a brand new world and made us masters of forces that are revolutionizing production. We want men not like dumb, driven cattle from those nations where the progressive thought of the times has scarcely made a beginning and where they see men as mere machines; we want men who have an appreciation of the responsibility brought about by the manifestation of the power of that individual. We have not that in this country to-day. We have men here to-day who are selfishly utilizing the enormous forces discovered by genius, and if we are not careful as statesmen, if we are not careful in our legislation, these very masters of the tremendous forces that have been made available to us will bring us under their domination and control by virtue of the power they have in multiplying their wealth....

We do not want to tangle the skein of America's progress by those who imperfectly understand the genius of our Government and the opportunities that lie about us. Let up keep what we have, protect what we have, make what we have the realization of the dream of those who wrote the Constitution.

I am more concerned about that than I am about whether a new railroad shall be built or whether there shall be diversified farming next year or whether a certain coal mine shall be mined. I would rather see American citizenship refined to the last degree in all that makes America what we hope it will be than to develop the resources of America at the expense of the citizenship of our country. The time has come when we should shut the door and keep what we have for what we hope our own people to be.

QUESTIONS

1. What are Senator Smith's main justifications for immigrant restriction?
2. Who is an "American," according to Senator Smith?
3. How would an antirestrictionist counter Smith's arguments?

22.3. KU KLUX KLAN, EXCERPTS FROM THE *KLAN MANUAL* (1925)

The Ku Klux Klan of the 1920s was explicitly anti-black, anti-Catholic, and anti-Jewish. These selections from the 1925 *Klan Manual* illuminate several of the Klan's objectives and methods.

OBJECTS AND PURPOSES (ARTICLE II, THE CONSTITUTION)

I. MOBILIZATION

This is its primary purpose: "To unite white male persons, native-born, Gentile citizens of the United States of America, who owe no allegiance of any nature or degree to any foreign government, nation, institution, sect, ruler, person, or people; whose morals are good; whose reputations and vocations are respectable; whose habits are exemplary; who are of sound minds and eighteen years or more of age, under a common oath into a brotherhood of strict regulations."

II. CULTURAL

The Knights of the Ku Klux Klan is a movement devoting itself to the needed task of developing a genuine spirit of American patriotism. Klansmen are to be examples of pure patriotism. They are to organize the patriotic sentiment of native-born white, Protestant Americans for the defense of distinctively American institutions. Klansmen are dedicated to the principle that America shall be made American through the promulgation of American doctrines, the dissemination of American ideals, the creation of wholesome American sentiment, the preservation of American institutions....

IV. BENEFICENT

"To relieve the injured and the oppressed; to succor the suffering and unfortunate, especially widows and orphans."

The supreme pattern for all true Klansmen is their Criterion of Character, Jesus Christ, "who went about doing good." The movement accepts the full Christian program of unselfish helpfulness, and will seek to carry it on in the manner commanded by the one Master of Men, Christ Jesus.

V. PROTECTIVE

1. The Home. "To Shield the Sanctity of the Home."

The American home is fundamental to all that is best in life, in society, in church, and in the nation. It is the most sacred of human institutions. Its sanctity is to be preserved, its interests are to be safeguarded, and its well-being is to be promoted. Every influence that seeks to disrupt the home must itself be destroyed. The Knights of the Ku Klux Klan would protect the home by promoting whatever would make for its stability, its betterment, its safety, and its inviolability.

2. Womanhood.

The Knights of the Ku Klux Klan declares that it is committed to "the sacred duty of protecting womanhood"; and announces that one of its purposes is "to shield...the chastity of womanhood."

The degradation of women is a violation of the sacredness of human personality, a sin against the race, a crime against society, a menace to our country, and a prostitution of all that is best, and noblest, and highest in life. No race, or society, or country, can rise higher than its womanhood.

Source: David Rothman and Sheila M. Rothman, eds., *Sources of the American Social Tradition*, vol. 2 (New York: Basic Books, 1975), 166–72.

3. The Helpless.

"To protect the weak, the innocent, and the defense-less from the indignities, wrongs, and outrages of the lawless, the violent, and the brutal."

Children, the disabled, and other helpless ones are to know the protective, sheltering arms of the Klan.

VI. RACIAL

"To maintain forever white supremacy." "To maintain forever the God-given supremacy of the white race."

Every Klansman has unqualifiedly affirmed that he will "faithfully strive for the eternal maintenance of white supremacy."

THE OATH OF ALLEGIANCE

This oath of allegiance is divided into four sections, and will be analyzed section by section.

I. OBEDIENCE

Every Klansman, by his own oath, is solemnly and unconditionally pledged:

1. To obey faithfully the Constitution and laws of the order.
2. To conform to all regulations, usages, and require-ments of the order.
3. To respect and support the Imperial Authority of the order.
4. To heed heartily.
5. The only qualification: "I having knowledge of same, Providence alone preventing." This is the only qualification that mitigates in any way the failure of any Klansman to keep any part of this section of the oath of allegiance.

II. SECRECY

1. *The Klansman's pledge of secrecy pertains to all matters connected with the Knights of the Ku Klux Klan.*

    (a) He is sworn to keep solemnly secret the symbols of the order. This means that he will not disclose the signs, words, or grip.
    (b) He is solemnly sworn to keep sacredly secret all information that he may receive concerning the order. The alien world is eager to learn all it can of the inner secrets and workings and plans of the organiza-tion. The Klansman who is enlightened as to these matters is obligated to keep his in-formation both sacred and secret.

2. *These matters must never be divulged to the alien.* Klans-men must not publish or cause to be published such secret matters to any person in the whole world, except such person be a member of the order in good and regular standing, and not even then unless it be for the best interests of the order....

III. FIDELITY

1. *Every Klansman is solemnly pledged to guard and fos-ter every interest of the order.*

    (a) He will protect the order in every respect. He will defend its honor. He will defend its principles. Every Klansman should be a propagator of the Knights of the Ku Klux Klan, disseminating its principles and pro-moting its growth.
    (b) He will maintain its social cast and dignity. Every Klan should be a body consisting of the best, most honorable, and outstanding men in every community. It is every Klans-man's duty to live up to the highest and noblest standards prevailing among men of this character.

2. *Every Klansman must be faithful in fulfilling all obli-gations to the order.* He has pledged himself to pay promptly all just and legal demands made upon him to defray the expenses of his Klan and of the order, when same are due and called for. He will pay his dues, and will meet such other just demands as may be laid upon him, withholding nothing that rightfully belongs to the order....

IV. KLANNISHNESS

4. *Civic and Patriotic:*

    (a) Every true Klansman is loyally patriotic. This means he is devoted to:

        (1) The government of the United States of America.

(2)   His state.

(3)   His flag.

(4)   The Constitution of the United States.

(5)   Constitutional laws.

(6)   Law enforcement.

(b)   The true Klansman is pledged to absolute devotion to American principles. Before the sacred altar of the Klan, face to face with the Stars and Stripes, and beneath the holy light of the Fiery Cross, he pledged himself in these words; "I swear that I will most zealously and valiantly shield and preserve, by any and all justifiable means and methods, the sacred Constitutional rights and privileges of…"

(1)   Free public schools.

(2)   Free speech and free press.

(3)   Separation of church and state.

QUESTIONS

1.   How did the Ku Klux Klan define "pure patriotism"?

2.   Who is an "American," according to the Klan?

3.   What did the Klan fear most in the 1920s? How did the Klan address these fears?

22.4. VISUAL DOCUMENT: *FLESH AND THE DEVIL* MOVIE POSTER (1926)

Hollywood-produced movies became a major source of entertainment at home and abroad in the 1920s. Silent film stars attracted devoted audiences, which grew even larger after the institution of sound motion pictures in 1927.

QUESTIONS

1.   What does this poster suggest about movies and movie idols in the 1920s?

2.   How have ads for movies changed since the 1920s? How have they remained the same?

Source: FLESH AND THE DEVIL, Greta Garbo, John Gilbert, 1926/Everett Collection

22.5. CLARENCE DARROW AND WILLIAM JENNINGS BRYAN, EXCERPTS FROM THE SCOPES TRIAL (1925)

During the trial of John Thomas Scopes, who had been charged with violating Tennessee's law prohibiting the teaching of evolution, three-time democratic presidential candidate William Jennings Bryan, an ardent opponent of the scientific theory of evolution, joined the prosecution team. Clarence Darrow, a prominent defense attorney, called Bryan to testify. Their exchange over the factual validity of the Bible captured wide public attention.

[MR. DARROW]: But the Bible you have offered in evidence says 2,340 something, so that 4,200 years ago there was not a living thing on the earth, excepting the people on the ark and the animals on the ark and the fishes?

[MR. BRYAN]: There have been living things before that.

Q: I mean at that time.

A: After that.

Q: Don't you know there are any number of civilizations that are traced back to more than 5,000 years?

A: I know we have people who trace things back according to the number of ciphers they have. But I am not satisfied they are accurate.

Q: You are not satisfied there is any civilization that can be traced back 5,000 years?

A: I would not want to say there is because I have no evidence of it that is satisfactory.

Q: Would you say there is not?

A: Well, so far as I know, but when the scientists differ from 24,000,000 to 306,000,000 in their opinion as to how long ago life came here, I want them to be nearer, to come nearer together, before they demand of me to give up my belief in the Bible.

Q: Do you say that you do not believe that there were any civilizations on this earth that reach back beyond 5,000 years?

A: I am not satisfied by any evidence that I have seen....

Q: When was that flood?

A: I would not attempt to fix the date. The date is fixed, as suggested this morning.

Q: About 4004 B.C.?

A: That has been the estimate of a man that is accepted today. I would not say it is accurate.

Q: That estimate is printed in the Bible?

A: Everybody knows, at least, I think most of the people know, that was the estimate given.

Q: But what do you think that the Bible, itself, says? Don't you know how it was arrived at?

Source: Robert D. Marcus and David Burner, eds., *America Firsthand: Readings from Reconstruction to the Present*, vol 1, 4th ed. (Boston: Bedford, 1997), 154, 157–63.

A:	I never made a calculation.
Q:	What do you think?
A:	I do not think about things I don't think about.
Q:	Do you think about things you do think about?
A:	Well, sometimes.
THE BAILIFF:	Let us have order.
MR. DARROW:	Mr. Bryan, you have read these dates over and over again?
A:	Not very accurately; I turn back sometimes to see what the time was.
Q:	You want to say now you have no idea how these dates were computed?
A:	No, I don't say, but I have told you what my idea was. I say I don't know how accurate it was.
Q:	You say from the generation of man—
GEN. STEWART:	I am objecting to his cross-examining his own witness.
MR. DARROW:	He is a hostile witness.
THE COURT:	I am going to let Mr. Bryan control—
THE WITNESS:	I want him to have all the latitude he wants, for I am going to have some latitude when he gets through.
MR. DARROW:	You can have latitude and longitude.
THE COURT:	Order.
GEN. STEWART:	The witness is entitled to be examined as to the legal evidence of it. We were supposed to go into the argument today, and we have nearly lost the day, your Honor.
MR. MCKENZIE:	I object to it.
GEN. STEWART:	Your Honor, he is perfectly able to take care of this, but we are attaining no evidence. This is not competent evidence.
THE WITNESS:	These gentlemen have not had much chance—they did not come here to try this case. They came
	here to try revealed religion. I am here to defend it, and they can ask me any question they please.
THE COURT:	All right.
MR. DARROW:	Great applause from the bleachers.
THE WITNESS:	From those whom you call "yokels."
MR. DARROW:	I have never called them yokels.
THE WITNESS:	That is the ignorance of Tennessee, the bigotry.
MR. DARROW:	You mean who are applauding you?
THE WITNESS:	Those are the people whom you insult.
MR. DARROW:	You insult every man of science and learning in the world because he does not believe in your fool religion.
THE COURT:	I will not stand for that.
MR. DARROW:	For what he is doing?
THE COURT:	I am talking to both of you....
Q:	I ask for a direct answer.
A:	I do not ask to expect to find out all those things, ad I do not expect to find out about races.
Q:	I didn't ask you that. Now, I ask you if you know if it was interesting enough or important enough for you to try to find out about how old these ancient civilizations were?
A:	No; I have not made a study of it.
Q:	Don't you know that the ancient civilizations of China are 6,000 or 7,000 years old, at the very least?
A:	No; but they would not run back beyond the creation, according to the Bible, 6,000 years.
Q:	You don't know how old they are, is that right?
A:	I don't know how old they are, but probably you do. [*Laughter in the courtyard.*] I think you would give preference to anybody who opposed the Bible, and I give preference to the Bible.

Q: I see. Well, you are welcome to your opinion. Have you any idea how old the Egyptian civilization is?

A: No.

Q: Do you know of any record in the world, outside of the story of the Bible, which conforms to any statement that it is 4,200 years ago or thereabouts that all life was wiped off the face of the earth?

A: I think they have found records.

Q: Do you know of any?

A: Records reciting the flood, but I am not an authority on the subject.

Q: Now, Mr. Bryan, will you say if you know of any record, or have ever heard of any records, that describe that a flood existed 4,200 years ago, or about that time, which wiped all life off the earth?

A: The recollection of what I have read on that subject is not distinct enough to say whether the records attempted to fix a time, but I have seen in the discoveries of archaeologists where they have found records that described the flood.

Q: Mr. Bryan, don't you know that there are many old religions that describe the flood?

A: No, I don't know.

Q: You know there are others beside the Jewish?

A: I don't know whether these are the record of any other religion or refer to this flood.

Q: Don't you ever examine religion so far to know that?

A: Outside of the Bible?

Q: Yes.

A: No; I have not examined to know that, generally.

Q: You have never examined any other religions?

A: Yes, sir.

Q: Have you ever read anything about the origins of religions?

A: Not a great deal.

Q: You have never examined any other religion?

A: Yes, sir.

Q: And you don't know whether any other religion ever gave a similar account of the destruction of the earth by the flood?

A: The Christian religion has satisfied me, and I have never felt it necessary to look up some competing religions.

Q: Do you consider that every religion on earth competes with the Christian religion?

A: I think everybody who does not believe in the Christian religion believes so—

Q: I am asking what you think?

A: I do not regard them as competitive because I do not think they have the same sources we have.

Q: You are wrong in saying "competitive"?

A: I would not say competitive, but the religious unbelievers.

Q: Unbelievers of what?

A: In the Christian religion.

Q: What about the religion of Buddha?

A: I can tell you something about that, if you want to know.

Q: What about the religion of Confucius or Buddha?

A: Well, I can tell you something about that, if you would like to know.

Q: Did you ever investigate them?

A: Somewhat.

Q: Do you regard them as competitive?

A: No, I think they are very inferior. Would you like for me to tell you what I know about it?

Q:	No.
A:	Well, I shall insist on giving it to you.
Q:	You won't talk about free silver, will you?
A:	Not at all....

QUESTIONS

1. How would you describe the tone of the exchange between Darrow and Bryan?
2. How does this exchange encapsulate the tensions between modernism and fundamentalism?

22.6. IRÉNÉE DUPONT AND THE ASSOCIATION AGAINST THE PROHIBITION AMENDMENT, EXCERPTS FROM ANTI-PROHIBITION STATEMENTS (c. 1928)

Prohibition, popular at first, soon generated widespread opposition and calls for its repeal. In the first document below, Irénée DuPont, a wealthy industrialist whose family was the principal owner of the DuPont Chemical Corporation, explains why he went from being a supporter to an opponent of Prohibition. One of the few antiprohibitionists to mention the taxation implications of the Prohibition law in the mid-1920s, DuPont was clearly troubled that legitimate industries were carrying a tax burden avoided by bootleggers. The second document presents an excerpt from a resolution adopted by the Association Against the Prohibition Amendment in the spring of 1928 calling for repeal of the Eighteenth Amendment.

DUPONT ON REASONS TO OPPOSE PROHIBITION

First: It is not producing total abstinence but on the contrary is increasing the abuse of liquor, especially among young people.

Second: It is transferring an enormous revenue which could be collected by the Government in the form of a tax to the bootlegger and corrupt dry agent.

Third: It is an infringement on state rights and it is preferable that the several states govern themselves wherever possible.

Fourth: but not last, it is the opening wedge to a breaking down of our whole theory of Government by legislating through the Constitution....

The corporations of this country are being taxed 13% of their net profits, which is substantially in lieu of the tax on liquor which should flow to the Government....In 1914...we had become a temperate country; drinking in the upper classes had nearly vanished and was no longer a problem industrially. It was then almost impossible for minors to buy liquor; certainly they didn't do it....Today it is notorious that a minor can get all the bootleg liquor he wants without regulation. Prohibition...has driven the saloon off the sidewalk but has put it in the cellar where it is out of sight....Personally, I would rather a few habitual drunkards die of their own volition by the use of alcoholic beverages than to have one man accidentally killed by the route of denatured alcohol.

Source: David E. Kyvig. *Repealing National Prohibition* (Kent, OH: Kent State University Press, 2000), 79–80, 97.

RESOLUTION OF THE ASSOCIATION AGAINST THE PROHIBITION AMENDMENT

RESOLVED, That we shall work, first and foremost, for the entire repeal of the Eighteenth Amendment to the Constitution of the United States, to the end of casting out this solitary, sumptuary statute, the intrusion of which into constitutional realms has so severely hurt our country. The question of whether prohibition or regulation is the more effective relation of government to the liquor traffic is utterly subordinate to the distortion of our Federal Constitution by compelling it to carry the burden of a task which is an affair for the police power of each of our forty-eight separate and sovereign states, and never should be the business of the Federal Government.

QUESTIONS

1. Summarize the main arguments for ending Prohibition.
2. How would a Prohibitionist counter these arguments?

CHAPTER 23

A NEW DEAL FOR AMERICANS, 1931–1939

23.1. E. J. SULLIVAN, "THE 1932ND PSALM" (1932)

Shortly before the November 1932 presidential election, as the Depression grew worse, a despond-ent citizen named E. J. Sullivan published a parody of the 23rd Psalm. His words reflected growing anxiety about the nation's economy and ridiculed Herbert Hoover's response to the crisis.

Hoover is my shepherd, I am in want.
He maketh me to lie down on park benches
He leadeth me by still factories
He restoreth my doubt in the Republican Party.
He guided me in the path of the unemployed for his party's sake.
Yea, though I walk through the alley of soup kitchens, I am hungry.
I do not fear evil, for thou art against me.
Thy Cabinet and thy Senate, they do discomfort me.
Thou didst prepare a reduction in my wages.

In the presence of my creditors thou anointed my income with taxes,
So my expense overruneth my income.
Surely poverty and hard times will follow me
All the days of the Republican administration.
And I shall dwell in a rented house forever.
Amen.

QUESTIONS

1. What real economic hardships does the author of this parody identify?
2. Why did the psalm attack Herbert Hoover?

Source: Robert McElvaine, *The Depression and New Deal: A History In Documents* (New York: Oxford University Press, 2003), 28.

23.2. MR. AND MRS. W. L. HANNON, "LETTER TO MRS. ROOSEVELT" (1939)

During the New Deal, hundreds of thousands of ordinary Americans wrote to Franklin and Eleanor Roosevelt to share their fears and hopes. Many of them recounted the impact of programs such as the Farm Security Administration on their lives. The Roosevelt Presidential Library preserved this letter sent by Mr. and Mrs. W. L. Hannon of Eldorado, Kansas, to the First Lady in 1939.

Eldorado, Kansas

Dear Mrs. Roosevelt:

I take this liberty to tell you of the work of the Farm Security Administration in Kansas.

Many things have been said and printed against the New Deal which made me wonder why more hasn't been said and printed for the New Deal then I thought we accept all the benefactions of the New Deal without saying much about it and many times receiving these merciful benefactions and at the same time saying much against it.

I wish to write the best I can with the limited talents I possess of our actual experience and for no other reason than to show our gratitude.

In 1932 we were prosperous farmers with youth, health, and ambition. We worked hard and long hours, met all our debts promptly, and were able to accumulate a reasonable amount each year. We made well on cattle. This fired our ambition. We decided to double our herd. We would surely be able to buy the much longed for farm home.

We awoke one morning to find we owed money we never had possessed. We felt a little dazed but on every hand was consoled with the good news (it couldn't last) and by all means hold on to those cattle until prices returned.

Well the trials and tribulations of holding on to those cattle for return prices would fill a book. Droughts set in in earnest. The grass would die. Five years we had insufficient feed. I can say for endurance we couldn't be beat, for the cattle nearly died of starvation and old age before we decided prosperity wasn't just around the corner. I might add the thought of meeting a deficit at the bank had something to do with our endurance.

Finally the bankers and ourselves decided we couldn't await prosperity any longer. A sale was called. We still had a deficit of three thousand dollars and without cattle. We managed to pay rent, support our family, but could not pay interest, say nothing about the principal.

We felt a strict obligation to our debts but it began to look like we had met with the impossible. We realized interest was compounding, the principal was mounting and try our best nothing we could do about it, with crop failures and ruinous prices.

Our bankers were caught as we were facing the impossible it became too heavy a burden for them to bear. They brought in a collector to take his place, who made it his business to collect regardless. We would turn our Gov. crop checks and sell off stock not ready for market to meet his demands. Finally, we realized there was nothing more to give in his greedy taking. he had killed the goose that lay the golden egg. I am still surprised in this day of specialized training that a man so incompetent should be placed in this position. I can now see where a collector should be a man of tact and should be able to pass a high intelligence test.

We farmers of this community, while not highly educated, had common sense enough to note his

Source: Letter from Mr. and Mrs. W. L. Hannon to Eleanor Roosevelt, 1939, Folder FSA-1939, Official File 1568, The Franklin D. Roosevelt Library.

egotism and lack of sympathy and also that he would have starved to death on a farm if compelled to live by his own efforts. Farmers are a little different from other classes. They do with out rather than face debt so we all felt as if we had committed the unpardonable sin. It was a skeleton in the closet. No soldier ever fought a braver battle to keep the neighbors from knowing things were not as they should be. We went with aching teeth and flirted with death rather than consult a Dr. I might add of all the many sacrifices we made our children's education was the last denial but even that came to pass.

By this time a farmer with a relative who had money would borrow or beg to pay this collector to have a chance to recuperate but alas for ourselves and many like us who had no one to turn to. We were facing the possibility of being sold out as we had signed over everything we possessed to protect the bank against this cattle loss.

We were farmers, knew no other trade, and by this time the trained city worker could not find work. We realized we had no chance in town. We were desperate. My husband's health broke under the strain of worry and overwork. I realized this was the last straw with my husband bedfast I went to this collector and asked him if we could just keep enough stock to keep off relief and plant another crop and he could take the rest. He said he would take it all and if relief was the only thing left why thousands were taking it so we would not matter. Sick and discouraged I do not like to think what might have happened had we not the Gov. to turn to.

The Gov. granted our loan, got us out from under this tyrant, reestablished us—now the result.

With peace of mind my husband's health is restored and this is no more important than his restored courage. He has taken a new lease on life, making plans in a bigger, better way and may I say here I think the loan worth the price from no other standpoint than the fact it installs a bookkeeping which is going to make a business man of the farmer. We profit from its benefits each month and instead of trying to destroy us the Gov. loan seeks to aid us in every way.

Not a day of my life I do not thank God for President Roosevelt and his leaders who have made such a sacrifice to help the oppressed.

Oh yes! They wonder how he carries on so well and still laughs so heartily and call him America's showman No. I. They well know what he has to content with, but the one thing they do not know is that each night as he lays these terrific burdens down he is consoled and strengthened by the fact that he has given courage and hope to thousands upon thousands and that he has fought for the oppressed with a courage no other human has ever shown. These facts account for the fact he carries on so well and can still laugh so heartily.

From a grateful farmer and his wife to whom the Farm Security Administration has given health, happiness and courage.

Mr. and Mrs. W. L. Hannon
Route 3
Eldorado, Kansas

QUESTIONS

1. How did the Depression hurt Kansas farmers?
2. What relief did New Deal programs provide to farmers?

23.3. U.S. CONGRESS, EXCERPTS FROM THE NATIONAL LABOR RELATIONS ACT (1935)

In 1935, Congress passed the National Labor Relations Act, sponsored by Senator Robert Wagner of New York. This legislation codified the right of workers to organize unions and bargain collectively with employers. The law, which was passed through presidential support and strenuous organizational efforts by groups such as the Congress of Industrial Organizations (CIO), resulted in millions of workers in the automobile, steel, coal, rubber, and electrical industries joining unions.

An Act
To diminish the causes of labor disputes burdening or obstructing interstate and foreign commerce, to create a National Labor Relations Board, and for other purposes.

FINDINGS AND POLICY

Sec. 1. The denial by employers of the right of employees to organize and the refusal by employers to accept the procedure of collective bargaining lead to strikes and other forms of industrial strife or unrest, which have the intent or the necessary effect of burdening or obstructing commerce by (a) impairing the efficiency, safety, or operation of the instrumentalities of commerce; (b) occurring in the current of commerce; (c) materially affecting, restraining, or controlling the flow of raw materials or manufactured or processed goods from or into the channels of commerce; or the prices of such materials or goods in commerce; or (d) causing diminution of employment and wages in such volume as substantially to impair or disrupt the market for goods flowing from or into the channels of commerce.

The inequality of bargaining power between employees who do not possess full freedom of association or actual liberty of contract, and employers who are organized in the corporate or other forms of ownership association substantially burdens and affects the flow of commerce, and tends to aggravate recurrent business depressions, by depressing wage rates and the purchasing power of wage earners in industry and by preventing the stabilization of competitive wage rates and working conditions within and between industries.

Experience has proved that protection by law of the right of employees to organize and bargain collectively safeguards commerce from injury, impairment, or interruption, and promotes the flow of commerce by removing certain recognized sources of industrial strife and unrest, by encouraging practices fundamental to the friendly adjustment of industrial disputes arising out of differences as to wages, hours, or other working conditions, and by restoring equality of bargaining power between employers and employees....

Sec. 7. Employees shall have the right to self-organization, to form, join, or assist labor organizations, to bargain collectively through representatives of their own choosing, and to engage in concerted activities, for the purpose of collective bargaining or other mutual aid or protection.

Sec. 8. It shall be an unfair labor practice for an employer—

Source: National Labor Relations Act; 29 U.S.C. §§ 151–169. National Labor Relations Board Website, www.nlrb.gov/national-labor-relations-act.

(1) To interfere with, restrain, or coerce employees in the exercise of the rights guaranteed in Section 7.

(2) To dominate or interfere with the formation or administration of any labor organization or contribute financial or other support to it....

(3) By discrimination in regard to hire or tenure of employment or any term or condition of employment to encourage or discourage membership in any labor organization: Provided, That nothing in this Act...or in any other statute of the United States, shall preclude an employer from making an agreement with a labor organization (not established, maintained, or assisted by any action defined in this Act as an unfair labor practice) to require as a condition of employment membership therein, if such labor organization is the representative of the employees as provided in Section 9(a), in the appropriate collective bargaining unit covered by such agreement when made.

(4) To discharge or otherwise discriminate against an employee because he has filed charges or given testimony under this Act.

(5) To refuse to bargain collectively with the representatives of his employees, subject to the provisions of Section 9(a).

REPRESENTATIVES AND ELECTIONS

Sec. 9. (a) Representatives designated or selected for the purposes of collective bargaining by the majority of the employees in a unit appropriate for such purposes, shall be the exclusive representatives of all the employees in such unit for the purposes of collective bargaining in respect to rates of pay, wages, hours of employment, or other conditions of employment: Provided, That any individual employee or a group of employees shall have the right at any time to present grievances to their employer....

LIMITATIONS

Sec. 13. Nothing in this Act shall be construed so as to interfere with or impede or diminish in any way the right to strike.

QUESTIONS

1. What support for labor unions did this law provide?
2. How did this support mark a change in government policy toward organized labor?

23.4. VISUAL DOCUMENT: SOCIAL SECURITY BOARD, "A MONTHLY CHECK TO YOU" POSTER (1936)

During 1936, American workers were encouraged by posters such as this one to sign up for their first Social Security card. A hallmark New Deal reform, Social Security held out the promise of a dignified retirement for the elderly and assistance to disabled workers.

QUESTIONS

1. What benefits did Social Security provide to most working Americans?

2. Who was excluded from Social Security coverage?

Source: The Granger Collection, NYC.

23.5. VISUAL DOCUMENTS: DOROTHEA LANGE, PHOTOGRAPHS OF MIGRATORY WORKERS IN CALIFORNIA (1936–1939)

Between 1935 and 1942, the Farm Security Administration hired some of the nation's most talented photographers, including Dorothea Lange, Sheldon Dick, Ben Shawn, and Walker Evans, to chronicle the lives of ordinary workers, migrant laborers, and rural farmers facing hard times.

Mexican Migratory Field Worker's Home on the Edge of a Frozen Pea Field, Imperial Valley, California, 1937.

Source: Dorothea Lange/U.S. Farm Security Administration/Library of Congress, Prints and Photographs Division.

Pea Pickers in California, 1936.

Migratory Workers in California, 1936–1939.

QUESTIONS

1. Why did Farm Security Administration photographers memorialize the poorest of the poor?

2. Who was the audience for these photographs?

CHAPTER 24

ARSENAL OF DEMOCRACY: THE WORLD AT WAR, 1931–1945

24.1. FRANKLIN D. ROOSEVELT AND WINSTON CHURCHILL, THE ATLANTIC CHARTER (AUGUST 14, 1941)

In August 1941, four months before Japan's attack on Pearl Harbor, President Franklin Roosevelt and British Prime Minister Winston Churchill issued the Atlantic Charter. Reflecting Roosevelt's vision of a reformed world order, the charter spoke of bringing democracy, self-determination, and disarmament to the world following the defeat of the Axis powers.

The President of The United States of America and the Prime Minister, Mr. *Churchill*, representing His Majesty's Government in The United Kingdom, being met together, deem it right to make known certain common principles in the national policies of their respective countries on which they base their hopes for a better future for the world.

1. Their countries seek no aggrandizement, territorial or other.
2. They desire to see no territorial changes that do not accord with the freely expressed wishes of the peoples concerned.
3. They respect the right of all peoples to choose the form of government under which they will live; and they wish to see sovereign rights and self-government restored to those who have been forcibly deprived of them.
4. They will endeavor, with due respect for their existing obligations, to further the enjoyment by all States, great or small, victor or vanquished, of access, on equal terms, to the trade and to the raw materials of the world which are needed for their economic prosperity.
5. They desire to bring about the fullest collaboration between all nations in the economic field with the object of securing, for all, improved labor standards, economic advancement and social security.

Source: Declaration by Franklin D. Roosevelt and Winston Churchill, August 14, 1941. President's Secretary's File (PSF) Box 1, Folder 7. Courtesy of the Franklin D. Roosevelt Presidential Library and Museum Website, http://docs.fdrlibrary.marist.edu/PSF/BOX1/a07p01.html (2009).

6. After the final destruction of the Nazi tyranny, they hope to see established a peace which will afford to all nations the means of dwelling in safety within their own boundaries, and which will afford assurance that all the men in all the lands may live out their lives in freedom from fear and want.
7. Such a peace should enable all men to traverse the high seas and oceans without hindrance.
8. They believe that all of the nations of the world, for realistic as well as spiritual reasons, must come to the abandonment of the use of force. Since no future peace can be maintained if land, sea or air armaments continue to be employed by nations which threaten, or may threaten, aggression outside of their frontiers, they believe, pending the

establishment of a wider and permanent system of general security, that the disarmament of such nations is essential. They will likewise aid and encourage all other practicable measures which will lighten for peace-loving peoples the crushing burden of armaments.

Franklin D. Roosevelt
Winston S. Churchill

August 14, 1941

QUESTIONS

1. What pledge did Roosevelt offer to colonial peoples?
2. What proposals does the document make to ensure postwar peace?

24.2. WESTERN DEFENSE COMMAND, "INSTRUCTIONS TO ALL PERSONS OF JAPANESE ANCESTRY LIVING IN THE FOLLOWING AREA" (APRIL 30, 1942)

Following the Japanese attack on the Pacific Fleet at Pearl Harbor, newspapers, politicians, and some military officials along the West Coast stoked popular fears of Japanese invasions abetted by Japanese-Americans. About 110,000 Americans of Japanese ancestry, most of them citizens, were forced to leave California and other states in the West and were placed in internment camps for most of the war years. The Western Defense Command issued the following order in April 1942 that applied to the areas around San Francisco.

WESTERN DEFENSE COMMAND AND FOURTH ARMY WARTIME CIVIL CONTROL ADMINISTRATION

Presidio of San Francisco, California

INSTRUCTIONS TO ALL PERSONS OF JAPANESE ANCESTRY LIVING IN THE FOLLOWING AREA:

All of that portion of the County of Alameda, State of California, within that boundary beginning at the

Source: U.S. Army, Western Defense Command, *Final Report, Japanese Evacuation from the West Coast, 1942* (Washington, DC: U.S. Army, 1943), 99–100.

point at which the southerly limits of the City of Berkeley meet San Francisco Bay; thence easterly and following the southerly limits of said city to College Avenue; thence southerly on College Avenue to Broadway; thence southerly on Broadway to the southerly limits of the City of Oakland; thence following the limits of said city westerly and northerly, and following the shoreline of San Francisco Bay to the point of beginning.

Pursuant to the provisions of Civilian Exclusion Order No. 27, this Headquarters, dated April 30, 1942, all persons of Japanese ancestry, both alien and non-alien, will be evacuated from the above area by 12 o'clock noon, P.W.T., Thursday May 7, 1942.

No Japanese person living in the above area will be permitted to change residence after 12 o'clock noon, P.W.T., Thursday, April 30, 1942, without obtaining special permission from the representative of the Commanding General, Northern California Sector, at the Civil Control Station located at:

530 Eighteenth Street,
Oakland, California.

Such permits will only be granted for the purpose of uniting members of a family, or in cases of grave emergency.

The Civil Control Station is equipped to assist the Japanese population affected by this evacuation in the following ways:

1. Give advice and instructions on the evacuation.
2. Provide services with respect to the management, leasing, sale, storage or other disposition of most kinds of property, such as real estate, business and professional equipment, household goods, boats, automobiles and livestock.
3. Provide temporary residence elsewhere for all Japanese in family groups.
4. Transport persons and a limited amount of clothing and equipment to their new residence.

THE FOLLOWING INSTRUCTIONS MUST BE OBSERVED:

1. A responsible member of each family, preferably the head of the family, or the person in whose name most of the property is held, and each individual living alone, will report to the Civil Control Station to receive further instructions. This must be done between 8:00 A.M. and 5:00 P.M. on Friday, May 1, 1942, or between 8:00 A.M. and 5:00 P.M. on Saturday, May 2, 1942.

2. Evacuees must carry with them on departure for the Assembly Center, the following property:

   (a) Bedding and linens (no mattress) for each member of the family;
   (b) Toilet articles for each member of the family;
   (c) Extra clothing for each member of the family;
   (d) Sufficient knives, forks, spoons, plates, bowls and cups for each member of the family;
   (e) Essential personal effects for each member of the family.

All items carried will be securely packaged, tied and plainly marked with the name of the owner and numbered in accordance with instructions obtained at the Civil Control Station. The size and number of packages is limited to that which can be carried by the individual or family group.

3   No pets of any kind will be permitted.

4. No personal items and no household goods will be shipped to the Assembly Center.

5. The United States Government through its agencies will provide for the storage at the sole risk of the owner of the more substantial household items, such as iceboxes, washing machines, pianos and other heavy furniture. Cooking utensils and other small items will be accepted for storage if crated, packed and plainly marked with the name and address of the owner. Only one name and address will be used by a given family.

6. Each family, and individual living alone will be furnished transportation to the Assembly Center or will be authorized to travel by private automobile in a supervised group. All instructions pertaining to the movement will be obtained at the Civil Control Station.

Go to the Civil Control Station between the hours of 8:00 A.M. and 5:00 P.M., Friday, May 1,

1942, or between the hours of 8:00 A.M. and 5:00 P.M., Saturday, May 2, 1942, to receive further instructions.

J. L. DeWitt
Lieutenant General, U. S. Army
Commanding

April 30, 1942

QUESTIONS

1. How did the U.S. internment policy violate the basic rights of Japanese-Americans?
2. What arguments were made to justify internment?

24.3. ELEANOR ROOSEVELT, EXCERPT FROM "RACE, RELIGION, AND PREJUDICE" (MAY 11, 1942)

During World War II, no American worked harder than Eleanor Roosevelt to preserve and advance the New Deal reform agenda. Americans fought racist dictatorships in the war against Germany and Japan but lived in a largely segregated country that barred the entry of most Eastern Europeans and Jews, and all Asians. In this 1942 article, Mrs. Roosevelt spoke forcefully of the need to recognize the humanity of all peoples and assure their equality under the law. Even she, however, counseled patience by African Americans in asserting their full rights.

One of the phases of this war that we have to face is the question of race discrimination.

We have had a definite policy toward the Chinese and Japanese who wished to enter our country for many years, and I doubt very much if after this war is over we can differentiate between the peoples of Europe, the Near East and the Far East.

Perhaps the simplest way of facing the problem in the future is to say that we are fighting for freedom, and one of the freedoms we must establish is freedom from discrimination among the peoples of the world, either because of race, or of color, or of religion.

The people of the world have suddenly begun to stir and they seem to feel that in the future we should look upon each other as fellow human beings, judged by our acts, by our abilities, by our development, and not by any less fundamental differences.

Here in our own country we have any number of attitudes which have become habits and which constitute our approach to the Jewish people, the Japanese and Chinese people, the Italian people, and above all, to the Negro people in our midst.

Perhaps because the Negroes are our largest minority, our attitude towards them will have to be faced first of all. I keep on repeating that the way to face this situation is by being completely realistic. We cannot force people to accept friends for whom they have no liking, but living in a democracy it is entirely reasonable to demand that every citizen of that democracy enjoy the fundamental rights of a citizen.

Over and over again, I have stressed the rights of every citizen:

Equality before the law.
Equality of education.

Source: Eleanor Roosevelt, "Race, Religion, and Prejudice," *The New Republic*, May 11, 1942, 630.

Equality to hold a job according to his ability.

Equality of participation through the ballot in the government.

These are inherent rights in a democracy, and I do not see how we can fight this war and deny these rights to any citizen in our own land.

The other relationships will gradually settle themselves once these major things are part of our accepted philosophy.

It seems trite to say to the Negro, you must have patience, when he has had patience so long; you must not expect miracles overnight, when he can look back to the years of slavery and say—how many nights! he has waited for justice. Nevertheless, it is what we must continue to say in the interests of our government as a whole and of the Negro people; but that does not mean that we must sit idle and do nothing. We must keep moving forward steadily, removing restrictions which have no sense, and fighting prejudice. If we are wise we will do this where it is easiest to do it first,

and watch it spread gradually to places where the old prejudices are slow to disappear.

There is now a great group of educated Negroes who can become leaders among their people, who can teach them the value of things of the mind and who qualify as the best in any field of endeavor. With these men and women it is impossible to think of any barriers of inferiority, but differences there are and always will be, and that is why on both sides there must be tact and patience and an effort at real understanding. Above everything else, no action must be taken which can cause so much bitterness that the whole liberalizing effort may be set back over a period of many years.

QUESTIONS

1. What racial problems did Mrs. Roosevelt identify in American society?
2. Why did she believe it was vital to solve these problems?

24.4. VISUAL DOCUMENT: J. HOWARD MILLER, *WE CAN DO IT* ("ROSIE THE RIVETER") POSTER (1942)

As 16 million men entered military service between 1941 and 1945, American women faced greatly expanded opportunities and obligations. They worked in military production and became single parents, homemakers, breadwinners, and role models for their children. J. Howard Miller's *We Can Do It* poster has become an icon of the era. This determined, muscular defense worker, with rolled-up sleeves, was as ubiquitous during the war years as the recruiting poster of Uncle Sam declaring "I Want You."

QUESTION

1. How did poster art of wartime women mark a reversal of feminine stereotypes existing before the war? What new realities did they reflect?

Source: Courtesy of The Granger Collection.

J. Howard Miller, *We Can Do It* ("Rosie the Riveter") poster, War Production Co-ordinating Committee (1942).

24.5. FRANKLIN D. ROOSEVELT, EXCERPT FROM "AN ECONOMIC BILL OF RIGHTS" (JANUARY 11, 1944)

In his State of the Union Address to Congress and the American people on January 11, 1944, President Franklin Roosevelt outlined the framework for a new economic bill of rights. Government, he proclaimed, must actively promote full employment, a decent standard of living, health care, affordable housing, and a good education. Many of these ideas were incorporated into the GI Bill of Rights that benefited 16 million veterans and their families.

It is our duty now to begin to lay the plans and determine the strategy for the winning of a lasting peace and the establishment of an American standard of living higher than ever before known. We cannot be content, no matter how high that general standard of living may be, if some fraction of our people—whether it be one-third or one-fifth or one-tenth—is ill-fed, ill-clothed, ill-housed, and insecure.

This Republic had its beginning, and grew to its present strength, under the protection of certain inalienable political rights—among them the right of free speech, free press, free worship, trial by jury, freedom from unreasonable searches and seizures. They are our rights to life and liberty.

As our Nation has grown in size and stature, however—as our industrial economy expanded—these political rights proved inadequate to assure us equality in the pursuit of happiness.

We have come to a clear realization of the fact that true individual freedom cannot exist without economic security and independence. "Necessitous men are not free men." People who are hungry and out of a job are the stuff of which dictatorships are made.

In our day these economic truths have become accepted as self-evident. We have accepted, so to speak, a second Bill of Rights under which a new basis of security and prosperity can be established for all—regardless of station, race, or creed.

Among these are:

The right to a useful and remunerative job in the industries or shops or farms or mines of the Nation;

The right to earn enough to provide adequate food and clothing and recreation;

The right of every farmer to raise and sell his products at a return which will give him and his family a decent living;

The right of every businessman, large and small, to trade in an atmosphere of freedom from unfair competition and domination by monopolies at home or abroad;

The right of every family to a decent home;

The right to adequate medical care and the opportunity to achieve and enjoy good health;

The right to adequate protection from the economic fears of old age, sickness, accident, and unemployment;

The right to a good education.

All of these rights spell security. And after this war is won we must be prepared to move forward, in the implementation of these rights, to new goals of human happiness and well-being.

Source: Samual I. Rosenman, ed., The Public Papers and Addresses of Franklin D. Roosevelt, vol. 13 (New York: Harper and Bros., 1950), 40–42.

America's own rightful place in the world depends in large part upon how fully these and similar rights have been carried into practice for our citizens. For unless there is security here at home there cannot be lasting peace in the world.

QUESTIONS

1. How did Roosevelt propose expanding the concept of freedom contained in the Bill of Rights?
2. For what economic guarantees did he call?

CHAPTER 25

PROSPERITY AND LIBERTY UNDER THE SHADOW OF THE BOMB, 1945–1952

25.1. EXHIBITING THE ENOLA GAY

Few events in history have generated as much controversy as the decision to use the atomic bomb on human targets. In the 1990s, the Smithsonian Institution acquired funding to restore the *Enola Gay*, the B-29 that dropped the bomb on Hiroshima. The American Air Force Association helped raise funds to support the restoration and presentation of the plane. After the airplane's restoration, the Smithsonian designed an exhibition, "The Crossroads: The End of World War II, The Atomic Bomb and the Origins of the Cold War," around it. Before the exhibit's official opening in 1995, Pacific veterans and Republican leaders were given a sneak peak ahead of the public. Many came away dismayed at the impression left by an exhibit that included graphic details of the bomb's effect on the citizens of Hiroshima. Eight thousand veterans, with the support of conservatives in Congress, petitioned the Smithsonian to revise the exhibit and remove the disturbing content about bomb victims. The ensuing political fight was part of a larger "culture war" that pitted conservative politicians and pundits against historians. Ultimately, the exhibit was curtailed, eliminating most mentions of the politics of war and focusing on the mechanics of the airplane and its atomic payload. The director of the Smithsonian was fired, and a heated national debate about "who owns history" dominated the airwaves and front pages.

Sources: Text of first draft of Enola Gay Exhibit. Full text may be found in Philip Nobile, *Judgement at the Smithsonian* (New York: Marlow & Co., 1995); John T. Correll, "The Smithsonian and the Enola Gay," Air Force Association Special Report (March 15, 1994), http://www.afa.org/media/enolagay/03–001.asp.

TEXT OF FIRST DRAFT OF ENOLA GAY EXHIBIT

GROUND ZERO:

HIROSHIMA, 8:15 A.M., AUGUST 6, 1945

NAGASAKI, 11:02 A.M., AUGUST 9, 1945

Hiroshima, August 6, 1945

The mushroom cloud as seen 15 to 20 minutes after the explosion from the Mikumari Gorge, some 6.5 kilometers (4 miles) from ground zero.—Photograph by Seizo Yamada

"At first I saw rainbows, one over the other, then a mushroom cloud began to rise, and I heard the sound of a tremendous explosion."—Seizo Yamada, Hiroshima

(Artifacts in this section are preliminary; based on initial request to the Hiroshima and Nagasaki Museums.)

This wristwatch was smashed when its owner, Akito Kawagoe, was buried beneath the debris of the Futaba-No-Sato army barracks, 1.8 kilometers (1.1 miles) from the explosion. He escaped and survived.— Loaned by Akito Kawagoe and the Hiroshima Peace Memorial Museum

Broken wall clock, Nagasaki—Loaned by Nagasaki International Culture Hall

Hiroshima, 8:17. a.m., August 6, 1945

The base of the growing mushroom cloud as seen from near the Kanda Bridge , 8 kilometers (5 miles) from ground zero, two minutes after the explosion.— Photograph by Mitsuo Matsuhige

Hiroshima, 8:30 a.m., August 6, 1945

Gon'ichi Kimura was stationed at the Army Water Transport Headquarters, Ujina, about 4 kilometers (2.5 miles) south of ground zero. He snapped this photo of the cloud roughly 15 minutes after the explosion.— Photograph by Gon'ichi Kimura

Nagasaki, 11:12 a.m., August 9, 1945

This photograph of the Nagasaki cloud was taken from Koyagi Island in Nagasaki Harbor, 10 kilometers (6 miles) south of the explosion.

Nagasaki, 11:12 a.m., August 9, 1945

The Nagasaki cloud as seen from a spot only 8 kilometers (5 miles) from ground zero. Judging from the size and shape of the cloud, the photograph was taken about 10 minutes after the explosion. Twelve minutes after the blast, the top of the mushroom cloud had already reached an altitude of 12 kilometers (7.5 miles).

THE SMITHSONIAN AND THE ENOLA GAY

AT THE SMITHSONIAN, HISTORY GRAPPLES WITH CULTURAL ANGST.

The Smithsonian Institution acquired the *Enola Gay* —the B-29 that dropped the first atomic bomb—forty-four years ago. After a decade of deterioration in open weather, the aircraft was put into storage in 1960. Now, following a lengthy period of restoration, it will finally be displayed to the public on the fiftieth anniversary of its famous mission. The exhibition will run from May 1995 to January 1996 at the Smithsonian's National Air and Space Museum in Washington.

The aircraft will be an element in a larger exhibition called "The Crossroads: The End of World War II, the Atomic Bomb, and the Origins of the Cold War." The context is the development of the atomic bomb and its use against the Japanese cities of Hiroshima and Nagasaki in August 1945.

The *Enola Gay*'s task was a grim one, hardly suitable for glamorization. Nevertheless, many visitors may be taken aback by what they see. That is particularly true for World War II veterans who had petitioned the museum to display the historic bomber in a more objective setting.

The restored aircraft will be there all right, the front fifty-six feet of it, anyway. The rest of the gallery space is allotted to a program about the atomic bomb. The presentation is designed for shock effect. The museum's exhibition plan notes that parents might find some parts unsuitable for viewing by their children, and the script warns that "parental discretion is advised."

For what the plan calls the "emotional center" of the exhibit, the curators are collecting burnt watches, broken wall clocks, and photos of victims—which will be enlarged to life size—as well as melted and broken religious objects. One display will be a schoolgirl's lunch box with remains of peas and rice reduced to carbon. To ensure that nobody misses the point, "where possible, photos of the persons who owned or wore these artifacts would be used to show that real people stood behind the artifacts." Survivors of Hiroshima and Nagasaki will recall the horror in their own words.

The Air and Space Museum says it takes no position on the "difficult moral and political questions" involved. For the past two years, however, museum officials have been under fire from veterans groups who charge that the exhibition plan is politically biased.

CONCESSIONS TO BALANCE

The exhibition plan the museum was following as recently as November picked up the story of the war in 1945 as the end approached. It depicted the Japanese in a desperate defense of their home islands, saying little about what had made such a defense necessary. U.S. conduct of the war was depicted as brutal, vindictive, and racially motivated.

The latest script, written in January, shows major concessions to balance. It acknowledges Japan's "naked aggression and extreme brutality" that began in the 1930s. It gives greater recognition to U.S. casualties. Despite some hedging, it says the atomic bomb "played a crucial role in ending the Pacific war quickly." Further revisions to the script are expected.

The ultimate effect of the exhibition will depend, of course, on how the words are blended with the artifacts and audiovisual elements. And despite the balancing material added, the curators still make some curious calls.

"For most Americans," the script says, "it was a war of vengeance. For most Japanese, it was a war to defend their unique culture against Western imperialism." Women, children, and mutilated religious objects are strongly emphasized in the "ground zero" scenes from Hiroshima and Nagasaki. The museum says this is "happenstance," not a deliberate ideological twist. The Air and Space Museum is also taking flak from the other side. A prominent historian serving on an advisory group for the exhibition, for example, objects to the "celebratory" treatment of the *Enola Gay* and complains that the crew showed "no remorse" for the mission.

QUESTIONS

1. Do you agree with the American Air Force Association that the exhibit plan was "politically biased?"
2. Is there a way to present such a controversial topic without cultural or political bias?

25.2. FRIEDA S. MILLER, "WHAT'S BECOME OF ROSIE THE RIVETER?" (MAY 5, 1946)

The systematic removal of women from the industrial workforce was more than a practical response to the return of male veterans—it was a Cold War imperative. Cold War government propaganda stressed that American women could best fight the Communist ideological menace by being homemakers. Women's work in the Soviet Union and women's work in the United States became an important point of differentiation between the two systems. The Soviets celebrated women workers as symbols of socialist equality. American politicians pointed to Soviet women workers as an example of the backward Communist system that required all citizens to slave away in service of the state.

Source: Frieda S. Miller, "What's Become of Rosie the Riveter?" *New York Times*, May 5, 1946, SM11.

WHAT'S BECOME OF ROSIE THE RIVETER?

HER NUMBERS REDUCED BY MILLIONS SINCE JULY, SHE IS INVOLVED IN A TREMENDOUS RESHUFFLING

When a character captures the imagination of the American public, his ups and downs are followed with an interest that sometimes surpasses avidity. Thus it is with Rosie the Riveter, who symbolized to America the effort of all women workers toward winning the war.

Today, there is little doubt that Rosie and her industrial sisters are fading from the scene of heavy manufacturing. Since V-E Day, about a million women production workers have left the nation's aircraft plants, shipyards, ammunition factories and other industries that produced so prodigiously for war. The sharpest decline, of course, followed victory over Japan, but the trend had started even before V-E Day in the shipyards and aircraft plants, large wartime employers of women among the durable goods industries.

As a result of this exodus of women factory workers, the public is asking: Where have Rosie and the rest of the heroines of the war production front gone? What are they planning to do now that the men are taking over? Is it true that these women, despite their gallant war service, are finding factory doors to heavy industry closed to them?

Positive answers to all of the questions are not easy in a period of readjustment. Rosie and her sisters, like millions of men and women, have become involved in the most tremendous reshuffling of human resources, both occupationally and geographically, that the country ever has known. Some answers, however, have emerged with a certain clarity, and one of these is the whereabouts of Rosie the Riveter and the women for whom she became a wartime symbol.

Some of the former riveters and other industrial workers, wearied by the long grind of forty-eight hours and more per week and the exacting task of producing for war, are taking well-earned rests before putting out feelers about post-war jobs. Still others, particularly a number of the young women whose husbands have been demobilized from the armed services, have no definite plans. At the moment, they are waiting to see how their veteran husbands fare in the readjustments to civilian life.

If the ex-GI can bring home enough pay in his weekly envelope to support a wife and establish a home, the former Rosies will at least have the chance to devote their entire time to homemaking and some of them are sure to take it. On the other hand, if the husband wishes to continue his education, start in business for himself, or for some reason or another does not immediately resume his breadwinning role, the wife may find her pay check badly needed. In that even, she probably will seek another job, though the job in all likelihood will not be similar to her wartime occupation, as disappointing as that fact will be—and has been to other displaced women war workers.

Some of the wartime factory workers, of course, already have new jobs—in consumer-goods plants, laundries, stores, restaurants, hotels, beauty shops and other civilian services. From records of employment, however, this number is not large, for the employment of women in all types of work has decreased by more than 4 million since last July, or dropped from about $19\frac{1}{2}$ million to around $15\frac{1}{2}$ million. In view of this large decline, the number of women looking for work—about half a million, according to the latest estimate—is surprisingly small, only 40,000 more than last July.

In the light of the long-time trend of women's increasing participation in the work life of the nation, this appears to be accounted for not by the fact that women as workers are showing a tendency to withdraw from paid employment but by certain characteristics of the present transitional period. Important among these are: (1) The reabsorption of returning service men; (2) the indecision of some workers, both men and women, concerning their future plans; (3) the lack of job opportunities commensurate with the skills and wages of displaced women; (4) the desire of some displaced workers to take a rest before looking for jobs; and (5) the expected voluntary withdrawal of large numbers of women who were duration workers. Other factors contributing to the decline in the number of women workers during the period from last July to the present were the withdrawal of seasonal workers and teenagers.

Much has been written and said about the fact that reconverted heavy industries are closing their doors, for the most part, to the very women the depended on during the war. This frequently has been referred to as marking "the end of industry's courtship of women workers." Undoubtedly, heavy industry no longer is courting the riveters, the welders and machine operators who helped to make victory possible, and in this fact may be reflected some of the prejudice that has been leveled at women by certain sections of industry. The inference, however, that prejudice alone accounts for the trek of women from the war plants is both unfair and unsound.

Prior to the war, women were less than 1 per cent of the wage-earners in the ship-building industry. Women riveters, welders or crane operators would have been considered by some employers as fanciful as a tale from the "Arabian Nights." Yet, during the war, women production workers in commercial and Navy yards reached a peak of about 150,000. In the aircraft industry, which had only ,000 women factory workers the week before the Pearl Harbor attack, the number rose to over 360,000, and women became more than a third of all workers producing such giants of the air as Liberators, B-29's, and the swift fighters that helped to spell victory.

Today, with peace at hand, our nation no longer needs these ships of war or the vast army of men and women who produced them. Women, relatively speaking, were newcomers to the shipyards and aircraft plants and, as such, were the first to feel the impact of cutbacks. Additionally, there were scores of factories that owed their very existence to war. Foremost among these were the ammunition plants, in which women formed more than 41 per cent of all workers. Obviously, many of these factories have no peacetime future.

Women workers themselves, for the most part, are cognizant of the workings of the seniority system under which American industry operates. Since they generally were the last to come, it came as no surprise to them that they were the first to go. Most of them, however, liked the new and shining factories of which they became a part. They like the up-to-date equipment, the comfortable dressing rooms, the music that came to them through the loudspeaker system.

But more than the refinements, they liked the regular and higher pay that came in their weekly envelopes. It is in the pay that is being offered them with the current opening that they are most disappointed. This interest in the pay check is not peculiar to their sex. It is, as one woman riveter put it, "just the plain American desire to get ahead."

Women workers do not want to get ahead at the expense of veterans. In fact, they never have regarded their work as a substitute for that of men. Their won record of achievement over a long period of years obviates that need or desire. Even before the war, they were a fourth of all the nation's employed persons, and a half or more of those engaged in domestic service, medical and other health services, educational services, telephone services, hotels and lodging places, limited price variety stores, general merchandise stores, and in the manufacture of apparel and accessories, tobacco, knit goods and miscellaneous products made from textiles.

Contrary to the opinion held by many persons, even during the height of our spectacular war production, the bulk of the nation's employed women were hard at work on the kinds of jobs women always had performed. Unsung and unheralded, millions of women did their part for victory by staffing the stores, laundries, restaurants, consumer-goods plants and other establishments and industries that gave necessary underpinnings to war production. The needs of these women, as well as those of the displaced war workers, must be taken into account in the various plans that are made for women.

Rosie the Riveter and her industrial coworkers, as it was pointed out at a recent Women's Bureau conference on the post-war employment problems of women, upgraded themselves during the war. They would like to retain some, if not all, of the gains. Because expanding opportunities for women appear to be in the extension of established services and in the development of new services that post-war America will want and need rather than in the old-line industries in which men have predominated, the industrial workers' gains may not be measured in terms of retaining their war-acquired skills. If America accepts the challenge, they can be measured in other terms: Wages that permit them to maintain the standards of living they have achieved, hours of work that are conducive to health and decency standards, and working environments that are a far cry from those of some pre-war establishments.

Closely related to the question of wages is the matter of equal pay, or objective rates based on the content of the job rather than on the sex of the worker. As Senator Wayne Morse, co-author of the pending Federal equal-[ay legislation, has pointed out, the principle of equal pay goes far beyond being a matter of plain justice to women. Because it rests on a sound economic basis, such a practice promotes the general welfare of the community and the nation by promoting wage levels and sustaining the purchasing power of all concerned. Women's awareness of this fact is one of the reasons why they feel that we cannot afford the threat that unequal pay to them involves. They have a deep, natural interest in the welfare of their families and realize that every time a working man's income is reduced through the competition of workers who can be hired at lower rates than those prevailing, the family of the man inevitable suffers a lower standard of living.

These needs of women workers have long existed, and for just as many years they have been recognized by individuals and agencies interested in the welfare of the wage-earning woman. Through concerted action notable gains have been made in minimum-wage legislation, in State equal-pay laws, and through other measures sponsored by unions and progressive employers. A great deal, however, remains to be done before Rosie the Riveter, Winnie the Welder, and other women of the war sorority of industrial workers will be content to return to the woman-employing fields that are characterized by substandard wages and unreasonably long hours.

These changes are needed not only for the sake of Rosie and other returning war workers but for the benefit of the thousands of women who stuck to their jobs in the service industries throughout the war. The plight of Rosie and her highly praised war companions may serve, however, to focus public attention on the issue. Club women, unions and other champions of women already have made considerable progress in this direction, and a few individual communities—though not nearly enough—are including women in their programs for post-war workers.

Secretary of Labor Schwellenbach, in an address before key representatives of more than 70 organizations who attended a recent Women's Bureau conference on the employment problems of women summed up the needs of women workers and issued a challenge to post-war America when he said:

"Certain artificial restrictions that belong to a past age should not be allowed to handicap the contribution women can make....for instance, no bars should be erected against the employment of women, married or single, in work they can do under physically healthful conditions no pay scales should discriminate against them. As members of a free society, women should be enabled to choose the way of life that permits them to make their fullest contribution to the world's upbuilding."

QUESTIONS

1. What are some of the options indicated for the former "Rosies" in the post-war economy?
2. How does the article explain the striking decline in women workers?
3. Do the statistics on types of wartime employment change your perception of women workers during WWII?

25.3. VISUAL DOCUMENT: JOHN HERSEY, "HIROSHIMA" IN *THE NEW YORKER* (AUGUST 31, 1946)

THE NEW YORKER

A REPORTER AT LARGE

HIROSHIMA

I—A NOISELESS FLASH

AT exactly fifteen minutes past eight in the morning, on August 6, 1945, Japanese time, at the moment when the atomic bomb flashed above Hiroshima, Miss Toshiko Sasaki, a clerk in the personnel department of the East Asia Tin Works, had just sat down at her place in the plant office and was turning her head to speak to the girl at the next desk. At that same moment, Dr. Masakazu Fujii was settling down cross-legged to read the Osaka *Asahi* on the porch of his private hospital, overhanging one of the seven deltaic rivers which divide Hiroshima; Mrs. Hatsuyo Nakamura, a tailor's widow, stood by the window of her kitchen, watching a neighbor tearing down his house because it lay in the path of an air-raid-defense fire lane; Father Wilhelm Kleinsorge, a German priest of the Society of Jesus, reclined in his underwear on a cot on the top floor of his order's three-story mission house, reading a Jesuit magazine, *Stimmen der Zeit*; Dr. Terufumi Sasaki, a young member of the surgical staff of the city's large, modern Red Cross Hospital, walked along one of the hospital corridors with a blood specimen for a Wassermann test in his hand; and the Reverend Mr. Kiyoshi Tanimoto, pastor of the Hiroshima Methodist Church, paused at the door of a rich man's house in Koi, the city's western suburb, and prepared to unload a handcart full of things he had evacuated from town in fear of the massive B-29 raid which everyone expected Hiroshima to suffer. A hundred thousand people were killed by the atomic bomb, and these six were among the survivors. They still wonder why they lived when so many others

died. Each of them counts many small items of chance or volition—a step taken in time, a decision to go indoors, catching one streetcar instead of the next—that spared him. And now each knows that in the act of survival he lived a dozen lives and saw more death than he ever thought he would see. At the time, none of them knew anything.

THE Reverend Mr. Tanimoto got up at five o'clock that morning. He was alone in the parsonage, because for some time his wife had been commuting with their year-old baby to spend nights with a friend in Ushida, a suburb to the north. Of all the important cities of Japan, only two, Kyoto and Hiroshima, had not been visited in strength by *B-san*, or Mr. B, as the Japanese, with a mixture of respect and unhappy familiarity, called the B-29; and Mr. Tanimoto, like all his neighbors and friends, was almost sick with anxiety. He had heard uncomfortably detailed accounts of mass raids on Kure, Iwa-

---

TO OUR READERS

The New Yorker this week devotes its entire editorial space to an article on the almost complete obliteration of a city by one atomic bomb, and what happened to the people of that city. It does so in the conviction that few of us have yet comprehended the all but incredible destructive power of this weapon, and that everyone might well take time to consider the terrible implications of its use.

—THE EDITORS

---

kuni, Tokuyama, and other nearby towns; he was sure Hiroshima's turn would come soon. He had slept badly the night before, because there had been several air-raid warnings. Hiroshima had been getting such warnings almost every night for weeks, for at that time the B-29s were using Lake Biwa, northeast of Hiroshima, as a rendezvous point, and no matter what city the Americans planned to hit, the Super-fortresses streamed in over the coast near Hiroshima. The frequency of the warnings and the continued abstinence of Mr. B with respect to Hiroshima had made its citizens jittery; a rumor was going around that the Americans were saving something special for the city.

Mr. Tanimoto is a small man, quick to talk, laugh, and cry. He wears his black hair parted in the middle and rather long; the prominence of the frontal bones just above his eyebrows and the smallness of his mustache, mouth, and chin give him a strange, old-young look, boyish and yet wise, weak and yet fiery. He moves nervously and fast, but with a restraint which suggests that he is a cautious, thoughtful man. He showed, indeed, just those qualities in the uneasy days before the bomb fell. Besides having his wife spend the nights in Ushida, Mr. Tanimoto had been carrying all the portable things from his church, in the close-packed residential district called Naga-ragawa, to a rayon manufacturer in Koi, two miles from the center of town. The rayon man, a Mr. Matsui, had opened his then unoccupied estate to a large number of his friends and acquaintances, so that they might evacuate whatever they wished to a safe distance from the

---

The August 31, 1946, edition of *The New Yorker* was devoted entirely to an essay by journalist John Hersey that was based on interviews with Hiroshima survivors. The issue sold out within hours, the text was read over radio broadcasts, and a book-length version titled simply "Hiroshima" became an international best seller.

QUESTIONS

1. Hersey's simple account of the aftermath of the first atomic bomb was criticized by some as "one-sided" and unpatriotic. Why might this account be viewed this way?

2. Critics and readers lauded Hersey's article and book, which features only six people, for giving a human face to the final event of World War II. Why might readers in 1946 have appreciated this historical method? How might you explain the immense popularity of this book?

25.4. WINSTON CHURCHILL, EXCERPT FROM "THE SINEWS OF PEACE" (MARCH 5, 1946)

On March 5, 1946, Winston Churchill gave a speech at Westminster College in Fulton, Missouri, entitled "The Sinews of Peace." This speech included the memorable line: "an iron curtain has descended across the Continent."

Leslie Gilbert, "Peep Under the Iron Curtain" (1946). Associated Newspapers Ltd/Solo Syndication, London.

A shadow has fallen upon the scenes so lately lighted by the Allied victory. Nobody knows what Soviet Russia and its Communist international organization intends to do in the immediate future, or what are the limits, if any, to their expansive and proselytizing tendencies. I have a strong admiration and regard for the valiant Russian people and for my wartime comrade, Marshal Stalin. There is deep sympathy and goodwill in Britain—and I doubt not here also—towards the peoples of all the Russias and a resolve to persevere through many differences and rebuffs in establishing lasting friendships. We understand the Russian need to be secure on her western frontiers by the removal of all possibility of German aggression. We welcome Rus-

Source: Winston Churchill, "The Sinews of Peace," Westminster College, Fulton, Missouri, March 5, 1946. Courtesy NATO archives.

sia to her rightful place among the leading nations of the world. We welcome her flag upon the seas. Above all, we welcome, or should welcome, constant, frequent and growing contacts between the Russian people and our own people on both sides of the Atlantic. It is my duty however, for I am sure you would wish me to state the facts as I see them to you. It is my duty to place before you certain facts about the present position in Europe.

From Stettin in the Baltic to Trieste in the Adriatic an iron curtain has descended across the Continent. Behind that line lie all the capitals of the ancient states of Central and Eastern Europe. Warsaw, Berlin, Prague, Vienna, Budapest, Belgrade, Bucharest and Sofia, all these famous cities and the populations around them lie in what I must call the Soviet sphere, and all are subject in one form or another, not only to Soviet influence but to a very high and, in some cases, increasing measure of control from Moscow. Athens alone— Greece with its immortal glories—is free to decide its future at an election under British, American and French observation. The Russian-dominated Polish Government has been encouraged to make enormous and wrongful inroads upon Germany, and mass expulsions of millions of Germans on a scale grievous and undreamed-of are now taking place. The Communist parties, which were very small in all these Eastern States of Europe, have been raised to pre-eminence and power far beyond their numbers and are seeking everywhere to obtain totalitarian control. Police governments are prevailing in nearly every case, and so far, except in Czechoslovakia, there is no true democracy.

Turkey and Persia are both profoundly alarmed and disturbed at the claims which are being made upon them and at the pressure being exerted by the Moscow Government. An attempt is being made by the Russians in Berlin to build up a quasi-Communist party in their zone of occupied Germany by showing special favors to groups of left-wing German leaders. At the end of the fighting last June, the American and British Armies withdrew westward, in accordance with an earlier agreement, to a depth at some points of 150 miles upon a front of nearly four hundred miles, in order to allow our Russian allies to occupy this vast expanse of territory which the Western Democracies had conquered.

If now the Soviet Government tries, by separate action, to build up a pro-Communist Germany in their areas, this will cause new serious difficulties in the American and British zones, and will give the defeated Germans the power of putting themselves up to auction between the Soviets and the Western Democracies. Whatever conclusions may be drawn from these facts— and facts they are—this is certainly not the Liberated Europe we fought to build up. Nor is it one which contains the essentials of permanent peace.

The safety of the world, ladies and gentlemen, requires a new unity in Europe, from which no nation should be permanently outcast. It is from the quarrels of the strong parent races in Europe that the world wars we have witnessed, or which occurred in former times, have sprung. Twice in our own lifetime we have seen the United States, against their wished and their traditions, against arguments, the force of which it is impossible not to comprehend, twice we have seen them drawn by irresistible forces, into these wars in time to secure the victory of the good cause, but only after frightful slaughter and devastation have occurred. Twice the United States has had to send several millions of its young men across the Atlantic to find the war; but now war can find any nation, wherever it may dwell between dusk and dawn. Surely we should work with conscious purpose for a grand pacification of Europe, within the structure of the United Nations and in accordance with our Charter. That I feel opens a course of policy of very great importance.

QUESTIONS

1. How does this early speech point to growing tensions among former World War II allies?
2. How does Churchill use history to encourage Americans to take a more proactive approach to these growing tensions?

25.5. FRANKLIN D. ROOSEVELT, EXCERPTS FROM STATEMENT ON SIGNING THE G.I. BILL (JUNE 22, 1944)

As the war wound down, concern for returning soldiers came from every quarter. Memories of inadequate treatment for veterans of World War I still resonated. In 1944, Congress, with the support of liberals who saw it as a much-needed social welfare program and conservatives who considered it a patriotic vote of thanks, passed the Servicemen's Readjustment Act, also called the G.I. Bill.

Franklin Delano Roosevelt Signs the G.I. Bill, June 22, 1944. Courtesy of Franklin D. Roosevelt Presidential Library and Museum.

This bill, which I have signed today, substantially carries out most of the recommendations made by me in a speech on July 28, 1943, and more specifically in messages to the Congress dated October 27, 1943, and November 23, 1943:

1. It gives servicemen and women the opportunity of resuming their education or technical training after discharge, or of taking a refresher or retrainer course, not only without tuition charge up to $500 per school

Source: Franklin Delano Roosevelt Library, http://docs.fdrlibrary.marist.edu/odgist.html.

year, but with the right to receive a monthly living allowance while pursuing their studies.

2. It makes provision for the guarantee by the Federal Government of not to exceed 50 percent of certain loans made to veterans for the purchase or construction of homes, farms, and business properties.

3. It provides for reasonable unemployment allowances payable each week up to a maximum period of one year, to those veterans who are unable to find a job.

4. It establishes improved machinery for effective job counseling for veterans and for finding jobs for returning soldiers and sailors.

5. It authorizes the construction of all necessary additional hospital facilities.

6. It strengthens the authority of the Veterans Administration to enable it to discharge its existing and added responsibilities with promptness and efficiency.

With the signing of this bill a well-rounded program of special veterans' benefits is nearly completed. It gives emphatic notice to the men and women in our armed forces that the American people do not intend to let them down.

By prior legislation, the Federal Government has already provided for the armed forces of this war: adequate dependency allowances; mustering-out pay; generous hospitalization, medical care, and vocational rehabilitation and training; liberal pensions in case of death or disability in military service; substantial war risk life insurance, and guaranty of premiums on commercial policies during service; protection of civil rights and suspension of enforcement of certain civil liabilities during service; emergency maternal care for wives of enlisted men; and reemployment rights for returning veterans.

This bill therefore and the former legislation provide the special benefits which are due to the members of our armed forces—for they "have been compelled to make greater economic sacrifice and every other kind of sacrifice than the rest of us, and are entitled to definite action to help take care of their special problems." While further study and experience may suggest some changes and improvements, the Congress is to be congratulated on the prompt action it has taken.

There still remains one recommendation which I made on November 23, 1943, which I trust that the Congress will soon adopt—the extension of social security credits under the Federal Old-Age and Survivors' Insurance Law to all servicemen and women for the period of their service.

I trust that the Congress will also soon provide similar opportunities for postwar education and unemployment insurance to the members of the merchant marine, who have risked their lives time and again during this war for the welfare of their country.

But apart from these special benefits which fulfill the special needs of veterans, there is still much to be done.

As I stated in my message to the Congress of November 23, 1943, "What our servicemen and women want, more than anything else, is the assurance of satisfactory employment upon their return to civil life. The first task after the war is to provide employment for them and for our demobilized workers.... The goal after the war should be the maximum utilization of our human and material resources."

As a related problem the Congress has had under consideration the serious problem of economic reconversion and readjustment after the war, so that private industry will be able to provide jobs for the largest possible number. This time we have wisely begun to make plans in advance of the day of peace, in full confidence that our war workers will remain at their essential war jobs as long as necessary until the fighting is over.

The executive branch of the Government has taken, and is taking, whatever steps it can, until legislation is enacted. I am glad to learn that the Congress has agreed on a bill to facilitate the prompt settlement of terminated contracts. I hope that the Congress will also take prompt action, when it reconvenes, on necessary legislation which is now pending to facilitate the development of unified programs for the demobilization of civilian war workers, for their reemployment in peacetime pursuits, and for provision, in cooperation with the States, of appropriate unemployment benefits during the transition from war to peace. I hope also that the Congress, upon its return, will take prompt action on the pending legislation to facilitate the orderly disposition of surplus property.

A sound postwar economy is a major present responsibility.

QUESTIONS

1. Some historians believe that the G.I. Bill represents the most significant federal welfare program in American history. Is the G.I. Bill welfare?

2. Roosevelt mentions two motives for supporting this legislation—What are they?

25.6. W. E. B. DU BOIS, EXCERPTS FROM "AN APPEAL TO THE WORLD" (1947)

America's leading black intellectual, W. E. B. Du Bois, eloquently captured African Americans' concerns about the coming Cold War. In an address entitled "An Appeal to the World: A Statement on the Denial of Human Rights to Minorities and an Appeal to the United Nations for Redress," presented to the United Nations General Assembly in 1947, Du Bois presented research on the impact of segregation and the denial of voting rights on African Americans in the United States. Du Bois's appeal presented American racism and Cold War hypocrisy in rich detail, and with eloquence and insight not easily dismissed. Partly as a response to this plea for global recognition of American inequality, President Harry Truman created the first Civil Rights Commission. Du Bois followed his U.N. address with an equally eloquent attack on American foreign policy at the World Peace Congress in April 1949.

W. E. B. Du Bois and Paul Robeson, Salle Pleyel, Paris, World Peace Congress, 1949, © Bettmann/CORBIS

Source: Eric J. Sundquist, *The Oxford W. E. B. Du Bois Reader* (New York: Oxford University Press, 1996), 454–60.

There were in the United States of America, 1940, 12,865,518 citizens and residents, something less than a tenth of the nation, who form largely a segregated caste, with restricted legal rights, and many illegal disabilities. They are descendants of the Africans brought to America during the sixteenth, seventeenth, eighteenth and nineteenth centuries and reduced to slave labor. This group has no complete biological unity, but varies in color from white to black, and comprises a great variety of physical characteristics since many are the offspring of white European-Americans as well as of Africans and American Indians. There are a large number of white Americans who also descend from Negroes but who are not counted in the colored group nor subjected to caste restrictions because the preponderance of white blood conceals their descent.

The so-called American Negro group therefore, while it is in no sense absolutely set off physically from its fellow Americans, has nevertheless a strong, hereditary cultural unity, born of slavery, of common suffering, prolonged proscription and curtailment of political and civil rights; and especially because of economic and social disabilities. Largely from this fact, have arisen their cultural gifts to America—their rhythm, music and folk song; their religious faith and customs; their contribution to American art and literature; their defense of their country in every war, on land, sea and in the air; and especially the hard, continuous toil upon which the prosperity and wealth of this continent has largely been built.

The group has long been internally divided by dilemma as to whether its striving upward should be aimed at strengthening its inner cultural and group bonds, both for intrinsic progress and for offensive power against caste; or whether it should seek escape wherever and however possible into the surrounding American culture. Decision in this matter has been largely determined by outer compulsion rather than inner plan; for prolonged policies of segregation and discrimination have involuntarily welded the mass almost into a nation within a nation with its own schools, churches, hospitals, newspapers and many business enterprises.

The result has been to make American Negroes to a wide extent provincial, introvertive, self-conscious and narrowly race-loyal; but it has also inspired them to frantic and often successful effort to achieve, to deserve, to show the world their capacity to share modern civilization. As a result there is almost no area of American civilization in which the Negro has not made creditable showing in the face of all his handicaps.

If, however, the effect of the color caste system on the North American Negro has been both good and bad, its effect on white America has been disastrous. It has repeatedly led the greatest modern attempt at democratic government to deny its political ideals, to falsify its philanthropic assertions and to make its religion to a great extent hypocritical. A nation which boldly declared "That all men are created equal," proceeded to build its economy on chattel slavery; masters who declared race mixture impossible, sold their own children into slavery and left a mulatto progeny which neither law nor science can today disentangle; churches which excused slavery as calling the heathen to god, refused to recognize the freedom of converts or admit them to equal communion. Sectional strife over the profits of slave labor and conscientious revolt against making human beings real estate led to bloody civil war, and to a partial emancipation of slaves which nevertheless even to this day is not complete. Poverty, ignorance, disease and crime have been forced on these unfortunate victims of greed to an extent far beyond any social necessity; and a great nation, which today ought to be in the forefront of the march toward peace and democracy, finds itself continuously making common cause with race hate, prejudiced exploitation and oppression of the common man. Its high and noble words are turned against it, because they are contradicted in every syllable by the treatment of the American Negro for three hundred and twenty-eight years....

Today the paradox again looms after the Second World War. We have recrudescence of race hate and caste restrictions in the United States and of these dangerous tendencies not simply for the United States itself but for all nations. When will nations learn that their enemies are quite as often within their own country as without? It is not Russia that threatens the United States so much as Mississippi; not Stalin and Molotov but Bilbo and Rankin; internal injustice done to one's brother is far more dangerous than the aggression of strangers from abroad....

All these are but passing incidents, but they show clearly that a discrimination practiced in the United States against her own citizens and to a large extent a contravention of her own laws, cannot be persisted in, without infringing upon the rights of the peoples of the world and especially upon the ideals and the work of the United Nations.

QUESTIONS

1. Why do you think Du Bois took his arguments about American civil rights to world forums?
2. What is the relationship between the rhetoric of the Cold War and the civil rights movement?
3. Was Du Bois's strategy of strongly criticizing the United States in global forums wise?

CHAPTER 26

THE DYNAMIC 1950s

26.1. VISUAL DOCUMENTS: *TIME MAGAZINE,* "MAN OF THE YEAR" (JANUARY 6, 1958) AND HERBLOCK, *MR. ATOM—ISLAND FOOTPRINT* IN *THE WASHINGTON POST* (SEPTEMBER 24, 1949)

In 1957, scientists from around the world engaged in work on projects for the International Geophysical Year (IGY), a global celebration of modern technology. The United States planned to launch a three-pound satellite into the earth's orbit as part of the event. The IGY represented an opportunity for international cooperation in technology, especially in the new realm of space. Scientists were hopeful that space exploration might open new avenues for research cooperation during a period when secrecy and competition pervaded the development of weapons technology. This hope faded on October 4, 1957, with the stunning news of the successful launch and orbit of the Soviet satellite *Sputnik*. The launch of *Sputnik* was a shock to the Western world, a graphic illustration of Soviet technological advancement. As *Sputnik* circled the globe, it beamed a radio beep that could be captured by astonished Americans listening on their radios. Only the size of a basketball, the little beeping space ball caused an international uproar and instigated an unprecedented peacetime technological race.

In the United States, *Sputnik* raised concerns about a "science lag," an education crisis, and a "missile gap." The Soviet victory in the first battle of the space race forever linked the space race with the Cold War. *Sputnik* posed no danger, but it did raise the specter of a future in which nuclear missiles could rain down on America from space. Eisenhower responded by increasing federal science funding and working with Congress to create the National Aeronautics and Space Administration (NASA). Congress quickly passed the National Defense Education Act (NDEA), which provided federal funds to local school districts for the first time in the nation's history. Books like *Why Johnny Can't Read and Ivan Can* fueled fears about the baby boom generation's ability to compete with the Communists. Eisenhower's Soviet counterpart, Nikita Khrushchev, reveled in the public relations

Sources: Time Magazine, "Man of the Year" cover from *Time Magazine,* January 6, 1958. Copyright © Time Inc. Used under license. Herblock cartoon, *Mr. Atom—Island Footprint* in *The Washington Post,* September 24, 1949, copyright by The Herb Block Foundation.

victory. By 1960, the United States was spending billions on rocket science in a full-fledged "space race" with the Soviets.

The first image below is a 1958 cover of *Time* magazine depicting Nikita Khrushchev and the USSR's technological might. The second image, a 1949 Herblock cartoon for the *Washington Post* entitled "Mr. Atom—Island Footprint," shows a surprised U.S. atomic power confronting the reality, like Robinson Crusoe, that America was not alone in technological might. The successful Soviet test of an atomic weapon in 1949 ushered in a new era of weapons, placing science and technology at the heart of the Cold War.

Time Magazine, "Man of the Year" cover, January 6, 1958.

Herblock, *Mr. Atom—Island Footprint,* from the *Washington Post,* September 24, 1949. Graphite, ink, and opaque white over graphite underdrawing. Mr. Atom looking at a single footprint holding an umbrella with American flag.

QUESTIONS

1. What does the *Time* cover of Khrushchev as Man of the Year say about American perceptions of the USSR?

2. Herblock was one of the most insightful observers of Cold War culture. What does his cartoon suggest about why the United States was falling behind the Soviets?

26.2. KWAME NKRUMAH, EXCERPT FROM A SPEECH DELIVERED TO THE COUNCIL ON FOREIGN RELATIONS (1958)

In the aftermath of World War II and the collapse of the European colonial system, the map of the globe changed dramatically. Former colonies around the world sought and gained their independence from Western European colonial powers. This trend was particularly evident in Africa and Asia and figured heavily in U.S. foreign policy in the 1950s.

Kwame Nkrumah, the leader of Ghana, the first of the former British colonies in Africa to gain its independence (1957), at first attempted to gain support from both the former colonial power and the United States. In the early 1960s, Nkrumah increasingly turned to the Eastern Bloc for assistance. Below is an excerpt from a speech he delivered to the Council on Foreign Relations in New York in 1958.

The first [principle] is our desire to see Africa free and independent. The second is our determination to pursue foreign policies based upon non-alignment. The third is our urgent need for economic development. There is no area in Africa today where these three points are not on the agenda of politics. There is no need to underline for American readers the reason for Africa's rejection of colonial status. We believe, as do Americans, that to be self-governing is one of the inalienable rights of man. In Africa, if peoples are to be truly independent, their governments must reflect the fact that, in all parts of Africa, the overwhelming majority of the population are native-born Africans. Even in the countries of considerable European settlement, such as Southern Rhodesia, 90% of the people are African. When, therefore, at our recent African conference, we called for an end to colonialism, we were doing no more than stating our belief that the fact of a vast African majority should be accepted as a basis of government in Africa....

We asked for the fixing of the definite dates for early independence and called upon the administering powers to take rapid steps to implement the provisions of the United Nations Charter and the political aspirations of the people, namely self-determination and independence. These steps should, in my view, include a greatly accelerated and enlarged programme of education and technical training, the opening up systematically of new opportunities for Africans in agriculture and industry and rapid growth of African participation in the country's political life. Such timetables would restore what, we believe, is most lacking in Africa's plural societies—and that is the element of confidence and hope on the part of the African majority....

Non-alignment can only be understood in the context of the present atomic arms race and the atmosphere of the Cold War. There is a wise African proverb: "When the bull elephants fight, the grass is trampled down." When we in Africa survey the industrial and military power concentrated behind the two great powers in the Cold War, we know that no military or strategic act of ours could make one jot of difference to this balance of power, while our involvement might draw us into areas of conflict which so far have not spread below the Sahara. Our attitude, I imagine,

Source: Jussi Hanhimäki and Odd Arne Westad, eds., *The Cold War: A History in Documents and Eyewitness Accounts* (Oxford: Oxford University Press, 2003), 354–56.

is very much that of America looking at the disputes of Europe in the 19th century. We do not wish to be involved. In addition, we know that we cannot affect the outcome. Above all, we believe the peace of the world in general is served, not harmed by keeping one great continent free from the strife and rivalry of military blocs and cold wars.

But this attitude of non-alignment does not imply indifference to the great issues of our day. It does not imply isolationism. It is in no way anti-Western; nor is it anti-Eastern. The greatest issue of our day is surely to see that *there is a tomorrow*. For Africans especially there is a particular tragedy in the risk of thermo-nuclear destruction. One continent has come but lately to the threshold of the modern world. The opportunities of health and education and a wider vision which other nations take for granted are barely within the reach of our people. And now they see the risk that all this richness of opportunity may be snatched away by destructive war. In any war, the strategic areas of the world would be destroyed or occupied by some great power. It is simply a question of who gets there first—the Suez Canal, Afghanistan and Gulf of Aquaba are examples.

On this great issue, therefore, of war and peace, the people and government of Ghana put all their weight behind the peaceful settlement of disputes and seek conditions in which disputes do not become embittered to the point of violence. We are willing to accept every provision from the United Nations Charter. We go further and favour every extension of an international police force as an alternative to war. One of the most important roles of the smaller nations today is surely to use their influence in season and out of season to substitute the peaceful settlement of disputes and international policing of disturbed areas for the present disastrous dependence upon arms and force. For this reason, at our African conference, we underlined our demands for controlled disarmament, we deplored the use of the sale of arms as a means of influencing other nations' diplomacy and we urged that African states should be represented on all international bodies concerned with disarmament.

Thus it is not indifference that leads to a policy of non-alignment. It is our belief that international blocs and rivalries exacerbate and do not solve disputes and that we must be free to judge issues on their merits and to look for solutions that are just and peaceful, irrespective of the powers involved. We do not wish to be in the position of condoning imperialism or aggression from any quarter. Powers which pursue policies of goodwill, co-operation and constructive international action will always find us at their side. In fact, perhaps "non-alignment" is a mis-statement of our attitude. We are firmly aligned with all the forces in the world that genuinely make for peace....

The hopes and ambitions of the African people have been planted and brought to maturity by the impact of the Western civilization. The West has set the pattern of our hopes, and by entering Africa in strength, it has forced the patterns upon us. Now comes our response. We cannot tell our peoples that material benefits and growth and modern progress are not for them. If we do, they will throw us out and seek other leaders who promise more. And they will abandon us, too, if we do not in reasonable measure respond to their hopes. Therefore we have no choice. Africa has no choice. We have to modernise. Either we shall do so with your interest and support—or we shall be compelled to turn elsewhere. This is not a warning or a threat, but a straight statement of political reality.

And I also affirm, for myself and I believe for most of my fellow leaders in Africa, that we want close co-operation with our friends. We know you. History has brought us together. We still have the opportunity to build up a future on the basis of free and equal co-operation. This is our aim. This is our hope.

QUESTIONS

1. Why does Nkrumah wish to maintain links to the United States?
2. How does the Cold War look different from the vantage point of a Third World leader?

26.3. VISUAL DOCUMENTS: MARCH OF DIMES FUNDRAISING POSTER AND IMAGE OF IRON LUNGS IN GYM (1950s)

1950s efforts in applied science, especially in medicine, led to massive public health campaigns to eliminate infectious diseases. The dread disease of the age was polio. This insidious ailment struck children and teens seemingly at random and in their prime of life and health. Victims' symptoms ranged from partial disability to crippling effects so dire that patients were forced to be confined to a rudimentary artificial breathing device known as the "iron lung." In 1954, Dr. Jonas Salk perfected the polio vaccine and became an international hero.

Grassroots citizen activism played a large role in the successful search for a cure for polio. The National Foundation for Infantile Paralysis was founded in 1938 to continue fundraising efforts begun by President Franklin Roosevelt. Volunteers began collecting dimes to support research, and the Foundation was renamed the March of Dimes. Millions of people contributed dimes to support the research of Salk's team. This remarkable campaign featured affective posters of afflicted children and images of the dread Iron Lung. The March of Dimes set the model for fundraising for the rest of the century.

March of Dimes fundraising poster.

Sources: March of Dimes Poster © March of Dimes Foundation; Iron Lungs in Gym © Bettmann/CORBIS.

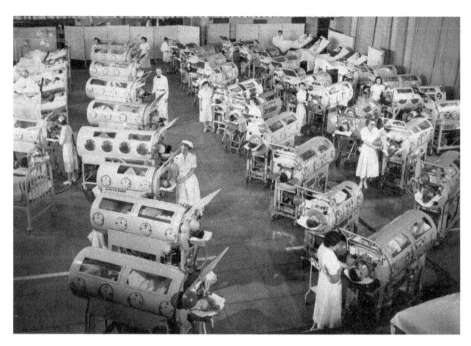

Iron lungs in gym.

QUESTIONS

1. The picture of the large room full of iron lungs struck fear into the hearts of parents. Take a close look at the photograph. Does this appear to be an actual functioning treatment facility? If not, why would the photograph be staged this way?

2. Can you point to efforts today that clearly benefited from the cause-oriented marketing strategy pioneered by the March of Dimes?

26.4. DWIGHT D. EISENHOWER, ADDRESS TO CONGRESS ON THE INTERSTATE HIGHWAY SYSTEM (FEBRUARY 22, 1955)

The 1956 Interstate and Defense Highways Act, the largest public works program in American history, drastically altered cities, transformed millions of acres of rural lands, isolated some towns while elevating others, linked states, and facilitated the growth of suburbs and the complex of industries that sustained them. Missouri is one of three states (along with Kansas and Pennsylvania) to claim to be the first to begin construction on an interstate highway project following passage of the act.

FOR RELEASE AT 12 NOON (E.S.T.)

February 22, 1955

CAUTION: The following message of the President scheduled for delivery to the Congress today, February 22, 1955, MUST BE HELD IN STRICT CONFIDENCE and no portion, synopsis or intimation may be given out or published UNTIL RELEASE TIME.

The same caution applies to all newspapers, radio and television commentators and news broadcasters, both in the United States and abroad.

PLEASE USE EXTREME CARE TO AVOID PREMATURE PUBLICATION OR ANNOUNCEMENT.

James C. Hagerty
Press Secretary to the President

THE WHITE HOUSE

TO THE CONGRESS OF THE UNITED STATES:

Our unity as a nation is sustained by free communication of thought and by easy transportation of people and goods. The ceaseless flow of information throughout the Republic is matched by individual and commercial movement over a vast system of interconnected highways criss-crossing the Country and joining at our national borders with friendly neighbors to the north and south.

Together, the uniting forces of our communication and transportation systems are dynamic elements in the very name we bear—United States. Without them, we would be a mere alliance of many separate parts.

The Nation's highway system is a gigantic enterprise, one of our largest items of capital investment. Generations have gone into its building. Three million, three hundred and sixty-six thousand miles of road, travelled by 58 million motor vehicles, comprise it. The replacement cost of its drainage and bridge and tunnel works is incalculable. One in every seven Americans gains his livelihood and supports his family out of it. But, in large part, the network is inadequate for the nation's growing needs.

In recognition of this, the Governors in July of last year at my request began a study of both the problem and methods by which the Federal Government might assist the States in its solution. I appointed in September the President's Advisory Committee on a National Highway Program, headed by Lucius D. Clay, to work with the Governors and to propose a plan of action for submission to the Congress. At the same time, a committee representing departments and agencies of the national Government was organized to conduct studies coordinated with the other two groups.

All three were confronted with inescapable evidence that action, comprehensive and quick and forward-looking, is needed.

Source: Message to the Congress regarding highways, February 22, 1955, Office of the Press Secretary to the President, Box 4, Press Releases Feb. 8–March 14, 1955, http://www.eisenhower.archives.gov/research/online_documents/interstate_highway_system/1955_02_22_Message_to_Congress.pdf.

First: Each year, more than 36 thousand people are killed and more than a million injured on the highways. To the home where the tragic aftermath of an accident on an unsafe road is a gap in the family circle, the monetary worth of preventing that death cannot be reckoned. But reliable estimates place the measurable economic cost of the highway accident toll to the Nation at more than $4.3 billion a year.

Second: The physical condition of the present road net increases the cost of vehicle operation, according to many estimates, by as much as one cent per mile of vehicle travel. At the present rate of travel, this totals more than $5 billion a year. The cost is not borne by the individual vehicle operator alone. It pyramids into higher expense of doing the nation's business. Increased highway transportation costs, passed on through each step in the distribution of goods, are paid ultimately by the individual consumer.

Third: In case of an atomic attack on our key cities, the road net must permit quick evacuation of target areas, mobilization of defense forces and maintenance of every essential economic function. But the present system in critical areas would be the breeder of a deadly congestion within hours of an attack.

Fourth: Our Gross National Product, about $357 billion in 1954, is estimated to reach over $500 billion in 1965 when our population will exceed 180 million and, according to other estimates, will travel in 81 million vehicles 814 billion vehicle miles that year. Unless the present rate of highway improvement and development is increased, existing traffic jams only faintly foreshadow those of ten years hence.

To correct these deficiencies is an obligation of Government at every level. The highway system is a public enterprise. As the owner and operator, the various levels of Government have a responsibility for management that promotes the economy of the nation and properly serves the individual user. In the case of the Federal Government, moreover, expenditures on a highway program are a return to the highway user of the taxes which he pays in connection with his use of the highways.

Congress has recognized the national interest in the principal roads by authorizing two Federal-aid systems, selected cooperatively by the States, local units and the Bureau of Public Roads.

The Federal-aid primary system as of July 1, 1954, consisted of 234,407 miles, connecting all the principal cities, county seats, ports, manufacturing areas and other traffic generating centers.

In 1944 the Congress approved the Federal-aid secondary system, which on July 1, 1954, totally 482,972 miles, referred to as farm-to-market roads—important feeders linking farms, factories, distribution outlets and smaller communities with the primary system.

Because some sections of the primary system, from the viewpoint of national interest are more important than others, the Congress in 1944 authorized the selection of a special network, not to exceed 40,000 miles in length, which would connect by routes, as direct as practicable, the principal metropolitan areas, cities and industrial centers, serve the national defense, and connect with routes of continental importance in the Dominion of Canada and the Republic of Mexico.

This National System of Interstate Highways, although it embraces only 1.2 percent of total road mileage, joins 42 State capital cities and 90 percent of all cities over 50,000 population. It carries more than a seventh of all traffic, a fifth of the rural traffic, serves 65 percent of the urban and 45 percent of the rural population. Approximately 37,600 miles have been designated to date. This system and its mileage are presently included within the Federal-aid primary system.

In addition to these systems, the Federal Government has the principal, and in many cases the sole, responsibility for roads that cross or provide access to Federally owned land—more than one-fifth the nation's area.

Of all these, the Interstate System must be given top priority in construction planning. But at the current rate of development, the Interstate network would not reach even a reasonable level of extent and efficiency in half a century. State highway departments cannot effectively meet the need. Adequate right-of-way to assure control of access; grade separation structures; relocation and realignment of present highways; all these, done on the necessary scale within an integrated system, exceed their collective capacity.

If we have a congested and unsafe and inadequate system, how then can we improve it so that ten years from now it will be fitted to the nation's requirements?

A realistic answer must be based on a study of all phases of highway financing, including a study of the costs of completing the several systems of highways, made by the Bureau of Public Roads in cooperation with the State highway departments and local units of government. This study, made at the direction of the 83rd Congress in the 1954 Federal-aid Highway Act, is the most comprehensive of its kind ever undertaken.

Its estimates of need show that a 10-year construction program to modernize all our roads and streets will require expenditure of $101 billion by all levels of Government.

The preliminary 10-year totals of needs by road systems are:

	(Billions)
Interstate (urban $11, rural $12 billion)	$23
Federal-aid Primary (urban $10, rural $20 billion)	30
Federal-aid Secondary (entirely rural)	15
Sub-total of Federal-aid Systems (urban $21, rural $47 billion)	68
Other roads and streets (urban $16, rural $17 billion)	33
Total of needs (urban $37, rural $64 billion)	$101

The Governor's Conference and the President's Advisory Committee are agreed that the Federal share of the needed construction program should be about 30 percent of the total, leaving to State and local units responsibility to finance the remainder.

The obvious responsibility to be accepted by the Federal Government, in addition to the existing Federal interest in our 3,366,000-mile network of highways, is the development of the Interstate System with its most essential urban arterial connections.

In its report, the Advisory Committee recommends:

1. That the Federal Government assume principal responsibility for the cost of a modern Interstate Network to be completed by 1964 to include the most essential urban arterial connections; at an annual average cost of $2.5 billion for the ten year period.

2. That Federal contributions to primary and secondary road systems, now at the rate authorized by the

1954 Act of approximately $525 million annually, be continued.

3. That Federal funds for that portion of the Federal-aid systems in urban areas not on the Interstate System, now approximately $75 million annually, be continued.

4. That Federal funds for Forest Highways be continued at the present $22.5 million per year rate.

Under these proposals, the total Federal expenditures through the ten year period would be:

	(Billions)
Interstate System	$25.000
Federal-aid Primary and Secondary	5.250
Federal-aid Urban	.750
Forest Highways	.225
	$31.225

The extension of necessary highways in the Territories and highway maintenance and improvement in National Parks, on Indian lands and on other public lands of the United States will continue to be treated in the budget for these particular subjects.

A sound Federal highway program, I believe, can and should stand on its own feet, with highway users providing the total dollars necessary for improvement and new construction. Financing of interstate and Federal-aid systems should be based on the planned use of increasing revenues from present gas and diesel oil taxes, augmented in limited instances with tolls.

I am inclined to the view that it is sounder to finance this program by special bond issues, to be paid off by the above-mentioned revenues which will be collected during the useful life of the roads and pledged to this purpose, rather than by an increase in general revenue obligations.

At this time, I am forwarding for use by the Congress in its deliberations the Report to the President made by the President's Advisory Committee on the National Highway Program. This study of the entire highway traffic problem and presentation of a detailed solution for its remedy is an analytical review of the major elements in a most complex situation. In addition, the Congress will have available the study made by the Bureau of Public Roads at the direction of the 83rd Congress.

These two documents together constitute a most exhaustive examination of the National highway system, its problems and their remedies. Inescapably, the vastness of the highway enterprise fosters varieties of proposals which must be resolved into a national highway pattern. The two reports, however, should generate recognition of the urgency that presses upon us; approval of a general program that will give us a modern safe highway system; realization of the rewards for prompt and comprehensive action. They provide a solid foundation for a sound program.

DWIGHT D. EISENHOWER
THE WHITE HOUSE,

February 22, 1955

QUESTIONS

1. Some historians have argued that interstates have done more to transform America than any other single phenomenon. Do you agree?
2. How does Eisenhower explain the connection between highways and national security?

26.5. BILLY GRAHAM, EXCERPTS FROM A RE-ENVISIONING OF JONATHAN EDWARDS' "SINNERS IN THE HANDS OF AN ANGRY GOD" FOR THE COLD WAR GENERATION (1949)

In late 1949, Christian evangelist Billy Graham initiated his first large-scale crusade in Los Angeles: an eight-week revival that, with the help of media giant William Randolph Hearst, launched Graham into America's religious spotlight. Graham often appropriated popular anticommunist rhetoric in his attempts to reinvigorate American society through vigorous preaching. Graham also drew on Jonathan Edwards's famous 200-year-old sermon, "Sinners in the Hands of an Angry God," in his attempt to reform Los Angeles and convert anxious listeners.

No one, save Christ. Hear no voice, save God's. We pray that this mighty sermon that thou didst use 200 years ago might be used again in this day to stir thy people, to convict sinners. And we pray tonight that we might see such an outbreak in this place that we prayed for and dreamed of and called upon God for. We pray that thou would vindicate thy word

tonight. And we pray that on this night might be the night on which all America is praying. In Jesus' name, Amen.

I've never stood before an audience in greater fear and trembling, and yet absolute dependence upon the Holy Spirit, as I now stand. And tonight, I covet, I request, the prayers of every child of God in this place.

Source: "Billy Graham and Sinners in the Hands of an Angry God: A Digital Exhibit." © *The Works of Jonathan Edwards Online,* Jonathan Edwards Center, 2008–2011. http://edwards.yale.edu/education/billy-graham.

Advertisement for Billy Graham's Los Angeles Crusade, 1949. AP Photo.

It was 200 years ago, it was the year 1740. It was a cold, blistery day in New England, in Northampton, Massachusetts, when an aging man stepped to the platform before a congregation of people. The people were expectant, there had been a semblance of revival throughout New England, people had been praying, souls were being saved, thousands of Christians were being stirred, revival fires were spreading, very much as they are at the present time across America. Jonathan Edwards had his Ph.D. from Yale University. He was later to become the eminent President of Princeton University. Jonathan Edwards was one of the greatest scholars that America ever produced, one of the greatest preachers, a man of tremendous conviction, a man that we look back on today and revere, and pray that God might raise up again such men on the American scene, that will not compromise, but will preach the word of God seriously, like Jonathan Edwards preached....

George Whitefield came over to stir the revival fires in that day. And what has been considered one of the greatest sermons ever preached by a man since the days of Pentecost, was one of the sermons that was used of God to shake New England in that day and age. The sermon was entitled "Sinners in the hands of an angry God." Jonathan Edwards stood before the crowd of people, hardly an eyelash moved, hardly a person moved a hand, and before he was through preaching, people gripped the front of the benches in front of them and screamed in mercy, and revival broke out that night.

Tonight, in the very strange providence of God, I'm doing something I've never done before in my ministry. I'm bringing to you that message that was preached 200 years ago by Jonathan Edwards, the president of Princeton University. I'm going to do as he did. He stepped to the platform, and with gestures he preached, but he read every word of it. It's a very brief sermon, it's not too long. I'm going to read it, and extemporize part of it, but I want you to feel the grip, I want you to feel the language. I'm asking tonight the same blessed Holy Ghost that moved in that day to move again tonight in 1949 and shake us out of our lethargy as Christians and convict sinners that we might come to repentance. So tonight, we take our text. I want you to see that scene, I want you to see the little lanterns. The little oil lanterns. I want you to see the candles in the windows. I want you to see the snow falling outside. I want you to see the people as they're sitting in this little auditorium. I want you to see this eminent man as he stands to his feet. And his opening words were these: "Let us turn to Deuteronomy 32:35." Deuteronomy 32:35. These words: "Their foot shall slide in due time." "Their foot shall slide in due time." And if you've ever listened in your life, I want you to listen tonight. I want you to listen to the text. I want you to listen to the message. "Their foot shall slide in due time."

I'll tell you tonight, the wrath of God is something. And God says, that judgment is coming upon this world. And God says, the wages of sin is death. And God says, the soul that sins shall die. Ladies and gentlemen, tonight, men and women, tonight every one of us are hanging over the pit of hell and the only thing that keeps us from dropping in is the mercy of Almighty God. And tonight, I'm glad to tell you something, because I'm glad to tell you this, that the Lord Jesus Christ died on the cross of Calvary, and that God loves you with an everlasting love, and the mercy of God is everlasting to everlasting. And I don't care who you are tonight, man, woman, boy, or girl, it makes no difference who you are tonight, the Lord Jesus Christ can cleanse you from sin, and you can be assured that you're going to heaven, and every man, woman, boy, and girl in this place to know they're saved before they leave this place.

Wouldn't it be wonderful to walk out with peace in your heart, and that you walk alone not be afraid of the next step, not be afraid that some place along the way tomorrow you're going to drop? Wouldn't it be wonderful to have that glorious peace and joy in your heart, knowing that your sins are cleansed, and you're ready to meet God? Well you can know it right now. Right this minute. You say, how long does it take? Only an instant. You say, what do I have to do? All you have to do is let Jesus in, right now where you sit. You can make certain that you are ready to meet the Lord God. Shall we pray? Nobody leaving, nobody moving. You can leave while we were speaking, but not now. Not a person. Every head bowed. Every eye closed. While our heads are bowed, our eyes are closed, nobody's looking, I wonder how many people down in this place will say, "Billy, I'm not certain that I'm saved, I'm not certain if I died I'd go to heaven, I'm not sure how I stand before God, but I'd like to settle it, I'd like to know how I stand, I'd like to be certain that I'm on the road to heaven, I'd like to be sure that Christ lives in my heart. I don't want any doubts, I don't want any uncertainty, I want to know tonight that I'm on the road to heaven." All over this place—outside, nobody moving—all over this place, lift your hand tonight and say, "I want to be sure."

QUESTIONS

1. How does Graham close the chronological gap between 1741 and 1949?

2. What, for Graham, is at the heart of both Edwards's sermon and Graham's redaction of the same sermon?

3. How might have the perceived Communist threat and the fear of atomic war impacted the audience who listened to Graham's call for conversion?

26.6. VISUAL DOCUMENTS: MOVIE POSTER FROM *GODZILLA* AND STILL FROM *THEM!* (1954)

The 1950s were the golden age of science fiction. In hundreds of pulp magazines, books, and films, science fiction exploited the technological enthusiasm and fears of the post-war world. Films like Gordon Douglas's *Them!* (1954) and *Godzilla* (1954) featured mutants of nuclear technology turning on humanity. Whether they feared or celebrated it, Americans could not escape the reshaping of U.S. culture and geography by new and improved technologies. Science fiction was popular because it was fun, but the widespread enthusiasm for the genre during this period demonstrated that behind the wild plots and crazy characters were real hopes and concerns for a world increasingly dominated by technologies that few understood.

Godzilla, 1954.

Sources: *Godzilla*, TOHO/THE KOBAL COLLECTION (1954); *Them!* WARNER BROS/THE KOBAL COLLECTION (1954).

Them! 1954.

QUESTIONS

1. Based on these images how might these fantastic scenes from a science fiction film reflect the 1950s?
2. How do you think historians can use fictional popular culture sources as evidence for real historical changes?

3. If you had to make a small interpretive museum card for these "artifacts" what would you say?

CHAPTER 27

THE OPTIMISM AND THE ANGUISH OF THE 1960s

27.1. HO CHI MINH, EXCERPTS FROM *DECLARATION OF INDEPENDENCE* (1945)

On September 2, 1945, Vietminh leader Ho Chi Minh declared the independence of the Democratic Republic of Viet Nam. He referred to the American Declaration of Independence and the French Declaration of the Rights of Man. During the American War in Vietnam, representatives of North Vietnam and the National Liberation Front often appealed to this Declaration of Independence. This declaration was issued the same day that Japan surrendered to the Allies, ending World War II.

All men are created equal; they are endowed by their Creator with certain unalienable Rights; among these are Life, Liberty, and the pursuit of Happiness.

This immortal statement was made in the Declaration of Independence of the United States of America in 1776. In a broader sense, this means: All the peoples on the earth are equal from birth, all the people have a right to live, to be happy and free.

The Declaration of the French Revolution made in 1791 on the Rights of Man and the Citizen also states: "All men are born free and with equal rights, and must always remain free and have equal rights."

Those are undeniable truths.

Nevertheless, for more than 80 years, the French imperialists, abusing the standard of Liberty, Equality, and Fraternity, have violated our Fatherland and oppressed our fellow citizens. They have acted contrary to the ideals of humanity and justice....

They have enforced inhuman laws; they have set up three distinct political regimes in the North, the Center, and the South of Vietnam in order to wreck our national unity....

They have built more prisons than schools....

They have drowned our uprisings in rivers of blood....

Source: Howard J. Langer, ed., *The Vietnam War: An Encyclopedia of Quotations* (Westport, CT: Greenwood Press, 2005), 19–20.

They have robbed us of our rice fields, our mines, our forests, and our raw materials....

The French have fled, the Japanese have capitulated. Emperor Bao Dai has abdicated. Our people have broken the chains which for nearly a century have fettered them and have won independence for the Fatherland....

For these reasons, we, members of the Provisional Government, representing the whole Vietnamese people, declare that from now on we break off all relations of a colonial character with France and we abolish all the special rights the French have unlawfully acquired in our Fatherland....

The whole Vietnamese people...are determined to fight to the bitter end against any attempt by the French colonialists to reconquer their country....

For these reasons, we, members of the Provisional Government of the Democratic Republic of Viet-Nam, solemnly declare to the world that Viet-Nam has the right to be a free and independent country.

QUESTIONS

1. What does this excerpt tell you about Vietnam in 1945?
2. Does this artifact change your understanding about the root causes for the long Vietnam conflict?

27.2. LYNDON B. JOHNSON, EXCERPTS FROM "PEACE WITHOUT CONQUEST" (APRIL 7, 1965)

In this address at Johns Hopkins University in April 1965, President Lyndon B. Johnson justified U.S. participation in the war in Vietnam. He placed the American war effort in the context of the Cold War, and he referred indirectly to his efforts to promote a Great Society at home.

Over this war—and all Asia—is another reality: the deepening shadow of Communist China. The rulers in Hanoi are urged on by Peking. This is a regime which has destroyed freedom in Tibet, which has attacked India, and has been condemned by the United Nations for aggression in Korea. It is a nation which is helping the forces of violence in almost every continent. The contest in Viet-Nam is part of a wider pattern of aggressive purposes.

WHY ARE WE IN VIET-NAM?

Why are these realities our concern? Why are we in South Viet-Nam?

We are there because we have a promise to keep. Since 1954 every American President has offered support to the people of South Viet-Nam. We have helped to build, and we have helped to defend. Thus, over many years, we have made a national pledge to help South Viet-Nam defend its independence.

And I intend to keep that promise.

To dishonor that pledge, to abandon this small and brave nation to its enemies, and to the terror that must follow, would be an unforgivable wrong.

We are also there to strengthen world order. Around the globe, from Berlin to Thailand, are people whose well-being rests, in part, on the belief that they

Source: John T. Woolley and Gerhard Peters, the American Presidency Project, Santa Barbara, CA, http://www.presidency.ucsb.edu/ws/?pid=26877.

can count on us if they are attacked. To leave Viet-Nam to its fate would shake the confidence of all these people in the value of an American commitment and in the value of America's word. The result would be increased unrest and instability, and even wider war.

We are also there because there are great stakes in the balance. Let no one think for a moment that retreat from Viet-Nam would bring an end to conflict. The battle would be renewed in one country and then another. The central lesson of our time is that the appetite of aggression is never satisfied. To withdraw from one battlefield means only to prepare for the next. We must say in southeast Asia—as we did in Europe—in the words of the Bible: "Hitherto shalt thou come, but no further."

There are those who say that all our effort there will be futile—that China's power is such that it is bound to dominate all southeast Asia. But there is no end to that argument until all of the nations of Asia are swallowed up.

There are those who wonder why we have a responsibility there. Well, we have it there for the same reason that we have a responsibility for the defense of Europe. World War II was fought in both Europe and Asia, and when it ended we found ourselves with continued responsibility for the defense of freedom.

OUR OBJECTIVE IN VIET-NAM

Our objective is the independence of South Viet-Nam, and its freedom from attack. We want nothing for ourselves—only that the people of South Viet-Nam be allowed to guide their own country in their own way.

We will do everything necessary to reach that objective. And we will do only what is absolutely necessary....I wish it were possible to convince others with words of what we now find it necessary to say with guns and planes: Armed hostility is futile. Our resources are equal to any challenge. Because we fight for values and we fight for principles, rather than territory or colonies, our patience and our determination are unending....Such peace demands an independent South Viet-Nam—securely guaranteed and able to shape its own relationships to all others—free from outside interference—tied to no alliance—a military base for no other country.

These are the essentials of any final settlement....But we will always oppose the effort of one nation to conquer another nation.

We will do this because our own security is at stake.

But there is more to it than that. For our generation has a dream. It is a very old dream. But we have the power and now we have the opportunity to make that dream come true.

For centuries nations have struggled among each other. But we dream of a world where disputes are settled by law and reason. And we will try to make it so.

For most of history men have hated and killed one another in battle. But we dream of an end to war. And we will try to make it so.

For all existence most men have lived in poverty, threatened by hunger. But we dream of a world where all are fed and charged with hope. And we will help to make it so....I know this will not be easy. I know how difficult it is for reason to guide passion, and love to master hate. The complexities of this world do not bow easily to pure and consistent answers.

But the simple truths are there just the same. We must all try to follow them as best we can....Every night before I turn out the lights to sleep I ask myself this question: Have I done everything that I can do to unite this country? Have I done everything I can to help unite the world, to try to bring peace and hope to all the peoples of the world? Have I done enough?

QUESTIONS

1. What is the most important reason given for U.S. involvement in Vietnam?
2. Does this document reflect an understanding of the reasons Vietnam declared its independence in 1945?

27.3. BENJAMIN SPOCK AND MICHAEL ZIMMERMAN, EXCERPTS FROM "HOW WE GOT INVOLVED" (1968)

A large movement opposing U.S. involvement in Vietnam arose after President Johnson escalated the war. In the essay below, two antiwar activists, Benjamin Spock and Michael Zimmerman, explain why the United States should not be supporting the government of the Republic of South Vietnam.

So we first got involved in Vietnam for the same reasons nations have always interfered in business of other peoples: they had something and we wanted it.

What mainly mattered to our leaders was that the Vietnamese people were led by communists, and we feared that, if they won, our businessmen might not be allowed to get what they wanted from that part of the world.

THE GENEVA CONFERENCE

In May 1954, the Vietnamese nationalists utterly defeated the 15,000-man French force at Dien Bien Phu in one of the major battles of modern history. But the Vietnamese were to lose at the conference table, and afterward, much of what they had won on the battlefield.

Even in 1954 there were men in the United States who wanted to send American boys in to stave off the impending French defeat. Admiral Arthur B. Radford, who was the Chairman of the Joint Chiefs of Staff, Secretary of State John Foster Dulles, and Vice-President Richard M. Nixon were among them. There was even talk of using atomic bombs....

THE U.S. INSTALLS A PUPPET

General Walter Bedell Smith, the United States delegate to the final session of the General Conference, read an official American declaration on July 21, 1954, in which the United States promised "it will refrain from the threat or the use of force to disturb" the Agreement. The Declaration seemed to endorse the 1956 reunifying election: "In the case of nations now divided against their will, we shall continue to seek to achieve unity through free elections." ...

It was not difficult for our government to see to it that the election did not take place. We swiftly selected a new ruler for South Vietnam. Our choice: Ngo Dinh Diem, a Vietnamese aristocrat who had been living in Ossining, New York. Diem had no following in the land of his birth. His main support came from the United States.

"Secretary of State John Foster Dulles picked him," reported *Look* magazine (January 28, 1964). "Senator Mike Mansfield endorsed him, Francis Cardinal Spellman praised him, Vice-President Richard M. Nixon liked him, and President Dwight D. Eisenhower O.K'.d him."

Source: Benjamin Spock and Mitchell Zimmerman, *Dr. Spock on Vietnam* (New York: Dell Publishing Co., Inc., 1968), 15–26. Copyright © 1968 by Dr. Benjamin Spock and Mitchell Zimmerman. Used by permission of Dell Books, a division of Bantam Doubleday Dell Publishing Group, Inc. Also see George Katsiasficas, ed., *Vietnam Documents: American and Vietnamese Views of the War* (Armonk, NY: M. E. Sharpe, 1992), 37–43.

The rights of the people of South Vietnam—and the promises made to them at Geneva—were ignored.

Our leaders made the decision without consulting us. Most Americans no more knew that we had installed Diem, and were supporting his government, than they knew we had underwritten the cost of the war for the French for the previous four years.

Once our government had decided to establish South Vietnam as an American bastion, it had to violate the key terms of the Geneva Agreement.

The free election promised for July 1956 for the purpose of reunifying Vietnam was canceled by Diem, with the backing of the United States.

Since Diem could only be sure of keeping the South Vietnamese under his control by force, the United States had to supply him with military assistance, again violating the Geneva Agreement.... We were not aiding an independent country with our guns and ammunition. We were equipping an American Foreign Legion, organized by our man Diem, to hold onto what we regarded as our territory. According to Joseph Buttinger, who was with the International Rescue Committee in Vietnam, Diem himself repeatedly remarked, "that the borders of the United States extend to the 17th parallel," the northern boundary of South Vietnam.

In fact, down to the present day most of the expenses of the South Vietnamese Army—weapons, uniforms, salaries—have been paid for by the United States of America....

Despite the scuttling of the Geneva Agreement by the United States and Diem, North Vietnam did not attack South Vietnam. The North Vietnamese were bitter over the U.S.–Diem denial of peaceful reunification, but they were also tired of war, and more interested in rebuilding their country in the North than in liberating the South.

But the South Vietnamese people had reasons of their own to rise up against the U.S.–Diem government.

QUESTIONS

1. This document argues that the "Vietnamese people had reasons of their own to rise up against the U.S." How do the authors explain these reasons?

2. What is the core objective expressed in this document?

3. How does it differ from the perspective in LBJ's statement?

27.4. VISUAL DOCUMENT: DAVID LEVINE, "VIETNAM: THE TURNING POINT" (MAY 12, 1966)

In the spring of 1966, President Lyndon B. Johnson opened his shirt to show reporters the scar from his recent gallbladder surgery. As opposition to the war mounted, David Levine drew a widely reproduced cartoon indicating that the president's real wound was thousands of miles away in Vietnam.

QUESTIONS

1. How does this cartoon visually capture a growing critique of the war in Vietnam?

2. Cartoons often outlast other forms of political communication. In what ways does a simple cartoon like this help us understand important historical debates?

Source: David Levine, "Vietnam: The Turning Point," *The New York Review of Books*, May 12, 1966. Walter Daran/Time & Life Pictures/Getty Images.

27.5. HENRY KISSINGER, EXCERPT FROM *YEARS OF UPHEAVAL* (1982)

In the excerpt drawn from his memoirs below, Henry Kissinger explains the reasoning behind the policy of détente with the Soviet Union. He shows how the policy lost public support from an unlikely coalition of political conservatives and liberals.

Détente was thus built on the twin pillars of resistance to Soviet expansionism and a willingness to negotiate on concrete issues, on the concept of deterrence and a readiness to explore the principles of coexistence. In Jordan and Cienfuegos in 1970; in the India-Pakistan war of 1971; most recently in the alert at the end of the October 1973 war, the Nixon Administration had vigorously opposed geopolitical challenges by the Soviet Union and its allies. We fought for a strong defense policy over bitter Congressional opposition. Simultaneously, beginning with the Berlin agreement of 1971, we also explored the prospects of negotiation. By the Moscow summit of 1972 our strategy was clearly visible; by early spring 1973 a number of agreements in arms control and technical cooperation had been achieved and others were on the horizon. None of them caused us to imagine that tensions with our adversary had ended; those who made that the test of our policy misconceived its design or misrepresented its purpose. We slackened neither our determination to maintain the military balance nor to resist Soviet expansionism. What we were prepared to do was to reduce the risks of competition and to elaborate criteria for coexistence. We had learned that in a democracy, the prerequisite for effective prolonged struggle is the continued demonstration of the willingness to end it. And we were convinced, finally, that the corrosive effect of a long period of peace on the cohesion of the Soviet system would be much greater than on ours.

A chief executive with the prestige that Nixon had earned with the foreign policy successes of his first term might have brought off this pedagogical effort. The realities of the nuclear age and the imperatives of protracted competition could have been presented in a patient, serious, open public dialogue such as transformed American isolationism in the aftermath of World War II. But the bitter divisions of Vietnam and the ugly suspicions of Watergate produced a domestic climate ill suited for any thoughtful discussion.

As a result, conservatives who hated Communists and liberals who hated Nixon came together in a rare convergence, like an eclipse of the sun. Conservatives were uneasy with the number of agreements being signed with a declared adversary. They did not believe America could remain vigilant while seeming "progress" was being made under the aegis of détente. They were convinced that American preparedness could be honed only by ideological militance. They wanted uncompromising verbal hostility; they sometimes seemed to prize rhetorical intransigence more than toughness in substance.

The liberal case was more complex. The Nixon Administration was pursuing arms control, East-West trade, and other negotiations that liberals had been urging for decades. But the blood feud with Nixon ran too deep. If Nixon was for détente, so the subconscious thinking seemed to run, perhaps the Cold War wasn't all bad! At the same time many liberals who had fought bitterly against American overseas involvement—especially in Indochina—discovered during the Middle East war the peril to free nations if the United States abdicated its concern for regional balances of power against countries armed by the Soviets.

QUESTIONS

1. How does this document from 1982 reflect a new historical perspective on Cold War conflicts?
2. What is the emerging liberal-conservative consensus that Kissinger highlights?

Source: Henry Kissinger, *Years of Upheaval* (Boston: Little, Brown and Co., 1982), 982–83.

27.6. SENATOR SAM ERVIN, COMMENTS ON WATERGATE (1973)

North Carolina Democratic Senator San Ervin chaired the Senate Watergate committee. During the committee's televised hearings in the summer of 1973, Ervin explained why the issues in the Watergate scandal were so important.

I think... they were unable to accept the risk that people should exercise freedom for themselves. The First Amendment was written giving the rights of freedom of speech and freedom of thought, freedom of the press and freedom to protest to government, to make America a free society....

I think one of the unfortunate things which have arisen in recent years is that too many men in power have too little commitment to freedom and actually fear the exercise of freedom by other people, especially people whose actions or thoughts are displeasing to them....

I love my country. I venerate the office of the President, and I have the best wishes for the success of the incumbent of that office, because he is the only president this country has at this time.

But beyond that, the President of the United States, by reason of the fact that he holds the highest office in the gift of the American people, owes an obligation to furnish a high standard of leadership to this nation and his constitutional duties, in my opinion, and undoubtedly his duty of affording moral leadership to the country, place upon him some obligation in these circumstances.

And I don't think the people of the United States are interested so much in abstruse arguments about the separation of powers or executive privilege as they are in finding the answer to that question.

I deeply regret that this situation has arisen, because I think that the Watergate tragedy is the greatest tragedy this country has ever suffered. I used to think the Civil War was our country's greatest tragedy, but I do remember that there were some redeeming features in the Civil War in that there was some spirit of sacrifice and heroism displayed on both sides. I see no redeeming features in Watergate.

QUESTIONS

1. How does the author make the case for the broader significance of Watergate?
2. What is the most important consequence according to the author?

Source: Paul R. Clancy, *Just a Country Lawyer: A Biography of Sam Ervin* (Bloomington, IN: Indiana University Press, 1974), 264–5, 279–80.

27.7. VISUAL DOCUMENT: HERBLOCK, *NIXON HANGING BETWEEN THE TAPES* IN *THE WASHINGTON POST* (MAY 24, 1974)

As the Watergate scandal intensified, President Richard M. Nixon responded to reports that he had paid only a few hundred dollars in income taxes with the remark, "I am not a crook." *Washington Post* cartoonist Herblock, a longtime Nixon critic, mocked his defense.

QUESTIONS

1. Can you point to the different historical issues addressed by this simple cartoon?

2. How does Herblock use visual clues to help address complicated debates about presidential power and authority?

Source: Caroline and Erwin Swann Collection of Caricature & Cartoon (Library of Congress)

CHAPTER 28

THE VIETNAM ERA, 1961–1975

28.1 SARGENT SHRIVER, "LETTER TO THE EDITOR" ON THE JOBS CORPS (MARCH 21, 1965)

Many Great Society programs drew criticism for their high costs. In this letter to the editor of the *Washington Post*, Sargent Shriver, the Director of the Office of Economic Opportunity, the government's coordinating body for the War on Poverty, defends the Job Corps, a program designed to employ and train poor and poorly educated young people.

JOB CORPS COSTS

A news report in your paper recently made an adverse comparison between the total costs to the Government of providing 12 months of basic vocational and citizenship training to our disadvantaged youths in residential training centers under the United States Job Corps and the costs only to the student of an academic year at Harvard University.

The dollar costs in these two cases are not comparable, and not much else in the comparison is relevant. The comparison, in fact, is superficial, invidious and inaccurate.

Harvard students are among the most brilliant, self-reliant, and highly trained youth our Nation can produce. Thousands of dollars have been invested in their education before they ever get to Harvard. Most of them come from good schools and good families, and have lived in communities where much training and preparation has been given to them. The very atmosphere they breathe is helpful to them. They are getting advanced training at the top of our academic system.

Job Corps enrollees come from situations exactly the opposite. They have gotten the worst and cheapest training. Very little has been invested in them by their impoverished parents or by society. They frequently come from broken homes and physical environments conducive to everything but good work habits and good citizenship. The fact is that not only are they not qualified for Harvard; they are unqualified for any kind of job with a real future in America today.

Source: *Washington Post*, March 21, 1965, E6.

These differences would lead an objective critic to anticipate much higher costs for producing useful citizens out of Job Corps enrollees. Surprisingly, the Job Corps costs are significantly lower, per person, per year than the Harvard costs.

At Harvard, according to a study made by Seymour Harris, the noted Harvard economist, in an article entitled *The Economics of Harvard*, the tuition actually charged the student is only one third the educational cost to the University. The cost of tuition and room and board to the student at Harvard is $2890, according to the 1964 Official Register. Add to this cost to the student the factors outlined by Seymour Harris and you get $6410 per annum as the cost of an academic-year Harvard education.

On the other hand, the total cost to the Government for a Job Corps enrollee for nine months is only $4650—about two thirds of the cost of a Harvard education, and this figure includes $1500 for allowances, travel, clothing and major medical expenses, which are not even included in the Harvard costs cited above. When these items are excluded, the cost of nine months in the Job Corps is only $3100, less than half the cost of nine months at Harvard.

Furthermore, these cost estimates for Job Corps are figured on present enrollment plans and include initial startup expenses. Once the program is in full-scale operation at full strength, these costs could easily drop substantially.

The real test for both a Harvard education and a Job Corps education is not how much it costs, however, but how successful the graduates are. No one doubts that it is worth the cost of a Harvard education to produce outstanding businessmen, top college professors and leading Senators. I think it makes just as good sense to take a boy or girl who was born and raised in poverty and, as a result, faces adult life without the education and training needed to get a job, and provide that education and training through the Job Corps.

The real question for taxpayers to decide is not whether the Job Corps costs more or less than a Harvard education, but whether it is worth investing tax revenues in education and training to keep these young men and women off tomorrow's relief rolls, and out of tomorrow's courts, and get them into tomorrow's ranks of productive citizens and taxpayers. That is what the Job Corps is all about.

SARGENT SHRIVER,
Director, Office of Economic Opportunity.
Washington.

QUESTIONS

1. What broader point is Shriver making about the U.S. economy at this moment in history?
2. Who seems to be the audience for this defense?
3. Why does the author think Job Corps is worthwhile?

28.2 STUDENTS FOR A DEMOCRATIC SOCIETY, *THE PORT HURON STATEMENT* (1962) AND AN APPEAL TO STUDENTS (1964)

In 1962, University of Michigan student Tom Hayden drafted the Port Huron Statement, the first official document of the newly formed Students for a Democratic Society (SDS). In it, SDS criticized hypocritical and unjust aspects of post–World War II U.S. society.

Sources: Students for a Democratic Society, *The Port Huron Statement* (1962) (Chicago: Charles S. Kerr Publishing, 1999), 7–8.

SDS's presence grew on campuses across the country in 1964 and 1965. Copies of the Port Huron Statement circulated widely, along with appeals to join SDS. The appeal to students appeared on the back cover of the second printing of the Port Huron Statement (December 1964).

THE PORT HURON STATEMENT

INTRODUCTION: AGENDA FOR A GENERATION

We are people of this generation, bred in at least modest comfort, housed now in universities, looking uncomfortably to the world we inherit.

When we were kids the United States was the wealthiest and strongest country in the world; the only one with the atom bomb, the least scarred by modern war, an initiator of the United Nations that we thought would distribute Western influence throughout the world. Freedom and equality for each individual, government of, by, and for the people—these American values we found good, principles by which we could live as men. Many of us began maturing in complacency.

As we grew, however, our comfort was penetrated by events too troubling to dismiss. First, the permeating and victimizing fact of human degradation, symbolized by the Southern struggle against racial bigotry, compelled most of us from silence to activism. Second, the enclosing fact of the Cold War, symbolized by the presence of the Bomb, brought awareness that we ourselves, and our friends, and millions of abstract "others" we knew more directly because of our common peril, might die at any time. We might deliberately ignore, or avoid, or fail to feel all other human problems, but not these two, for these were too immediate and crushing in their impact, too challenging in the demand that we as individuals take the responsibility for encounter and resolution.

While these and other problems either directly oppressed us or rankled our consciences and became our subjective concerns, we began to see complicated and disturbing paradoxes in our surrounding America. The declaration "all men are created equal..." rang hollow before the facts of Negro life in the South and the big cities of the North. The proclaimed peaceful intentions of the United States contradicted its economic and military investments in the Cold War status quo.

We witnessed, and continue to witness, other paradoxes. With nuclear energy whole cities can easily be powered, yet the dominant nation-states seem more likely to unleash destruction greater than that incurred in all wars of human history. Although our own technology is destroying old and creating new forms of social organization, men still tolerate meaningless work and idleness. While two-thirds of mankind suffers undernourishment, our own upper classes revel amidst superfluous abundance. Although world population is expected to double in forty years, the nations still tolerate anarchy as a major principle of international conduct and uncontrolled exploitation governs the sapping of the earth's physical resources. Although mankind desperately needs revolutionary leadership, America rests in national stalemate, its goals ambiguous and tradition-bound instead of informed and clear, its democratic system apathetic and manipulated rather than "of, by, and for the people."

APPEAL TO STUDENTS

Students for a Democratic Society!

SDS is a movement of young people who study and participate in daily struggles for social change. Committed to change in many spheres of society, SDS members, in chapters, projects, and as individuals:

- Organize the dispossessed in community movements for economic gains. During the summer of 1964, one hundred and fifty students provided the full-time staffs for 10 community projects in the urban North—40 of them continuing full-time in the fall. Movements of welfare mothers, the unemployed, tenants, and others have been organized around their particular grievances.
- Participate in activity for peace through protest, research, education, and community organization.

SDS organized protests and proposed peaceful solutions during the Cuba and Vietnam crises; sponsors peace research among students; and is undertaking pilot efforts to organize defense workers for economic conversion.

- Work for civil rights through direct action, publication, and support of the Student Nonviolent Coordinating Committee. SDS projects in Chester, Pa., and Newark, N.J., serve as models for Negro movements in the North due to their mass support.
- Inject controversy into a stagnant educational system. SDS participated in the mass demonstrations and organized national support for free speech at Berkeley; pioneered in the introduction of peace courses into college curricula; and initiated the union organization of student employees at the U. of Michigan.

- Support political insurgents, such as Noel Day in Boston, in the fight for a government that would promote social justice. SDS produces studies of the political and electoral situation.

Won't you join?

QUESTIONS

1. How does the first statement explain the reasons for growing concern among young Americans?
2. Both of these documents point to a change that prompted some university students to question what they thought about their country. What was this change?
3. What is the relationship between the various activities stated in the SDS document?

28.3. CESAR CHAVEZ, SPEECH AT HARVARD UNIVERSITY (MARCH 1970)

In March 1970 Cesar Chavez, organizer of the four-year-old Delano Grape Strike, tells an audience at Harvard University of the hardships encountered by the men and women who were trying to organize California's farm workers.

You know, we have had a long historical struggle in the fields of California to form unions. Very little has been recorded, very little has been written about it, because in most cases this struggle has been waged by immigrant groups. In many cases those groups made very little achievement, but for the last seven years there have been basic struggles to organize, and for seven years these attempts have been thwarted and broken by the overwhelming power of the employer groups.

Today in Delano we have a group of men and women who have done outstanding work to try and liberate themselves through their collective action to get those things in life that other workers have had so long. They have gone to great expense and personal selfless dedication and work just to stay alive as a group. We ourselves frequently ask: What causes a man to give up his paycheck for forty-eight months—forty-nine months now—however small it may be, for the right to have a living? Or what would cause a woman striker to picket and demonstrate, peacefully and nonviolently, and then be arrested as a common criminal? Or what would cause men and women in the struggle to suffer the painful separation from family and be sent across the country to all the major cities and Canada,

Source: Cesar Chavez, *An Organizer's Tale: Speeches* (New York: Penguin, 2008), 88–90.

to bring the word of the boycott and the struggle of the farm workers? We often ask ourselves: What would cause teenage boys and girls to [go to] school without a new pair of shoes or go to school with the same old clothes and do without noon lunch? What causes this greatest personal sacrifice? Why are they going insane? Or what would cause still little children who are too small to understand the struggle, to do without milk, to do without the basic necessities of life because their parents are involved in what is getting to be perhaps the longest and, perhaps, we hope, the most successful strike of farm workers ever in the history of our country? We say that what causes this is what causes other people in other parts of the world and in our own country—a spirit of independence and freedom, the spirit that they want to change things and that they want to be independent and they want to be able to run their own lives. This is the cause why these workers are so willing to bear the sacrifices and all the personal suffering that go with the strike and boycott.

You know, organizing farm workers is very different from organizing any other workers in the country today. Here we don't have any rules, any regulations. We don't have any prescribed methods, no precedents. There is no law for farm labor organizing, save the law of the jungle. The citizens and their rights for seven years have been ignored and the employers have seen to it that they don't survive. Agriculture in this country is not a family with a small plot of land. That is not agriculture, that is not where the fruits and the vegetables, the nuts and the grapes are produced. They [are] produced in large factory farms, huge corporate farms. They themselves have adopted a new name: they call themselves "agrobusiness."

It is against agro-business, in such combinations as they have going now with the Defense Department, that we have to deal. For we had cut the sales of grapes nationally thirty percent. The Defense Department, on the other hand, is increasing its purchases to the extent that they are now shipping to Vietnam eight hundred percent more grapes than they were in the beginning of the boycott....

But it is no joke that the Defense Department is in a deal with agro-business for the sole purpose of breaking the strike. And the eight hundred percent only takes us to the end of the last fiscal year. As the report comes from the first quarter of this new fiscal year; we don't know what the percentage may be. We can very well guess that it will probably be about a thousand percent. That means they are sending to Vietnam now about eight pounds of grapes per man. Imagine what happens over there when a fellow doesn't like grapes gets that much!

But in the face of this overwhelming power, enough to wipe out literally any attempt of a group of people to organize, we will continue to work, we will continue to spread our strike and boycott to many parts of the world. We have been able to enlist the support of the transport workers throughout the world, the support of the metal-workers, all the labor movements in Canada and the labor movement here, the church supporting us in a manner to be marvelled at, and the liberal community. But it was not like this always. There was a time at the beginning of the strike when people were afraid of us. There was a time at the beginning of the strike when we stood alone with the workers and when no one dared to come near us. No one dared to come near us because we were being red-baited. And it did not come to be what it is today, except for today, thank God—and we thank them a million times—the students who came to our support right from the beginning. So there is sympathy of the worker in this struggle for students whoever they may be.

QUESTIONS

1. How does Chavez relate his struggle with historic issues?
2. What does Chavez mean when he says that the protestors were being "red-baited?"
3. How does this struggle for workers' rights compare to the privileged student protest goals explained in the SDS documents?

28.4. STOKELY CARMICHAEL, EXCERPTS FROM *STOKELY SPEAKS* (1965)

The publishers of Black Power advocate Stokely Carmichael's book *Stokely Speaks* printed a widely circulated photo of him raising a gun. The dedication page placed Black Power in an international context. In an excerpt from the book, Carmichael charges that racism deeply permeates U.S. society.

This book is dedicated to President Ahmed Sékou Touré and Mme. Touré and to my brothers and sisters in Guinea who have suffered much to maintain Africa's dignity and sustain Africa's will to survive.

I maintain that every civil rights bill in this country was passed for white people, not for black people. For example, I am black. I know that. I also know that while I am black I am a human being. Therefore I have the right to go into any public place. White people didn't know that. Every time I tried to go into a public place they stopped me. So some boys had to write a bill to tell that white man, "He's a human being; don't stop him." That bill was for the white man, not for me. I knew I could vote all the time and that it wasn't a privilege but my right. Every time I tried I was shot, killed or jailed, beaten or economically deprived. So somebody had to write a bill to tell white people, "When a black man comes to vote, don't bother him." That bill was for white people. I know I can live anyplace I want to live. It is white people across this country who are incapable of allowing me to live where I want. You need a civil rights bill, not me. The failure of the civil rights bill isn't because of Black Power or because of the Student Nonviolent Coordinating Committee or because of the rebellions that are occurring in the major cities. That failure is due to the whites' incapacity to deal with their own problems inside their own communities.

And so in a sense we must ask, How is it that black people move? And what do we do? But the question in a much greater sense is, How can white people who are the majority, and who are responsible for making democracy work, make it work? They have failed miserably on this point. They have never made democracy work, be it inside the United States, Vietnam, South Africa, the Philippines, South America, Puerto Rico, or wherever America has been. We not only condemn the country for what it has done internally, but we must condemn it for what it does externally. We see this country trying to rule the world, and someone must stand up and start articulating that this country is not God, and that it cannot rule the world.

The white supremacist attitude, which you have either consciously or subconsciously, is running rampant through society today. For example, missionaries were sent to Africa with the attitude that blacks were automatically inferior. As a matter of fact, the first act the missionaries did when they got to Africa was to make us cover up our bodies, because they said it got them excited. We couldn't go bare-breasted any more because they got excited! When the missionaries came to civilize us because we were uncivilized, to educate us because we were uneducated, and to give us some literate studies because we were illiterate, they charged a price. The missionaries came with the Bible, and we had the land; when they left, they had the land, and we still have the Bible. That's been the rationalization

Source: Stokely Carmichael, *Stokely Speaks: Black Power to Pan-Africanism* (New York: Random House, 1971), 47–49.

for Western civilization as it moves across the world—stealing, plundering and raping everybody in its path. Their one rationalization is that the rest of the world is uncivilized and they are in fact civilized. But the West is un-civ-i-lized. And that still runs on today, you see, because now we have "modern-day missionaries," and they come into our ghettos—they Head Start, Upward Lift, Bootstrap, and Upward Bound us into white society. They don't want to face the real problem. A man is poor for one reason and one reason only—he does not have money. If you want to get rid of poverty, you give people money. And you ought not to tell me about people who don't work, and that you can't give people money if they don't work, because if that were true, you'd have to start stopping Rockefeller, Kennedy, Lyndon Baines Johnson, Lady Bird Johnson, the whole of Standard Oil, the Gulf Corporation, all of them, including probably a large number of the board of trustees of this university. The question, then, is not whether or not one can work; it's *Who has power to make his or her acts legitimate?* That is all. In this country that power is invested in the hands of white people, and it makes their acts legitimate.

QUESTIONS

1. Why do you think the author concludes with a discussion of money and power?
2. At a time when most Americans were celebrating the civil rights movement, Carmichael's speech points to his own doubts. Why does he question the legal assault on segregation?

28.5. VISUAL DOCUMENT: TOMI UNGERER, *BLACK POWER WHITE POWER* (1967)

Artist Tomi Ungerer captures some of the upheaval in race relations that occurred in the midst of the Black Power movement and the white backlash to the push for civil rights.

QUESTIONS

1. What different issues do you see in this image?

2. How does this poster relate to Carmichael's statements in the previous document?

Source: Musée Tomi Ungerer - Centre International de l'Illustration, Strasbourg, Photo M. Bertola, © Diogenes Verlag, Zürich.

28.6. VISUAL DOCUMENT: ASSOCIATED PRESS, *BLACK POWER PROTEST AT THE 1968 MEXICO CITY OLYMPICS* (1968)

At the 1968 Olympic Games in Mexico City, U.S. athletes Tommie Smith (center) and John Carlos (right) raised their fists in the Black Power salute after winning the gold and bronze medals. Their demonstration led to their expulsion from the Games and subsequent ostracism by U.S. track and field officials.

QUESTIONS

1. Why do you think this simple act of protest became an icon of changing views of civil rights?

2. Does the act captured in this photo seem to merit the very strong reaction and punishment? Why do you think officials reacted as they did?

Source: AFP/Getty Images

28.7. TIMOTHY LEARY, EXCERPTS FROM *"PLAY-BOY* INTERVIEW: TIMOTHY LEARY—A CASUAL CONVERSATION" (1966)

In a 1966 *Playboy Magazine* interview, Timothy Leary praised psychedelic drugs for their value in opening new areas of human consciousness. He urged young people to "turn on, tune in, drop out," a phrase which soon became symbolic of the larger counterculture.

PLAYBOY: [A]ccording to a spokesman for the student left, many former campus activists who've gone the LSD route are "more concerned with what's happening in their heads than what's happening in the world." Any comment?

LEARY: There's a certain amount of truth in that. The insight of LSD leads you to concern yourself more with internal or spiritual values; you realize that it doesn't make any difference what you do on the outside unless you change the inside. If all the Negroes and left-wing college students in the world had Cadillacs and full control of society, they would still be involved in an anthill social system unless they opened themselves up first.

PLAYBOY: Aren't these young ex-activists among an increasing number of students, writers, artists and musicians whom one critic has called "the psychedelic dropouts," LSD users who find themselves divested of motivation, unable to readjust to reality or to resume their roles in society?

LEARY: There is an LSD dropout problem, but it's nothing to worry about. It's something to cheer. The lesson I have learned from over 300 LSD sessions, and which I have been passing on to others, can be stated in six syllables: Turn on, tune in, drop out. "Turn on" means to contact the ancient energies and wisdoms that are built into your nervous system. They provide unspeakable pleasure and revelation. "Tune in" means to harness and communicate these new perspectives in a harmonious dance with the external world. "Drop out" means to detach yourself from the tribal game. Current models of social adjustment—mechanized, computerized, socialized, intellectualized, televised, Sanforized—make no sense to the new LSD generation, who see clearly that American society is becoming an air-conditioned anthill. In every generation of human history, thoughtful men have turned on and dropped out of the tribal game, and thus stimulated the larger society to lurch ahead. Every historical advance has resulted from the stern pressure of visionary men who have declared their independence from the game: "Sorry, George III, we don't buy your model. We're going to try something new"; "Sorry, Louis XVI, we've got a new idea. Deal us out"; "Sorry, L.B.J., it's time to mosey on beyond the Great Society." The reflex reaction of society to the creative dropout is panic and irritation. If anyone questions the social order, he threatens the whole shaky edifice. The automatic, angry reaction to the creative dropout is that he will become a parasite on the hard-working, conforming citizen. This is not true. The LSD experience does not lead to passivity and withdrawal; it spurs a driving hunger to communicate in new forms, in better ways, to express a more harmonious message, to live a better life. The LSD cult has already wrought revolutionary changes in American culture. If you were to conduct a poll of the creative

Source: "Playboy Interview: Timothy Leary—A Casual Conversation," *Playboy* 13, no. 9 (September 1966): 93–113.

young musicians in this country, you'd find that at least 80 percent are using psychedelic drugs in a systematic way. And this new psychedelic style has produced not only a new rhythm in modern music but a new decor for our discotheques, a new form of film making, a new kinetic visual art, a new literature, and has begun to revise our philosophic and psychological thinking.

Remember, it's the college kids who are turning on the smartest and most promising of the youngsters. What an exciting prospect: a generation of creative youngsters refusing to march in step, refusing to go to offices, refusing to sign up on the installment plan, refusing to climb aboard the treadmill.

PLAYBOY: What will they do?

LEARY: Don't worry. Each one will work out his individual solution. Some will return to the establishment and inject their new ideas. Some will live underground as self-employed artists, artisans and writers. Some are already forming small communities out of the country. Many are starting schools for children and adults who wish to learn the use of their sense organs. Psychedelic businesses are springing up: bookstores, art galleries. Psychedelic industries may involve more manpower in the future than the automobile industry has produced in the last 20 years. In our technological society of the future, the problem will be not to get people to work, but to develop graceful, fulfilling ways of living a more serene, beautiful and creative life. Psychedelics will help to point the way.

QUESTIONS

1. What is Leary's argument about the importance of drugs?
2. In what ways does he believe that drug use will simply become part of modern life?

CHAPTER 29

CONSERVATISM RESURGENT, 1974–1989

29.1. PHYLLIS SCHLAFLY, EXCERPTS FROM "WHAT'S WRONG WITH 'EQUAL RIGHTS' FOR WOMEN?" (FEBRUARY 1972)

Phyllis Schlafly, a conservative activist since the early 1960s, grabbed national attention in the 1970s through her opposition to the proposed Equal Rights Amendment to the Constitution. She attacked feminists as "women's libbers" who were antireligion, anti-free enterprise, and a threat to traditional American values. Schlafly's efforts contributed to the failure of the amendment to win ratification by enough state legislatures.

Of all the classes of people who ever lived, the American woman is the most privileged. We have the most rights and rewards, and the fewest duties. Our unique status is the result of a fortunate combination of circumstances.

1. We have the immense good fortune to live in a civilization which respects the family as the basic unit of society. This respect is part and parcel of our laws and our customs. It is based on the fact of life—which no legislation or agitation can erase—that women have babies and men don't.

If you don't like this fundamental difference, you will have to take up your complaint with God because He created us this way. The fact that women, not men, have babies is not the fault of selfish and domineering men, or of the establishment, or of any clique of conspirators who want to oppress women. It's simply the way God made us.

Our Judeo-Christian civilization has developed the law and custom that, since women must bear the physical consequences of the sex act, men must be required to bear the other

Source: Phyllis Schlafly, "What's Wrong with 'Equal Rights' for Women?" *Phyllis Schlafly Report* 5, no. 7 (February 1972): 1–4.

consequences and pay in other ways. These laws and customs decree that a man must carry his share by physical protection and financial support of his children and of the woman who bears his children, and also by a code of behavior which benefits and protects both the woman and the children.

THE GREATEST ACHIEVEMENT OF WOMEN'S RIGHTS

This is accomplished by the institution of the family. Our respect for the family as the basic unit of society, which is ingrained in the laws and customs of our Judeo-Christian civilization, is the greatest single achievement in the entire history of women's rights. It assures a woman the most precious and important right of all—the right to keep her own baby and to be supported and protected in the enjoyment of watching her baby grow and develop....

Do we want financial security? We are fortunate to have the great legacy of Moses, the Ten Commandments, especially this one: "Honor thy father and thy mother that thy days may be long upon the land." Children are a woman's best social security—her best guarantee of social benefits such as old age pension, unemployment compensation, workman's compensation, and sick leave. The family gives a woman the physical, financial and emotional security of the home—for all her life.

THE FINANCIAL BENEFITS OF CHIVALRY

2. The second reason why American women are a privileged group is that we are the beneficiaries of a tradition of special respect for women which dates from the Christian Age of Chivalry. The honor and respect paid to Mary, the Mother of Christ, resulted in all women, in effect, being put on a pedestal....

In other civilizations, such as the African and the American Indian, the men strut around wearing feathers and beads and hunting and fishing (great sport for men!), while the women do all the hard, tiresome drudgery including the tilling of the soil (if any is done), the hewing of wood, the making of fires, the carrying of water, as well as the cooking, sewing and caring for babies.

This is not the American way because we were lucky enough to inherit the traditions of the Age of Chivalry. In America, a man's first significant purchase is a diamond for his bride, and the largest financial investment of his life is a home for her to live in. American husbands work hours of overtime to buy a fur piece or other finery to keep their wives in fashion, and to pay premiums on their life insurance policies to provide for her comfort when she is a widow (benefits in which he can never share).

THE REAL LIBERATION OF WOMEN

3. The third reason why American women are so well off is that the great American free enterprise system has produced remarkable inventors who have lifted the backbreaking "women's work" from our shoulders....

The real liberation of women from the backbreaking drudgery of centuries is the American free enterprise system which stimulated inventive geniuses to pursue their talents—and we all reap the profits. The great heroes of women's liberation are not the straggly-haired women on television talk shows and picket lines, but Thomas Edison who brought the miracle of electricity to our homes to give light and to run all those labor-saving devices—the equivalent, perhaps, of a half-dozen household servants for every middle-class American woman. Or Elias Howe who gave us the sewing machine which resulted in such an abundance of readymade clothing. Or Clarence Birdseye who invented the process for freezing foods. Or Henry Ford, who mass-produced the automobile so that it is within the price-range of every American, man or woman.

THE FRAUD OF THE EQUAL RIGHTS AMENDMENT

In the last couple of years, a noisy movement has sprung up agitating for "women's rights." Suddenly, everywhere we are afflicted with aggressive females on television talk shows yapping about how mistreated American women are, suggesting that marriage has put us in some kind of "slavery," that housework is menial and degrading, and—perish the thought—that women are discriminated against. New "women's liberation" organizations are popping up, agitating and demonstrating, serving demands on public officials, getting wide press coverage always, and purporting to speak for some 100,000,000 American women.

It's time to set the record straight. The claim that American women are downtrodden and unfairly treated is the fraud of the century. The truth is that American women never had it so good. Why should we lower ourselves to "equal rights" when we already have the status of special privilege?...

WOMEN'S LIBBERS DO NOT SPEAK FOR US

The "women's lib" movement is not an honest effort to secure better jobs for women who want or need to work outside the home. This is just the superficial sweet-talk to win broad support for a radical "movement." Women's lib is a total assault on the role of the American woman as wife and mother, and on the family as the basic unit of society.

Women's libbers are trying to make wives and mothers unhappy with their career, make them feel that they are "second-class citizens" and "abject slaves." Women's libbers are promoting free sex instead of the "slavery" of marriage. They are promoting Federal "day-care centers" for babies instead of homes. They are promoting abortions instead of families....

Modern technology and opportunity have not discovered any nobler or more satisfying or more creative career for a woman than marriage and motherhood. The wonderful advantage that American women have is that we can have all the rewards of that number-one career, and still moonlight with a second one to suit our intellectual, cultural or financial tastes or needs.

And why should the men acquiesce in a system which gives preferential rights and lighter duties to women? In return, the men get the pearl of great price: a happy home, a faithful wife, and children they adore.

If the women's libbers want to reject marriage and motherhood, it's a free country and that is their choice. But let's not permit these women's libbers to get away with pretending to speak for the rest of us. Let's not permit this tiny minority to degrade the role that most women prefer. Let's not let these women's libbers deprive wives and mothers of the rights we now possess.

Tell your Senators NOW that you want them to vote NO on the Equal Rights Amendment. Tell your television and radio stations that you want equal time to present the case FOR marriage and motherhood.

QUESTIONS

1. What faults does Schlafly identify in the women's liberation movement?
2. How does she defend traditional female roles?

29.2. PAUL WEYRICH, EXCERPT FROM "BUILDING THE MORAL MAJORITY" (AUGUST 1979)

In 1979, Paul Weyrich joined other conservative Christians, Catholic and Protestant, in founding the Moral Majority. The group sought to rally religious conservatives behind Republican candidates and make the Republican Party more responsive to their moral and religious concerns. In this article published in 1979, Weyrich explained the importance of creating a lobbying group that brought together formerly antagonistic groups of Christians through their opposition to abortion, gay rights, and the defense of traditional values.

Source: Paul Weyrich, "Building the Moral Majority," *Conservative Digest*, August 1979, 18–19.

The family will be to the decade of the 1980s what environmentalism and consumerism have been to the 1970s and what the Vietnam war was to the 1960s.

It is possible that the enemies of the family and society may at last have set up a situation where the majority in this nation who still subscribe to moral principles and traditional values can unite into a cohesive political movement to change the direction of the country.

There was, in fact, a moral majority of sorts who were in power in this country for many years, into the early part of this century. But the Scopes trial and the revolt against Prohibition swept these fundamentalists, if you will, out of power, and they have been on the defensive ever since, until recent times.

Television and the new breed of religious leader, exemplified by the Rev. Jerry Falwell and by Pat Robertson of the 700 Club, have given life and effectiveness to the Word of God as articulated by these men, who are not ashamed to pronounce that the Bible is the unerring truth. Unlike many of their predecessors, these "electronic preachers" understand the linkage between the religious and moral issues and the politics of our time.

Meanwhile, the Second Vatican Council of the Catholic Church has produced a whole new dimension which its modernist advocates did not intend. The liberal Catholic promoters of the excesses of Vatican II had a vision of a one-world Church, void of doctrine and beliefs, united at last with the "near beer" versions of mainline Protestantism. It is true, of course, that since Vatican II the social gospel advocates in the Catholic and Protestant churches have been working ever more closely together. But the "ecumaniacs" had not counted on a reverse coalition. Now, however, the true-believing Gospel-oriented Catholics, having been told by the hierarchy that they should seek accommodation with their Protestant brethren, have taken to working with fundamentalist/evangelical Protestants in, for example, the right-to-life movement rather than with liberal Protestants in boycotting grapes with Cesar Chavez.

The alliance has produced great results. The media often portray the right-to-life movement as a tool of the Catholic bishops. Movement insiders know it is a truly grassroots effort and that if anything the Catholic bishops have hindered its success. Any typical right-to-life gathering these days is a microcosm of the moral majority, with urban ethnic Catholics, Gospel-believing Protestants, Mormons and Orthodox Jews working together.

The upshot of this new alliance is that hundreds of thousands, perhaps millions, of lives have been saved because of the visibility of the issue. We never hear about these lives. They don't make the statistical counts. These are the babies born of the mothers who have heard the message that abortion is murder.

Because of the strong political reaction against abortion, the necrophiliac agenda for euthanasia, limiting the number of children a family may have (population control) and other overt antifamily schemes has been slowed down considerably.

And the movement has given teenagers of this generation a cause, something more important than themselves, for which to work. In this "era of the self," no other political movement has managed to accomplish anything like it.

What the right-to-life movement has managed to put together on the abortion issue is only a sample of what is to come when the full range of family and educational issues becomes the focus of debate in the 1980s.

The homosexual rights advocates, genetic engineers and militant secular humanists who insist on their religion in the schools had better understand what is happening.

The threat to the family has caused leaders of various denominations to put aside their sectarian differences and, for the first time in decades, agree on basic principles worth fighting for. This is no false unity based on papering over doctrinal differences. The various leaders of the individual communities have given up none of their beliefs in order to cooperate. Rather, the pro-family movement is a recognition that the moral majority must be put together as a coalition—because our very right to worship as we choose, to bring up our families in some kind of moral order, to educate our children free from the interference of the state, to follow the commands of Holy Scripture and the Church are at stake. These leaders have concluded it is better to argue about denominational differences at another time. Right now, it is the agenda of those opposed to the Scriptures and the Church which has bought us together....

The alliance of which Falwell spoke has great potential and political implications. Clear-cut moral choices can be offered the American voter for the first time in decades. The alliance on family issues is bound to begin to look at the morality of other issues such as SALT and the unjust power that has been legislated for union bosses.

What is more, all of this occurs at a time when the political parties have declined to the point where, in certain parts of the country, they are no longer taken seriously.

It is a coalition which can work. It can be the basis for a Christian democratic movement rooted in the authentic Gospel, not the social gospel.

Each part of the coalition brings something useful. The fundamentalist/evangelical Protestants bring a knowledge of and devotion to the Bible which no politician can shake. In addition, they have mastered the use of television and radio for their efforts, and this will make communications easier. The Catholics and Eastern Orthodox bring philosophical underpinnings which can help make the coalition impervious to attack, so that this alliance will not be swept away as happened earlier in this century. The Catholics also bring with them their rich cultural traditions from places like Ireland and Italy which can serve well during these times of attack on the family. The Mormons bring a superb knowledge of organization and outreach, and the Orthodox Jews bring not only family tradition but the ability to be productively aggressive.

QUESTIONS

1. How did controversies over abortion rights and school prayer create, as Weyrich saw it, a basis for political alliance between evangelical Protestants and Catholics?

29.3. JIMMY CARTER, EXCERPTS FROM "THE CRISIS OF CONFIDENCE" (JULY 15, 1979)

In a speech he delivered on July 15, 1979, President Jimmy Carter addressed the economic problems and low morale that afflicted the nation. Although he did not use the term, an aide described it as an overview of the "malaise" dragging down the national spirit, and that term stuck. Carter's opponents used it to criticize him for "blaming Americans" for the problems they experienced.

It's clear that the true problems of our Nation are much deeper—deeper than gasoline lines or energy shortages, deeper even than inflation or recession....

I know, of course, being President, that government actions and legislation can be very important. That's why I've worked hard to put my campaign promises into law—and I have to admit, with just mixed success. But...all the legislation in the world can't fix what's wrong with America. So, I want to speak to you first tonight about a subject even more serious than energy or inflation. I want to talk to you right now about a fundamental threat to American democracy....

Source: Presidential Papers of the Presidents of the United States: Jimmy Carter, 1979, vol. 2 (Washington, DC: US Government Printing Office, 1980), 1235–41.

The threat is nearly invisible in ordinary ways. It is a crisis of confidence. It is a crisis that strikes at the very heart and soul and spirit of our national will. We can see this crisis in the growing doubt about the meaning of our own lives and in the loss of a unity of purpose for our Nation.

The erosion of our confidence in the future is threatening to destroy the social and the political fabric of America.

The confidence that we have always had as a people is not simply some romantic dream or a proverb in a dusty book that we read just on the Fourth of July.... Confidence has defined our course and has served as a link between generations. We've always believed in something called progress. We've always had a faith that the days of our children would be better than our own.

Our people are losing that faith, not only in government itself but in the ability as citizens to serve as the ultimate rulers and shapers of our democracy....

In a nation that was proud of hard work, strong families, close-knit communities, and our faith in God, too many of us now tend to worship self-indulgence and consumption. Human identity is no longer defined by what one does, but by what one owns. But we've discovered that owning things and consuming things does not satisfy our longing for meaning. We've learned that piling up material goods cannot fill the emptiness of lives which have no confidence or purpose....

These changes did not happen overnight. They've come upon us gradually over the last generation, years that were filled with shocks and tragedy.

We were sure that ours was a nation of the ballot, not the bullet, until the murders of John Kennedy and Robert Kennedy and Martin Luther King, Jr. We were taught that our armies were always invincible and our causes were always just, only to suffer the agony of Vietnam. We respected the Presidency as a place of honor until the shock of Watergate.

We remember when the phrase "sound as a dollar" was an expression of absolute dependability, until 10 years of inflation began to shrink our dollar and our savings. We believed that our Nation's resources were limitless until 1973, when we had to face a growing dependence on foreign oil....

Looking for a way out of this crisis, our people have turned to the Federal Government and found it isolated from the mainstream of our Nation's life....

What you see too often in Washington and elsewhere around the country is a system of government that seems incapable of action....

Often you see paralysis and stagnation and drift. You don't like it, and neither do I. What can we do?

First of all, we must face the truth, and then we can change our course. We simply must have faith in each other, faith in our ability to govern ourselves, and faith in the future of this Nation. Restoring that faith and that confidence to America is now the most important task we face. It is a true challenge of this generation of Americans....

We are at a turning point in our history. There are two paths to choose. One is a path I've warned about tonight, the path that leads to fragmentation and self-interest. Down that road lies a mistaken idea of freedom, the right to grasp for ourselves some advantage over others. That path would be one of constant conflict between narrow interests ending in chaos and immobility. It is a certain route to failure.

All the traditions of our past, all the lessons of our heritage, all the promises of our future point to another path, the path of common purpose and the restoration of American values. That path leads to true freedom for our Nation and ourselves. We can take the first steps down that path as we begin to solve our energy problem.

Energy will be the immediate test of our ability to unite this Nation, and it can also be the standard around which we rally....

Little by little we can and we must rebuild our confidence. We can spend until we empty our treasuries, and we may summon all the wonders of science. But we can succeed only if we tap our greatest resources—America's people, America's values, and America's confidence.

QUESTIONS

1. What faults of American society does Carter identify?
2. How does he propose to boost American spirits?

29.4. VISUAL DOCUMENTS: RONALD REAGAN IMAGERY

As a candidate for president and throughout his first term, Reagan spoke in strident tones about the Communist threat, the need to rearm America, and his determination to roll back Soviet influence in the third world. His unapologetic, muscular patriotism was displayed in White House photographs and in his fans' identification of him with action hero "Rambo." In 1988, near the end of his presidency, as relations with the Soviet Union improved, he visited Moscow and posed for a picture near the Kremlin.

Second Lt. Charles A. Preysler, U.S. Army, Guard Post Commander, points out positions to President Ronald Reagan, from the south side of the DMZ in South Korea, November 13, 1983. AP Photo/Scott Stewart.

Sources: AP Photo/Scott Stewart; MAI/Landov.

Ronald Reagan posing with Mikhail Gorbachev near the Kremlin. MAI/Landov.

QUESTIONS

1. How did Reagan use imagery to appeal to patriotic sentiment?

2. How did his supporters use popular culture to boost his Superman image?

29.5. RONALD REAGAN, EXCERPTS FROM SPEECH TO THE NATIONAL ASSOCIATION OF EVANGELICALS (MARCH 1983)

Reagan's speech to the National Association of Evangelicals in March 1983 provided him with the opportunity to link his strident anticommunism and evangelical faith to social issues such as his opposition to abortion, high taxes, and "activist" federal judges. Government policies, he argued, must be consistent with precepts contained in the Bible.

I want you to know that this administration is motivated by a political philosophy that sees the greatness of America in you, her people, and in your families, churches, neighborhoods, communities—the institutions that foster and nourish values like concern for others and respect for the rule of law under God.

Now, I don't have to tell you that this puts us in opposition to, or at least out of step with, a prevailing attitude of many who have turned to a modern-day secularism, discarding the tried and time-tested values upon which our very civilization is based. No matter how well intentioned, their value system is radically different from that of most Americans. And while they proclaim that they're freeing us from superstitions of the past, they've taken upon themselves the job of superintending us by government rule and regulation. Sometimes their voices are louder than ours, but they are not yet a majority....

Let me state the case as briefly and simply as I can. An organization of citizens, sincerely motivated and deeply concerned about the increase in illegitimate births and abortions involving girls well below the age of consent, some time ago established a nationwide network of clinics to offer help to these girls and, hopefully, alleviate this situation. Now, again, let me say, I do not fault their intent. However, in their well-intentioned effort, these clinics have decided to provide advice and birth control drugs and devices to underage girls without the knowledge of their parents....

Is all of Judeo-Christian tradition wrong? Are we to believe that something so sacred can be looked upon as a purely physical thing with no potential for emotional and psychological harm? And isn't it the parents' right to give counsel and advice to keep their children from making mistakes that may affect their entire lives?...

More than a decade ago, a Supreme Court decision literally wiped off the books of 50 States statutes protecting the rights of unborn children. Abortion on demand now takes the lives of up to 1½ million unborn children a year. Human life legislation ending this tragedy will some day pass the Congress, and you and I must never rest until it does. Unless and until it can be proven that the unborn child is not a living entity, then its right to life, liberty, and the pursuit of happiness must be protected.

You may remember that when abortion on demand began, many, and, indeed, I'm sure many of you, warned that the practice would lead to a decline in respect for human life, that the philosophical premises

Source: Remarks at the Annual Convention of the National Association of Evangelicals in Orlando, Florida, March 8, 1983. Ronald Reagan Presidential Library, National Archives and Records Administration, http://www.reagan.utexas.edu/archives/speeches/1983/30883b.htm.

used to justify abortion on demand would ultimately be used to justify other attacks on the sacredness of human life—infanticide or mercy killing. Tragically enough, those warnings proved all too true. Only last year a court permitted the death by starvation of a handicapped infant....

Recent legislation introduced in the Congress by Representative Henry Hyde of Illinois not only increases restrictions on publicly financed abortions, it also addresses this whole problem of infanticide. I urge the Congress to begin hearings and to adopt legislation that will protect the right of life to all children, including the disabled or handicapped.

Now, I'm sure that you must get discouraged at times, but you've done better than you know, perhaps. There's a great spiritual awakening in America, a renewal of the traditional values that have been the bedrock of America's goodness and greatness.

One recent survey by a Washington-based research council concluded that Americans were far more religious than the people of other nations; 95 percent of those surveyed expressed a belief in God and a huge majority believed the Ten Commandments had real meaning in their lives. And another study has found that an overwhelming majority of Americans disapprove of adultery, teenage sex, pornography, abortion, and hard drugs. And this same study showed a deep reverence for the importance of family ties and religious belief.

I think the items that we've discussed here today must be a key part of the Nation's political agenda. For the first time the Congress is openly and seriously debating and dealing with the prayer and abortion issues—and that's enormous progress right there. I repeat: America is in the midst of a spiritual awakening and a moral renewal. And with your Biblical keynote, I say today, "Yes, let justice roll on like a river, righteousness like a never-failing stream."...

And this brings me to my final point today. During my first press conference as President, in answer to a direct question, I pointed out that, as good Marxist-Leninists, the Soviet leaders have openly and publicly declared that the only morality they recognize is that which will further their cause, which is world revolution. I think I should point out I was only quoting Lenin, their guiding spirit, who said in 1920 that they repudiate all morality that proceeds from supernatural ideas—that's their name for religion—or ideas that are outside class conceptions. Morality is entirely subordinate to the interests of class war. And everything is moral that is necessary for the annihilation of the old....

They must be made to understand we will never compromise our principles and standards. We will never give away our freedom. We will never abandon our belief in God. And we will never stop searching for a genuine peace. But we can assure none of these things America stands for through the so-called nuclear freeze solutions proposed by some....

Yes, let us pray for the salvation of all of those who live in that totalitarian darkness—pray they will discover the joy of knowing God. But until they do, let us be aware that while they preach the supremacy of the state, declare its omnipotence over individual man, and predict its eventual domination of all peoples on the Earth, they are the focus of evil in the modern world....

I believe we shall rise to the challenge. I believe that communism is another sad, bizarre chapter in human history whose last pages even now are being written. I believe this because the source of our strength in the quest for human freedom is not material, but spiritual. And because it knows no limitation, it must terrify and ultimately triumph over those who would enslave their fellow man.

QUESTIONS

1. What specific evils did Reagan associate with Communism?
2. Why did Reagan believe that religious faith was an antidote to Communism?

CHAPTER 30

AFTER THE COLD WAR, 1988–2000

30.1. APPLE COMPUTER COMPANY AND COMPUTERWORLD, "INTRODUCING MACINTOSH" ADVERTISEMENT (1984) AND EXCERPTS FROM "STEVE JOBS: ORAL HISTORY" (APRIL 20, 1995)

In 1984 Apple Computer Company introduced the Macintosh, or Mac, a personal computer designed for easy use and graphic publication. The first document below is an advertisement for the Mac around the time of its release. In the second document from a decade later, Steve Jobs, one of the inventors of the Mac and founders of Apple, explains aspects of the innovative culture of Silicon Valley.

INTRODUCING MACINTOSH. WHAT MAKES IT TICK. AND TALK.

Well, to begin with, 110 volts of alternating current.

Secondly, some of the hottest hardware to come down the pike in the last 3 years.

Some hard facts may be in order at this point:

Macintosh's brain is the same blindingly-fast 32-bit microprocessor we gave our other brainchild, the Lisa™ Personal Computer. Far more powerful than the 16-bit 8088 found in current generation computers.

Its heart is the same Lisa Technology of windows, pull-down menus, mouse commands and icons. All of

which make that 32-bit power far more useful by making the Macintosh™ Personal Computer far easier to use than current generation computers. In fact, if you can point without hurting yourself, you can use it.

NOW FOR SOME SMALL TALK.

Thanks to its size, if you can't bring the problem to a Macintosh, you can always bring a Macintosh to the problem. (It weighs 9 pounds less than the most popular "portable.")

Another miracle of miniaturization is Macintosh's built-in 3½" drive. Its disks store 400K—more than conventional 5¼" floppies. So while they're big enough

---

Sources: Personal Computing, April 1984, 196–97; Computerworld Honors Program International Archives, "Steve Jobs: Oral History," interview with Daniel S. Morrow, April 20, 1995.

to hold a desk full of work, they're small enough to fit in a shirt pocket. And, they're totally encased in a rigid plastic so they're totally protected.

AND TALK ABOUT PROGRAMMING.

There are already plenty of programs to keep a Macintosh busy. Like MacPaint,™ a program that, for the first time, lets a personal computer produce virtually any image the human hand can create. There's more software on the way from developers like Microsoft,* Lotus,™ and Software Publishing Corp., to mention a few.

And with Macintosh BASIC, Macintosh Pascal and our Macintosh Toolbox for writing your own mouse-driven programs, you, too, could make big bucks in your spare time.

You can even program Macintosh to talk in other languages, like Yiddish or Serbo-Croation, because it has a built-in polyphonic sound generator capable of producing high quality speech or music.

ALL THE RIGHT CONNECTIONS

On the back of the machine, you'll find built-in RS232 and RS422 AppleBus serial communication ports. Which means you can connect printers, modems and other peripherals without adding $150 cards. It also means that Macintosh is ready to hook in to a local area network. (With AppleBus, you will be able to interconnect up to 16 different Apple computers and peripherals.)

Should you wish to double Macintosh's storage with an external disk drive, you can do so without paying for a disk controller card—that connector's built-in, too.

There's also a built-in connector for Macintosh's mouse, a feature that costs up to $300 on computers that can't even run mouse-controlled software.

ONE LAST POINTER.

Now that you've seen some of the logic, the technology, the engineering genius and the software wizardry that separates Macintosh from conventional computers, we'd like to point you in the direction of your nearest authorized Apple dealer.

Over 1500 of them are eagerly waiting to put a mouse in your hand. As one point-and-click makes perfectly clear, the real genius of Macintosh isn't its

32-bit Lisa Technology, or its 3½" floppy disks, or its serial ports, or its software, or its polyphonic sound generator.

The real genius is that you don't have to be a genius to use a Macintosh.

You just have to be smart enough to buy one.

Soon there'll be just two kinds of people. Those who use computers. And those who use Apples.

STEVE JOBS: ORAL HISTORY

SJ: Apple was this incredible journey. I mean we did some amazing things there. The thing that bound us together at Apple was the ability to make things that were going to change the world. That was very important. We were all pretty young. The average age in the company was mid-to-late twenties. Hardly anybody had families at the beginning and we all worked like maniacs and the greatest joy was that we felt we were fashioning collective works of art much like twentieth century physics.

Something important that would last, that people contributed to and then could give to more people; the amplification factor was very large....

From almost the beginning at Apple we were, for some incredibly lucky reason, fortunate enough to be at the right place at the right time. The contributions we tried to make embodied values not only of technical excellence and innovation—which I think we did our share of—but innovation of a more humanistic kind.

The things I'm most proud about at Apple is where the technical and the humanistic came together, as it did in publishing for example. The Macintosh basically revolutionized publishing and printing. The typographic artistry coupled with the technical understanding and excellence to implement that electronically—those two things came together and empowered people to use the computer without having to understand arcane computer commands....

DSM: You used an interesting word in describing what you were doing. You were talking about art, not engineering, not science. Tell me about that.

SJ: I actually think there's actually very little distinction between an artist and a scientist or engineer of the highest caliber. I've never had a distinction in my mind between those two types of people. They've just been to me people who pursue different paths but basically kind of headed to the same goal which is to express something of what they perceive to be the truth around them so that others can benefit by it.

DSM: And the artistry is in the elegance of the solution, like chess playing or mathematics?

SJ: . . . If you study these people a little bit more what you'll find is that in this particular time, in the 70's and the 80's the best people in computers would have normally been poets and writers and musicians. Almost all of them were musicians. A lot of them were poets on the side. They went into computers because it was so compelling. It was fresh and new. It was a new medium of expression for their creative talents. The feelings and the passion that people put into it were completely indistinguishable from a poet or a painter. Many of the people were introspective, inward people who expressed how they felt about other people or the rest of humanity in general into their work, work that other people would use.

QUESTIONS

1. What, to judge from the Macintosh ad, were the characteristics and values of someone who would buy and use a Mac?
2. What, according to Jobs, was the purpose of work for those who created the culture of innovation that led to Apple and Silicon Valley? Does the Macintosh ad reflect these individuals' concept of work's purpose? If so, how so? If not, why not?

30.2. JOSEPH PERKINS, "OP-ED" (OCTOBER 21, 1994) AND *THE NEW YORK TIMES*, "WHY PROPOSITION 187 WON'T WORK" (NOVEMBER 20, 1994)

In 1994 California voters passed Proposition 187, a measure denying government services to undocumented immigrants. Although courts later invalidated Proposition 187, the initiative ignited a nationwide debate over immigration.

JOSEPH PERKINS: OP-ED

No one has been harder on California Gov. Pete Wilson than yours truly. But I have to give the devil his due for his principled stand on illegal immigration.

Specifically, I am referring to the governor's unequivocal support for a state ballot measure that would deny California's 1.6 million illegal immigrants taxpayer-funded education, nonemergency health care, welfare benefits and other public social services.

Wilson has been accused of, among other things, "scapegoating," "xenophobia" and "racism." But this is a patently absurd charge. Proposition 187, titled the "Save Our State" initiative, is favored by Californians across the board.

Sources: Joseph Perkins, "Op-ed," *San Diego Union Tribune*, October 21, 1994; *New York Times*, "Why Proposition 187 Won't Work" [editorial], November 20, 1994.

This was borne out by a recent Los Angeles Times survey, which showed that the ballot initiative is supported by a majority of Republicans and Democrats, conservatives and liberals, whites and, most telling of all, Hispanics.

California's legal residents recognize that the financially-strapped state no longer can afford to generously proffer government benefits to persons who steal across this country's border.

As it is, illegal immigrants are eligible for almost as many publicly-funded services as U.S. citizens. Indeed, they can cross the border and have babies at American hospitals at taxpayer expense. They can enroll their kids in American schools tuition-free. They can even get welfare benefits in their children's name.

As Wilson has repeatedly mentioned, illegal immigrants cost his state a net of $5 billion annually. That works out to more than $400 a year added to each California family's tax burden.

The illegal immigrants, themselves, are not to be faulted for taking advantage of Yankee largess. We have only ourselves to blame for devaluing U.S. citizenship, for conferring upon those who come here illegally the same rights and privileges as those who are either native-born Americans or who legally immigrated to this country.

Indeed, nothing is more ludicrous than the designation of so-called "citizen children." These are babies who become U.S. citizens through accident of birth; whose illegal-immigrant mothers happen to bring them into the world in an American maternity ward.

The babies are Americanized by virtue of the 14th Amendment's guarantee that any person born on U.S. soil is automatically a citizen. But when the amendment was ratified in 1868, neither Congress nor the state legislatures were even remotely thinking about future illegal immigrants.

They were thinking about former slaves who were brought to this country against their will, on whose backs the South's agrarian economy was built. Black men and women who were third- and fourth-generation residents of this country, who had no first-hand memories of their native land, but who nonetheless were disenfranchised by their new homeland.

To equate the citizenship rights of emancipated slaves with those of babies born to illegal immigrants is to trivialize the history of slavery in this country.

The emancipated slaves earned their U.S. citizenship by virtue of their longevity in this country and their uncompensated labors. The babies of illegal immigrants have done nothing to merit citizenship, except be born at U.S. taxpayer expense.

The 14th Amendment needs to be rewritten by Congress. American citizenship no longer should be routinely bestowed upon a baby that happens to be born here, but whose parents are foreign citizens. Let the child apply for naturalization at the age of 18. If he or she becomes a U.S. citizen then, it will be by intent rather than by default, the way it is now....

America continues to admit more foreign immigrants than all the other countries in the world combined. As most of these immigrants ultimately settle in California, at considerable expense to the state's taxpayers, it hardly is xenophobic or racist if California residents vote to deny publicly-funded benefits and services to immigrants who have entered the country illegally.

NEW YORK TIMES: WHY PROPOSITION 187 WON'T WORK

Proposition 187, the California ballot initiative that deprives illegal immigrants of state services, has quickly been revealed as the inhumane headache its opponents promised it would be.

Already a host of examples of the new measure's inevitable consequences have shown how unlikely it is that its supporters really thought much before casting their votes.

Did they, for example, intend to deprive a child who is a legal resident of treatment for lead poisoning—because his illegal mother is too frightened to bring him to the clinic? One health worker has already encountered this situation, although the law has yet to go into effect.

Did Californians, when they voted to deny illegal immigrants non-emergency medical care, think about the consequences of having people go untreated for communicable diseases, thereby putting whole communities at risk? And did Californians really want the people who run child-welfare agencies to abandon children already abandoned by their parents, or to evict abused children now in foster care?

Health care workers, educators and other public servants are having to think about such issues now.

That is one reason why the Los Angeles City Council and school district have vowed not to comply with 187; it is one reason why school principals around the state have rushed to reassure their pupils that they have no intention of playing enforcer for the Immigration and Naturalization Service; it is one reason why staffs at health clinics have vowed to give up state funding rather than turn away people in need....

Californians are learning that getting tough with illegal immigrants may sound wonderful in the abstract but it is heartbreaking, and tortuously complicated, in practice. Both because of its inhumanity and its impracticality, Proposition 187 invites massive civil disobedience. It is a bad law, which, if the courts continue to rule wisely, will never have to be instituted.

QUESTIONS

1. On what grounds did each side base its case for or against Proposition 187?
2. What, according to Perkins, should make someone a citizen of the United States? What might be the implications of his goal to rewrite the 14th Amendment?

30.3. PRESIDENT CLINTON, EXCERPTS FROM "THE ERA OF BIG GOVERNMENT IS OVER" (JANUARY 23, 1996)

In the 1994 elections, Republicans gained control of both houses of Congress for the first time in 40 years. Democratic President Bill Clinton and the Republican congressional majority fought bitterly in 1995, leading to a shutdown of the federal government in the fall. In his 1996 State of the Union address, President Clinton agreed with Republicans that "the era of big government is over," but he also challenged Congress to balance the federal budget.

The state of the Union is strong. Our economy is the healthiest it has been in three decades. We have the lowest combined rates of unemployment and inflation in 27 years. We have completed—created nearly 8 million new jobs, over a million of them in basic industries like construction and automobiles. America is selling more cars than Japan for the first time since the 1970's. And for 3 years in a row, we have had a record number of new businesses started in our country.

Our leadership in the world is also strong, bringing hope for new peace. And perhaps most important, we are gaining ground in restoring our fundamental values. The crime rate, the welfare and food stamp rolls, the poverty rate, and the teen pregnancy rate are all down. And as they go down, prospects for America's future go up.

We live in an age of possibility. A hundred years ago we moved from farm to factory. Now we move to an age of technology, information, and global competition. These changes have opened vast new opportunities for our people, but they have also presented them with stiff challenges. While more Americans are living better, too many of our fellow citizens are working harder just to keep up, and they are rightly concerned about the security of their families.

Source: John T. Woolley and Gerhard Peters, *The American Presidency Project*, Santa Barbara, CA, http://www.presidency.ucsb.edu/ws/?pid=53091.

We must answer here three fundamental questions: First, how do we make the American dream of opportunity for all a reality for all Americans who are willing to work for it? Second, how do we preserve our old and enduring values as we move into the future? And third, how do we meet these challenges together, as one America?

We know big Government does not have all the answers. We know there's not a program for every problem. We know, and we have worked to give the American people a smaller, less bureaucratic Government in Washington. And we have to give the American people one that lives within its means. The era of big Government is over. But we cannot go back to the time when our citizens were left to fend for themselves.

Instead, we must go forward as one America, one nation working together to meet the challenges we face together. Self-reliance and teamwork are not opposing virtues; we must have both. I believe our new, smaller Government must work in an old-fashioned American way, together with all of our citizens through State and local governments, in the workplace, in religious, charitable, and civic associations. Our goal must be to enable all our people to make the most of their own lives, with stronger families, more educational opportunity, economic security, safer streets, a cleaner environment in a safer world....

Here, in this place, our responsibility begins with balancing the budget in a way that is fair to all Americans. There is now broad bipartisan agreement that permanent deficit spending must come to an end.

I compliment the Republican leadership and the membership for the energy and determination you have brought to this task of balancing the budget. And I thank the Democrats for passing the largest deficit reduction plan in history in 1993, which has already cut the deficit nearly in half in 3 years.

Since 1993, we have all begun to see the benefits of deficit reduction. Lower interest rates have made it easier for businesses to borrow and to invest and to create new jobs. Lower interest rates have brought down the cost of home mortgages, car payments, and credit card rates to ordinary citizens. Now, it is time to finish the job and balance the budget.

QUESTIONS

1. What, according to Clinton, was the proper role of government now that the era of big government was over?
2. This was Clinton's last State of the Union speech before the presidential election of 1996. In what ways does this speech reflect that impending event?

30.4. *THE ECONOMIST,* "THE END?" (FEBRUARY 11, 1999)

President Bill Clinton's involvement with Monica Lewinsky, a 21-year-old White House intern, captured public attention at home and abroad for a year beginning in January 1998. Britain's *Economist* newspaper expressed both the widespread fascination with the subject and the ultimate judgment that Clinton's critics went too far in impeaching the president.

As *The Economist* went to press, it was uncertain exactly how the Senate trial would be brought to its inevitably dismal end. But two things were clear. First, what has happened over the past year should never have happened at all; second, there is no guarantee that it will not happen again. The end of this awful tale still leaves in place the elements that spawned it: a diminished presidency, a bitterly divided Congress, an over-mighty prosecutor, and a media pack that is proud to seek out scandal wherever it can.

It was clear, if not from the start then soon after, that the president's impeachment should never have been undertaken. This huge, ponderous machine, whose workings paralyse normal government, should be activated only to remove a president who is agreed by both political parties and by the people to be a menace to the country. Bill Clinton's offences, perjury and obstruction of justice—not, it bears repeating, that he had a tawdry sexual fling—were in our view grave and shameful. Mr. Clinton disguised private lapses of behaviour with public lying, which had the public consequence of destroying the people's trust in him. To this, the proper response of a man of honour would have been to resign his office. But that was never the view of most Americans; still less did most Americans feel that these crimes justified the president's removal by another branch of government.

Since Mr. Clinton would not go, his political enemies determined to root him out, using impeachment to try to overturn, by a sort of constitutional *coup d'état,*

the result of two elections. This is not impeachment's purpose, and no one has emerged from the process untarnished: not the president, who refused even the courtesy of answering senators' questions, nor the Republican trial managers, who often exhibited pure vengeance, nor the Democrats, whose scramble to embrace their president suggests a wholesale abandonment of principle. It is expected (though nobody can be sure) that the Republicans will reap the whirlwind in the elections of 2000—that they, not the president or his Democrat apologists, will be blamed for taking the country through this horror. Even so, impeachment once devalued may be used this way again, not least by those who feel that vengeance and partisanship are most neatly countered by more of the same.

Morning-after Washington also bears the scars of other excesses. The scandal saw a sort of Faustian pact between the special prosecutor, Ken Starr, and the press, whereby each seemed to feed and encourage the prurient appetites of the other. Mr. Starr's powers to investigate the president had long been condemned as too far-reaching. But when the inquiry turned to sex, rather than obscure tracts of scrubland in Arkansas, the press became insatiable, and Mr. Starr obliged them with an extraordinary flood of detail. Where the Internet dared, the old press followed. Rumour was published before it had been verified; the prosecutor's office sprang leaks for which no apology was offered; and Congress, when the time came, pushed titillating material immediately and unthinkingly into the

Source: The Economist, "The End," February 11, 1999.

public domain. This howling after sex stoked the fires of Republican moralists, obscured the valid reasons for condemning this president, and made the public think one thing: this prosecution was unfair.

HUNGRY PRESS, HUNGRY PROSECUTOR

There is a grain of truth in that. No other president has faced a man of Mr. Starr's resources and persistence (a persistence that is still unsated); and none has had to deal with such a torrent of explicit revelations. Perhaps Mr. Clinton's successors will not have to. In the present mood of national regret, the overwhelming wish never to go through *that* again, the office of the special prosecutor may well be eliminated before the year is out. Yet something will have to replace it; the executive cannot go unwatched. The press will be restrained for a while, no doubt. Yet the modern trend to keep close tabs on the powerful, to comb through their private lives, to expose them and pull them down, is not about to disappear. Every would-be presidential contender now working the malls of New Hampshire must expect to have to defend himself.

The fact is that during the presidency of Bill Clinton, the perception of the office has changed and its authority has diminished. At this point in history, it is said, America does not require a leader to admire; prosperous and peaceful, it needs only a man who can steer straight, and Mr. Clinton can do that capably enough. Respect and special treatment are not necessary. This attitude was both confirmed and reflected during the Lewinsky affair, by the Supreme Court ruling that the Paula Jones civil suit could proceed against Mr. Clinton while he was in office. But this ruling was misguided; this, too, should not have happened. A president in office is not an ordinary man, but the head of state of the most powerful country on earth. He represents an entity to which, above all, the world looks for guidance. His accountability as a man before the law must always be balanced by a sense of the importance of the office he occupies.

QUESTIONS

1. Did someone or something, in the view of the *Economist*, bear a disproportionate share of the blame for the impeachment of Clinton? If so, who or what? If not, why not?
2. What did the *Economist* see as the likely future of American politics?

CHAPTER 31

21ST-CENTURY DANGERS AND PROMISES, 2000–PRESENT

31.1. AL QAEDA, FATWA AGAINST THE UNITED STATES (FEBRUARY 23, 1998)

In 1998, Osama bin Laden issued a *fatwa*, or religious decree, calling on Muslims to kill Americans and their allies. Few outside intelligence agencies paid close attention to bin Laden until Al Qaeda operatives flew airplanes into the World Trade Center and the Pentagon on September 11, 2001. The United States responded to these attacks with a global war on terror, which included prolonged and costly wars in Iraq and Afghanistan.

Praise be to God, who revealed the Book, controls the clouds, defeats factionalism, and says in His Book: "But when the forbidden months are past, then fight and slay the pagans wherever ye find them, seize them, beleaguer them, and lie in wait for them in every stratagem (of war)"; and peace be upon our Prophet, Muhammad Bin-'Abdallah, who said: I have been sent with the sword between my hands to ensure that no one but God is worshipped, God who put my livelihood under the shadow of my spear and who inflicts humiliation and scorn on those who disobey my orders.

The Arabian Peninsula has never—since God made it flat, created its desert, and encircled it with seas—been stormed by any forces like the crusader armies spreading in it like locusts, eating its riches and wiping out its plantations. All this is happening at a time in which nations are attacking Muslims like people fighting over a plate of food. In the light of the grave situation and the lack of support, we and you are obliged to discuss current events, and we should all agree on how to settle the matter.

No one argues today about three facts that are known to everyone; we will list them, in order to remind everyone:

First, for over seven years the United States has been occupying the lands of Islam in the holiest of places, the Arabian Peninsula, plundering its riches, dictating to its rulers, humiliating its people, terrorizing its neighbors, and turning its bases in the Peninsula into a spearhead through which to fight the neighboring Muslim peoples.

Source: "Al Qaeda's Fatwa," February 23, 1998, *Newshour with Jim Lehrer*, http://www.pbs.org/newshour/terrorism/international/fatwa_1998.html.

If some people have in the past argued about the fact of the occupation, all the people of the Peninsula have now acknowledged it. The best proof of this is the Americans' continuing aggression against the Iraqi people using the Peninsula as a staging post, even though all its rulers are against their territories being used to that end, but they are helpless.

Second, despite the great devastation inflicted on the Iraqi people by the crusader-Zionist alliance, and despite the huge number of those killed, which has exceeded 1 million...despite all this, the Americans are once against trying to repeat the horrific massacres, as though they are not content with the protracted blockade imposed after the ferocious war or the fragmentation and devastation.

So here they come to annihilate what is left of this people and to humiliate their Muslim neighbors. Third, if the Americans' aims behind these wars are religious and economic, the aim is also to serve the Jews' petty state and divert attention from its occupation of Jerusalem and murder of Muslims there. The best proof of this is their eagerness to destroy Iraq, the strongest neighboring Arab state, and their endeavor to fragment all the states of the region such as Iraq, Saudi Arabia, Egypt, and Sudan into paper statelets and through their disunion and weakness to guarantee Israel's survival and the continuation of the brutal crusade occupation of the Peninsula....

The ruling to kill the Americans and their allies—civilians and military—is an individual duty for every Muslim who can do it in any country in which it is possible to do it, in order to liberate the al-Aqsa Mosque and the holy mosque [Mecca] from their grip, and in order for their armies to move out of all the lands of Islam, defeated and unable to threaten any Muslim. This is in accordance with the words of Almighty God, "and fight the pagans all together as they fight you all together," and "fight them until there is no more tumult or oppression, and there prevail justice and faith in God."...

We—with God's help—call on every Muslim who believes in God and wishes to be rewarded to comply with God's order to kill the Americans and plunder their money wherever and whenever they find it. We also call on Muslim ulema, leaders, youths, and soldiers to launch the raid on Satan's U.S. troops and the devil's supporters allying with them, and to displace those who are behind them so that they may learn a lesson....

Almighty God also says: "O ye who believe, what is the matter with you, that when ye are asked to go forth in the cause of God, ye cling so heavily to the earth! Do ye prefer the life of this world to the hereafter? But little is the comfort of this life, as compared with the hereafter. Unless ye go forth, He will punish you with a grievous penalty, and put others in your place; but Him ye would not harm in the least. For God hath power over all things."

Almighty God also says: "So lose no heart, nor fall into despair. For ye must gain mastery if ye are true in faith."

QUESTIONS

1. What, in bin Laden's view, justified his fatwa against the United States?
2. What did bin Laden hope to achieve by issuing this fatwa?

31.2. KENNETH ADELMAN, "CAKEWALK IN IRAQ" (FEBRUARY 13, 2002)

Soon after the terror attacks of September 11, 2001, officials of the Bush administration advocated a U.S. assault on Iraq to destroy the regime of Saddam Hussein and create a democracy that would be a model for other states in the Arab Middle East. Critics of the plan advised caution, because they predicted that a war against Iraq would be prolonged and costly. Kenneth Adelman, a supporter of war with Iraq who had served as assistant to Defense Secretary Donald Rumsfeld from 1975 to 1977 and arms control director under President Ronald Reagan, explained in a *Washington Post* article why he believed such a war would be short and inexpensive.

Even before President Bush had placed Iraq on his "axis of evil," dire warnings were being sounded about the danger of acting against Saddam Hussein's regime. Two knowledgeable Brookings Institution analysts, Philip H. Gordon and Michael E. O'Hanlon, concluded that the United States would "almost surely" need "at least 100,000 to 200,000" ground forces [op-ed, Dec. 26, 2001]. Worse: "Historical precedents from Panama to Somalia to the Arab-Israeli wars suggest that…the United States could lose thousands of troops in the process."

I agree that taking down Hussein would differ from taking down the Taliban. And no one favors "a casual march to war." This is serious business, to be treated seriously.

In fact, we took it seriously the last time such fear-mongering was heard from military analysts—when we considered war against Iraq 11 years ago. Edward N. Luttwak cautioned on the eve of Desert Storm: "All those precision weapons and gadgets and gizmos and stealth fighters…are not going to make it possible to re-conquer Kuwait without many thousands of casualties." As it happened, our gizmos worked wonders. Luttwak's estimate of casualties was off by "many thousands," just as the current estimates are likely to be.

I believe demolishing Hussein's military power and liberating Iraq would be a cakewalk. Let me give simple, responsible reasons: (1) It was a cakewalk last time; (2) they've become much weaker; (3) we've become much stronger; and (4) now we're playing for keeps.

Gordon and O'Hanlon mention today's "400,000 active-duty troops in the Iraqi military" and especially the "100,000 in Saddam's more reliable Republican Guard and Special Republican Guard," which "would probably fight hard against the United States—just as they did a decade ago during Desert Storm." Somehow I missed that. I do remember a gaggle of Iraqi troops attempting to surrender to an Italian film crew. The bulk of the vaunted Republican Guard either hunkered down or was held back from battle.

Today Iraqi forces are much weaker. Saddam's army is one-third its size then, in both manpower and number of divisions. It still relies on obsolete Soviet tanks, which military analyst Eliot Cohen calls "death traps." The Iraqi air force, never much, is half its former size.

Iraqi forces have received scant spare parts and no weapons upgrades. They have undertaken little operational training since Desert Storm.

Meanwhile, American power is much fiercer. The advent of precision bombing and battlefield intelligence has dramatically spiked U.S. military prowess. The gizmos of Desert Storm were 90-plus percent dumb bombs. Against the Taliban, more than 80 percent were smart bombs. Unmanned Predators equipped with Hellfire missiles and Global Hawk

Source: Kenneth Adelman, "Cakewalk in Iraq," *Washington Post*, February 13, 2002, A27.

intelligence gathering did not exist during the first Iraqi campaign.

In 1991 we engaged a grand international coalition because we lacked a domestic coalition. Virtually the entire Democratic leadership stood against that President Bush. The public, too, was divided. This President Bush does not need to amass rinky-dink nations as "coalition partners" to convince the Washington establishment that we're right. Americans of all parties now know we must wage a total war on terrorism.

Hussein constitutes the number one threat against American security and civilization. Unlike Osama bin Laden, he has billions of dollars in government funds, scores of government research labs working feverishly on weapons of mass destruction—and just as deep a hatred of America and civilized free societies.

Once President Bush clearly announces that our objective is to rid Iraq of Hussein, and our unshakable determination to do whatever it takes to win, defections from the Iraqi army may come even faster than a decade ago.

Gordon and O'Hanlon say we must not "assume that Hussein will quickly fall." I think that's just what is likely to happen. How would it be accomplished?

By knocking out all his headquarters, communications, air defenses and fixed military facilities through precision bombing. By establishing military "no-drive zones" wherever Iraqi forces try to move. By arming the Kurds in the north, Shiites in the south and his many opponents everywhere. By using U.S. special forces and some U.S. ground forces with protective gear against chemical and biological weapons. By stationing theater missile defenses, to guard against any Iraqi Scuds still in existence. And by announcing loudly that any Iraqi, of any rank, who handles Hussein's weapons of mass destruction, in any form, will be severely punished after the war.

Measured by any cost-benefit analysis, such an operation would constitute the greatest victory in America's war on terrorism.

QUESTIONS

1. What promised to make war against Iraq a "cakewalk," in Adelman's view?
2. Adelman links a war on Iraq to a wider war on terrorism. What evidence does Adelman provide to establish such a link?

31.3. JUSTICE JOHN PAUL STEVENS, EXCERPTS FROM *HAMDAN V. RUMSFELD* (JUNE 29, 2006)

During the war on terror, U.S. forces captured hundreds of "enemy combatants" around the world and imprisoned then at a military base in Guantanamo Bay, Cuba. In 2006, the Supreme Court ruled that the military commission established by President George W. Bush to try captives was unconstitutional.

Justice Stevens announced the judgment of the Court and delivered the opinion of the Court with respect to Parts I through IV, Parts VI through VI-D-iii, Part VI-D-v, and Part VII, and an opinion with respect to Parts V and VI-D-iv, in which Justice Souter, Justice Ginsburg, and Justice Breyer join.

Petitioner Salim Ahmed Hamdan, a Yemeni national, is in custody at an American prison in

Source: Cornell University Law School Legal Information Institute (LLI), http://www.law.cornell.edu/supct/html/05–184. ZO.html.

Guantanamo Bay, Cuba. In November 2001, during hostilities between the United States and the Taliban (which then governed Afghanistan), Hamdan was captured by militia forces and turned over to the U. S. military. In June 2002, he was transported to Guantanamo Bay. Over a year later, the President deemed him eligible for trial by military commission for then-unspecified crimes. After another year had passed, Hamdan was charged with one count of conspiracy "to commit...offenses triable by military commission." App. to Pet. for Cert. 65a.

Hamdan filed petitions for writs of habeas corpus and mandamus to challenge the Executive Branch's intended means of prosecuting this charge. He concedes that a court-martial constituted in accordance with the Uniform Code of Military Justice (UCMJ), 10 U. S. C. §801 *et seq.* (2000 ed. and Supp. III), would have authority to try him. His objection is that the military commission the President has convened lacks such authority, for two principal reasons: First, neither congressional Act nor the common law of war supports trial by this commission for the crime of conspiracy—an offense that, Hamdan says, is not a violation of the law of war. Second, Hamdan contends, the procedures that the President has adopted to try him violate the most basic tenets of military and international law, including the principle that a defendant must be permitted to see and hear the evidence against him.

The District Court granted Hamdan's request for a writ of habeas corpus. 344 F. Supp. 2d 152 (DC 2004). The Court of Appeals for the District of Columbia Circuit reversed. 415 F. 3d 33 (2005). Recognizing, as we did over a half-century ago, that trial by military commission is an extraordinary measure raising important questions about the balance of powers in our constitutional structure, *Ex parte Quirin,* 317 U. S. 1, 19 (1942), we granted certiorari. 546 U. S. ____(2005).

For the reasons that follow, we conclude that the military commission convened to try Hamdan lacks power to proceed because its structure and procedures violate both the UCMJ and the Geneva Conventions. Four of us also conclude, see Part V, *infra,* that the offense with which Hamdan has been charged is not an "offens[e] that by...the law of war may be tried by military commissions." 10 U. S. C. §821....Common Article 3 obviously tolerates a great degree of flexibility in trying individuals captured during armed conflict; its requirements are general ones, crafted to accommodate a wide variety of legal systems. But *requirements* they are nonetheless. The commission that the President has convened to try Hamdan does not meet those requirements....We have assumed, as we must, that the allegations made in the Government's charge against Hamdan are true. We have assumed, moreover, the truth of the message implicit in that charge—viz., that Hamdan is a dangerous individual whose beliefs, if acted upon, would cause great harm and even death to innocent civilians, and who would act upon those beliefs if given the opportunity. It bears emphasizing that Hamdan does not challenge, and we do not today address, the Government's power to detain him for the duration of active hostilities in order to prevent such harm. But in undertaking to try Hamdan and subject him to criminal punishment, the Executive is bound to comply with the Rule of Law that prevails in this jurisdiction.

The judgment of the Court of Appeals is reversed, and the case is remanded for further proceedings.

It is so ordered.

The Chief Justice took no part in the consideration or decision of this case.

QUESTIONS

1. On what grounds did the Court find the military commission that was supposed to try Hamdan to be unconstitutional?

2. Did the Court majority balance of powers to be the most important issue at stake in the Hamdan case? If so, why? If not, why not?

31.4. POPE JOHN PAUL II, ROBERT AND MARY SCHINDLER, JUDGE GEORGE GREER, AND THE FLORIDA COURT OF APPEALS: OPINIONS ON TERRI SCHIAVO AND THE RIGHT TO DIE (2000s)

Arguments over the morality and legality of removing a feeding tube from Terri Schiavo became a flashpoint in the culture wars of the 1990s. Terri Schiavo's husband, Michael Schiavo, argued for the right to remove a feeding tube from his wife because she was in a persistent vegetative state. Her parents, Robert and Mary Schindler, argued that her Roman Catholic faith banned the use of any means to shorten life. Florida Judge George Greer repeatedly ruled in favor of Michael Schiavo, Terri's guardian.

POPE JOHN PAUL II

Faced with patients in similar clinical conditions, there are some who cast doubt on the persistence of the "human quality" itself, almost as if the adjective "vegetative" (whose use is now solidly established), which symbolically describes a clinical state, could or should be instead applied to the sick as such, actually demeaning their value and personal dignity. In this sense, it must be noted that this term, even when confined to the clinical context, is certainly not the most felicitous when applied to human beings....In opposition to such trends of thought, I feel the duty to reaffirm strongly that the intrinsic value and personal dignity of every human being do not change, no matter what the concrete circumstances of his or her life. *A man, even if seriously ill or disabled in the exercise of his highest functions, is and always will be a man*, and he will never become a "vegetable" or an "animal."...Even our brothers and sisters who find themselves in the clinical condition of a "vegetative state" retain their human dignity in all its fullness.

ROBERT AND MARY SCHINDLER

Mrs. Schiavo's medical condition in February 2000 was misrepresented to the trial court and to this court throughout these proceedings. They claim that she is not in a persistent vegetative state. What is more important, they maintain that current accepted medical treatment exists to restore her ability to eat and speak. The initial trial focused on what Mrs. Schiavo would have decided given her current medical condition and not on whether any available medical treatment could improve her condition. The Schindlers argue that in light of this new evidence of additional medical procedures intended to improve her condition, Mrs. Schiavo would now elect to undergo new treatment and would reverse the prior decision to withdraw life-prolonging procedures.

JUDGE GERGE GREER

[It is] beyond all doubt that [Mrs. Schiavo] is in a persistent vegetative state...per the specific testimony of

Sources: John Paul II, Address to the World Federation of Catholic Medical Associations and Pontifical Academy for Life Congress, March 2004, http://www.vatican.va/holy_father/john_paul_ii/speeches/2004/march/documents/hf_jp-ii_spe_20040320_congressfiamc_en.html; Kenneth W. Goodman, *The Case of Terri Schiavo: Ethics, Politics, and Death in the 21st Century* (New York: Oxford University Press, 2010), 27, 83, 171–73.

Dr. James Barnhill and corroborated by Dr. Vincent Gambone. The medical evidence before this court conclusively establishes that she has no hope of ever regaining consciousness and therefore capacity...The film offered into evidence by [the Schindlers] does nothing to change these medical opinions which are supported by the CAT scans in evidence. Mrs. Schindler has testified as her perceptions [*sic*] regarding her daughter and the court is not unmindful that *perceptions may become reality to the person having them.* But the overwhelming credible evidence is that Terri Schiavo has been totally unresponsive since lapsing into the coma almost ten years ago, that her movements are reflexive and predicated on brain stem activity alone, that she suffers from severe structural brain damage and to a large extent her brain has been replaced by spinal fluid, that with the exception of one witness whom the court finds to be so biased as to lack credibility, her movements are occasional and totally consistent with the testimony of the expert medical witnesses.

FLORIDA COURT OF APPEALS

The evidence is *overwhelming* that Theresa is in a permanent or persistent vegetative state. It is important to understand that a persistent vegetative state is not simply a coma. She is not asleep. She has cycles of apparent wakefulness and apparent sleep without any cognition or awareness. As she breathes, she often makes moaning sounds....Over the span of this last decade, Theresa's brain has deteriorated because of the lack of oxygen it suffered at the time of the heart attack.

QUESTIONS

1. For what reasons did Pope John Paul II and the Schindlers oppose the removal of Terri Schiavo's feeding tube? Why did Judge Greer and the Florida Court of Appeals refuse their claim?

2. What made this case so controversial and so reflective of the cultural divides then present in the United States?

31.5. *RICHMOND TIMES-DISPATCH*, EXCERPTS FROM "YOUNG VOTERS CONCERNED ABOUT ISSUES" (APRIL 20, 2008) AND *NEW YORK AMSTERDAM NEWS*, EXCERPTS FROM "YOUTH POLITICKING" (SEPTEMBER 18, 2008)

During the 2008 presidential election campaign, Illinois Senator Barack Obama aroused passionate support, especially among young people. His campaign slogans of "Hope" and "Change We Can Believe In" allowed many first-time voters to project their aspirations onto him.

Sources: Olympia Meola, "Young Voters Concerned about Issues," *Richmond Times-Dispatch*, April 20, 2008, A.21, http://www2.timesdispatch.com/news/2008/apr/20/-rtd_2008_04_20_0132-ar-138962/; Tobi Momoh, "Youth Politicking," *New York Amsterdam News*, September 18, 2008, 20.

YOUNG VOTERS CONCERNED ABOUT ISSUES

We gathered a diverse group of young voters to discuss their views on the 2008 presidential campaign. Here's what they said.

THE PANEL

Moderator: Cricket **White 57**, lives in Richmond.

Angela M. **Bitter 22**, VCU, Virginia Beach; Ramon **Bullard 20**, Univer; Melinda **Perron 18**, Randolph-Macon College, Virginia Beach; Galen **Pierce-Gardner 24**, VCU, Poquoson; Kristofer **Hutchinson 21**, Randolph-Macon, Richmond; Jessica **Lee 21**, VCU, Richmond; Hunter **Leemon 29**, works in real estate, Richmond; Jibran **Muhammad 23**, VCU, Falls Church; Ali **Shiflet 19**, Randolph-Macon College, Virginia Beach; Adam **Uddin 23**, VCU, Richmond; Matthew **Vinson 21**, J. Sargeant Reynolds, Montpelier; Gabriel **Walker 19**, VCU, Richmond; Earnest **White 23**, VCU, Richmond

YOUNG VOTERS' ENTHUSIASM

MUHAMMAD: You have an African-American running; you have the first female running for the office. So this is a historic event. Everybody's excited.

VINSON: There's a lot of major events, terrorist attacks, natural disasters. And so people are really looking for a leader that will provide…relief, and a plan.

LEE: The Bush years are definitively over. And then we have these two candidates [Obama and Clinton]….They represent something, I think, new, and which really excites people.

MUHAMMAD: I think it's minimizing when someone said, "Oh, they're just energized because of Barack Obama, or…after this thing is over, they won't get involved." No, they will get involved, because they're paying attention. Their friends are losing their lives [in Iraq], so they're paying attention.

UDDIN: I'm reluctant to actually say now that the youth vote and all this youth excitement is actually going to do something in the end. I remember a lot of people were really excited about the Puff Daddy "Vote or Die" campaign in 2004. Everybody thought everybody was going to come out in these giant numbers….If we have a brokered [Democratic] convention, I'm really scared

that…everybody's going to be disenchanted and it's going to be politics as usual.

PIERCE-GARDNER: I think students already have made a lasting mark in this election. They pretty much singlehandedly were responsible for [Obama's victory in] Iowa. And that has been the pivot point ever since with Barack Obama not letting himself be smothered in the cradle, as it were, by Hillary [Rodham Clinton].

BITTER: The Democrats have really, really been able to use this youth enthusiasm very, very well. And I don't think that the Republican Party has quite picked up on it the exact same way. I always feel like we're two steps behind when it comes to things like that.

LEEMON: I just think a lot of it has to do with the candidates….You can't lose sight of the fact that it's an African-American and a woman. And usually by this point, we're dealing with two middle-aged white men of Ivy League backgrounds.

COMPARING THE CANDIDATES

BITTER: What makes McCain stand out from the others is…that experience in national security….But on the other side, too, I really feel that there's a compassion on the part of Clinton and Obama that's very, very different from McCain.

PIERCE-GARDNER: Well, I think McCain is certainly older, both literally and in terms of his ideas. I think Obama has, obviously, great amounts of charisma. And his style is unique. I think he brings the ability to affect a 50-state electoral-map-changing strategy….I think Hillary has encyclopedic knowledge of policy, is obviously brilliant and capable. And then of course John McCain does have a great public-service record.

UDDIN: When they were my age, would I have hung out with them?…If we break it down, we've got John McCain, who went to the Naval Academy, ended up going to Vietnam. I don't see him as too likely of a candidate to hit him up for beer….Hillary went to Wesleyan, was president of the College Republicans. So I might see her as someone I would like to bring into the lifestyle but not necessarily anybody that I would ever hang out with. And then you've got Obama. Went to NYU, was studying constitutional law and, admittedly, in some of his books, he had a very free-loving time during his college time.

HUTCHINSON: First of all, to be very straightforward, I think all three of them would be phenomenal presidential candidates....I feel like, if we had to put a new president in right now, who could do it...I feel like [Clinton's] had eight years, she's already taken baby steps, in a way.

SHIFLET: McCain...[is] experienced with foreign policy and national defense. He's been in the military. He's gone to Vietnam. I just feel comfortable with that....I feel like [Obama] just would be great for the future. And then you have Clinton, who has done it before....Each one has something that they could bring to the table.

PERRON: I feel like...if [Obama] was my neighbor, I could give him the keys to my house and be like, "Oh, just water my plants while I'm gone." And I would not have any worry at all that he would do something weird in my house. I just see him being so great for the future. And he just really wants to do things differently. And I honestly think that he has, like, the best intentions at heart.

OPTIMISM

BULLARD: I'm very, very, very optimistic, especially when I think of Obama. When I think of it, it almost gives me flutters...in my heart when I think he actually could be there....We're almost going to change the White House....There's so many new possibilities on all levels, including foreign policy.

UDDIN: I guess the answer is kind of twofold. [In 2004] I was really excited about John Kerry coming in and no more four years of Bush. And I was let down. And...bouncing back from that, getting my political feet back, was a little hard.

PIERCE-GARDNER: I am young but still somewhat jaded to the process....But...the essence of America—and this is kind of cheesy sounding— is making the impossible possible. I mean that's what we're all about. And history shows that when we come together, we can achieve things that no other country can. So I think when you have the right leader, we can clean things up in four years, eight years.

YOUTH POLITICKING

This year's presidential election is one of excitement, as history may soon be made. There is a strong possibility that the nation will elect the first Black male as its president. From the get-go, the excitement of Senators Barack Obama and Hilary Clinton running for president made them the strongest two competitors for the Democratic election. Not only does the presidential [election] affect all classes, genders and segments of society, youths today are also involved in politics.

Sixteen-year-old Jordan Lewis of the Eagle Academy for Young Men has thorough knowledge of the presidential election. Very interested in politics and debate, Lewis speaks on the subject matter as if he had the ability to vote.

"Although Hilary had the experience of being in the White House, that's not the only thing you need to be a good president. Barack Obama is a great motivational speaker who can move a nation. This is one of the major changes from status quo. I believe he is the first African-American that has a chance to actually be president. His words are strong and intellectual. Obama is bright in the sense that he sparks change with his own talents," the savvy teen stated.

At 7 years old, Demi Cole spends some of his spare time watching the presidential conventions when he comes home from school. In a short interview with the Amsterdam News, he tells us what he thinks about the presidential election. "People are voting for Barack Obama. I like Barack Obama. I like him because he is a good person, he says nice things and he wants to help people. I like him a lot better than I like John McCain. And I like him because he's a Democrat."...

The crowd favorite has been Barack Obama and his wife Michelle. Some of the young people the AmNews spoke to say that she has been his secret weapon in the election and has increased Obama's chances of being the first Black president of the United States.

QUESTIONS

1. What made young Americans excited about the election of 2008? What explains their inclination to support Barack Obama in that contest?

2. In what ways did the young people interviewed for these stories understand politics and the potential impact of politics on their lives?